Studies in
the Sociology
of Social Problems

MODERN SOCIOLOGY

A Series of Monographs, Treatises, and Texts

Edited by
Gerald M. Platt

Studies in the Sociology of Social Problems

editors

Joseph W. Schneider
Drake University

John I. Kitsuse
University of California, Santa Cruz

Ablex Publishing Corporation
Norwood, New Jersey 07648

Library of Congress Cataloging in Publication Data
Main entry under title:

Studies in the sociology of social problems.

  (Modern sociology)
  Bibliography: p.
  Includes index.
  1. Sociology—Addresses, essays, lectures.   2. Social
problems—Addresses, essays, lectures.   I. Schneider,
Joseph W., 1943–   . II. Kitsuse, John I.
III. Series.
HM51.S929   1984   301   84-14549
ISBN 0-89391-053-8

Ablex Publishing Corporation
355 Chestnut Street
Norwood, New Jersey 07648

Contents

Contents

Introduction

Joseph W. Schneider

The sociology of social problems has been and continues to be something of an intellectual stepchild in the family of academic sociology. Were relative prestige studies done of sociological specialities, one suspects "social problems," if it could be found at all, would rank very low. This has been credited to the aridity of both theory and method in social problems writing, coupled with the doggedly difficult issue of how to study something the very definition of which seems to presuppose a moral stance. In short, the kinds of problems sociologists have faced in the study of social problems have been theoretical, methodological, and moral.

Theory in social problems typically has meant whatever implicit or, occassionally, explicit assumptions and related concepts one uses to study undesirable conditions. As such, it merely reflects those theories currently popular in the discipline that are then brought to bear in the analysis of these conditions. The same is true for methods. In short, there has been no theory and corresponding methodology *of* social problems as a sociological speciality distinct from various theories *in* research on problematic conditions. Moreover, as Richard Fuller (1938) lamented over forty years ago, teaching courses in social problems seems to require the instructor to be an "expert" on an endless variety of social conditions, kinds of actors, and situations. This has become more difficult as data and analyses accumulate. Textbooks for undergraduate courses on social problems reflect this in their "latest" official statistics on this or that kind of condition, with new editions necessary every few years to remain "current" in the market.

During the past decade, however, new developments in social problems sociology have renewed interest in the speciality as a bona fide intellectual and research enterprise. The most bold and systematic statement of this new view is found in Malcolm Spector and John I. Kitsuse's (1977) book, *Constructing Social Problems,* and has been extended in subsequent papers by each (Kitsuse, 1980; Spector, 1981). Spector and Kitsuse argue that social problems sociology involves a distinctive set of questions and research procedures that focus attention not on social conditions but on the full range of definitional activities that make such conditions problematic. Social problems, then, become "the activities of individuals or groups making assertions of grievances and claims with respect to some putative conditions" (Spector and Kitsuse, 1977: 75). Rather than becoming "experts" who document and analyze such conditions, and thus themselves participants in the social problem, sociologists study those who, through these definitional activities, make and pursue such "problems."

This particular collection of papers grew out of a session at the 1980 annual meetings of The Society for the Study of Social Problems, held in New York. The session, a product of an organizer's frantic call in search of any papers on social problems theory, was initially to be focused on methods in social problems research, and particularly research in this social definitional framework. As the date of the meeting drew closer, it became apparent that the papers would range rather widely around this methods focus, some being more about theory than methods, others being reports of studies of definitional processes that extend what we know about social problems theory and method.

This volume is the first in a series of publications on "advances" in sociological theory and research. We focus attention on the social definitional or constructionist perspective by collecting papers that variously take the assumptions and strategies of the work noted above as points of departure or contact. Of the eight chapters included, only one omits specific reference to this developing line of work. In this introduction, we say something about the substance and theme of each paper, and allude to general questions bearing on the definitional framework. Finally, we suggest how each paper contributes to our understanding of these more general issues in social definitional research on social problems.

At the core of these new developments in social problems sociology is the distinction between conditions and definitions about those conditions. In the first chapter, Naomi Aronson reviews recent developments in the sociology of knowledge and argues that these provide a firm foundation for the social definitional approach to understanding not only social problems sociology, but science in general. Fundamental to the *strong programme* in the sociology of knowledge is the absolute distinction between knowledge about the world and the world itself. Aronson points out how, in this view, *all* knowledge emerges from social interaction, is socially contingent, and that we should study not only the content of such knowledge, but how it is created.

This view of the nature and origins of knowledge does not allow science a special status as arbiter of truth. Rather, it becomes one among a number of ways in which "truth" statements about the world may be generated. The promising pursuit then is to examine the viability rather than the validity of these claims, and whether such claims are accepted, rejected, or altered as they move through various interactional networks. What science manipulates, then, are definitions about the natural world rather than that world. This is precisely the position Spector and Kitsuse adopt in their description of the social definitional stance.

Aronson argues that there is a striking but not particularly surprising parallel between science and social problems activities so defined, in that, at their core, both involve definitional processes. Moreover, she shows by examples from her own and previous research that such definitions become the grounds for a great deal of organizational activity; in short, that definitions have organizational consequences.

Beyond these "cognitive" internal claims, Aronson argues that science makes "interpretive" claims to relevant publics outside the scientific community. In so doing, these "statesmen" scientists become quite explicitly involved in social problems development in the society. Such claims-making activity, she argues, seeks to enhance the status of science and its political and economic security. By making claims for science as a tool to solve social problems, scientists continue scientific work in a way rarely appreciated.

What Aronson shows to be true for nutrition researchers in the 1890s and leukemia researchers between the years 1955 and 1975 is probably none the less true for social scientists and their various external audiences, as the national experiments of the "New Frontier," "Great Society," and "Reagonomics" suggest. Scientific work has important implications for the social construction of social problems. To the extent these interpretive claims succeed or fail, scientists expand or contract their control of resources and prerogatives in society generally and, more specifically, around one or another strategic research arena.

Another important question raised by the social definitional approach to social problems deals with the stance of the sociologist toward the subject matter and what this implies about his or her relationship to the lay audiences that consume this work. Joseph R. Gusfield, an early and insightful contributor to the definitional perspective on social problems, addresses this question in his essay, "On the Side: Practical Action and Social Constructivism in Social Problems Theory." In conventional approaches to social problems that focus on social conditions, sociologists assume the stance of expert technicians who can see, using their specially trained insight, social pathology, disorganization, latent dysfunctions, and their causes. Gusfield demonstrates, drawing from the work of William Ogburn and Robert and Helen Lynd, that the roots of American social problems writing grew deep in the soil of Enlightenment values of "progress" and a harmony between human, technological, and economic interests. Sociologists were "on the side" of society, which is to say they were "against" vested interests and institutions that resisted progress. This sociology of social problems saw itself as a vehicle for the application of science to the solution of such problems and toward a better life for all.

Gradually, however, this version of "proper" sociological involvement gave way to a less presumptuous view both of what social problems are and how the sociologist might be involved in them. Throughout the 1940s and 1950s, the model of the objective natural scientist gained great legitimacy in American sociology. To be a "scientist" was to be morally neutral toward one's subject matter, or at least to maintain such a public stance. Today there is considerably less consensus on these questions. The 1960s brought events that put this model of scientific work into both moral and intellectual disrepute. Value neutral sociology, and particularly of social problems, was seen to be impossible. Given this, the important question became, as Howard Becker (1967) put it, not whether to take sides but to decide "whose side" we are on, meaning from what perspective we see the events we presume to describe and analyze.

Gusfield details the history of these changing relationships between the social scientist as expert, the objects of study, and various external audiences. He argues that the rise of the social constructionist position in social problems returns us to the view that the scientist should be neutral, detached, and uninvolved in the social problems studied. His title, "On the Side," describes this view. The moral "starch" removed from their visions, these "new" sociologists of social problems not only do not take sides, they profess little if any concern over the outcome of the contest. It is not the outcome of the process that commands their interest, but the process itself.

But this focus on definitional process, treating, in Aronson's words, "all knowledge as contingent," is difficult to maintain even for those skilled in such analysis and conversant with the theoretical vision that guides it. There is perhaps no better example of this difficulty and the beguiling nature of our own commitments to notions of science as truth than Gusfield's present paper. While his title announces his intent, namely, to argue that social definitional sociologists stand "on the sidelines" of the controversies they study, he himself falls prey to the moral starch of positivist science. This is apparent in his discussion of the case of alcohol.

Having devoted much professional time and energy to the study of alcohol and the various professional and lay myths that surround it, Gusfield carries with him a view of what is "true," what is "fact," as he encounters claims made by various participants in this social problems drama. By making judgments about the truth value of some of these claims and then rejecting them on the grounds that they are not supported by "fact," Gusfield gives warrant to the procedures of science and the products they yield. In short, he gives his own and his fellow scientists' work a special status and then uses the criteria that define that status to judge other work, such as, for instance, claims by the National Council on Alcoholism or the National Highway Traffic Safety Administration, as "false" and less worthy. Gusfield comes at the end of his paper to contradict the Spector and Kitsuse position that he himself earlier approvingly cites.

Gusfield sees the social constructionist sociologist as social critic, able somehow to judge and debunk the claims of "social problems industry" personnel. But it is only if we are willing to grant the sociologist a special place, what Gusfield calls an "Olympian view," that such judgment qua truth is possible. Even though Gusfield argues that the moral starch of earlier social problems formulations has been washed away in the constructionist approach, he confounds his argument by identifying sociologists as cognoscenti having a favored stance from which to study social problems. Suddenly, the sociologist no longer stands on the side but is an active participant in the fray, assuming the familiar role of expert debunker and arbiter of truth.

We raise this criticism of Gusfield's argument with full appreciation of his dilemma and, more important, to point out how slippery are the distinctions that must be drawn to maintain a consistently definitional view. It may be that such definitions themselves become objects for claims by social problems sociologists. It is easy to recall the discomfort many felt in the 1960s when they attempted to defend their work as "value neutral." We believe, however, that qua sociologist of the social problems process, and quite aside from personal, even professional, decisions about commitment to values and ideals, it is essential to distinguish clearly the relationships between researcher and those studied.

We do not argue for a so-called "neutral," which is to say "special," position for the student of social problems. Indeed, Spector and Kitsuse reject such a notion. The posture and role of the sociologist as expert on social problems, however, *necessarily* renders him or her a participant among those seeking to define, defend, or solve some problematic condition. Whether or not such claims to expert status are warranted by other member-participants is an open question. The difficulty we find with Gusfield's discussion is that the cognoscenti he describes are not in fact "on the side" at all; sobering evidence of just how difficult it is to keep moral starch out of studying what are unequivocally moral phenomena.

Another issue brought forward by the definitional perspective on social problems turns on questions of data and method, specifically, "What materials are relevant as data?" "How are they to be used?" and "What meanings may the researcher attribute to these data?" Ronald J. Troyer, in "Better Read than Dead: Notes on Using Archival Materials in Social Problems and Deviance Research," and Gary T. Marx, in "Notes on the Discovery, Collection, and Assessment of Hidden and Dirty Data," offer discussions about data and method that bear on these questions. Both papers describe what their authors believe are neglected materials potentially valuable to social problems research.

Troyer gives attention to archival materials, much of which consist of numeric and classificatory data produced by various governmental agencies. From U.S. Census counts to state Bureau of Labor reports, annual reports of state institutions, and vital statistics, to local, city ordinances, court records, and newspapers, he reminds us of the vast resource this historical information represents, both for those wanting to study social problems as conditions ("social factists") and those who adopt a view of social problems as definitional activities ("social definitionists"). Troyer identifies these archival data, discusses how they are organized, where they are likely to be located, and how, with the help of a patient archivist, we can uncover them. He argues that these data, including the explanatory notes that accompany them, are relevant for both factists and definitionists, although the problems they present differ for each.

Marx is concerned not with data publicly available, but with what he calls *dirty* data that are "hidden" by organizations because such data are highly discrediting. Marx knows of these data and their significance from his work on agent-provocateurs, undercover police work, cover-ups, and the systematic attempt by powerful organizations to insure their power by maintaining secrecy. He wants us, moreover, not only to know about such things but to learn and use various methods to break through the secrecy that keeps them hidden. These inculde monitoring uncontrollable contingencies and accidents, using our own volition or that of "whistleblowers," and engaging in deception and outright coercion.

These methods are full of the kind of moral starch Gusfield wants to wash out of social problems research, and that Spector, Kitsuse, and others discourage. Marx rejects as pretense the notion that we can remain morally "on the side" in such research. We should know how to use the Freedom of Information Act, the Buckley Amendment, various state "sunshine laws," and the journalistic techniques of investigative reporting in the muckraking tradition (Marx himself has edited a 1971 volume called *Muckraking Sociology: Research As Social Criticism*). We should become sleuths for "residue elements," such as "signs of forced entry, missing documents, gaps on a tape . . . powder that can be seen only under untraviolet light, fingerprints . . ." and so on. He wants us, as social researchers, to help redress the abuses of power and privilege in American society. For those wanting to put such starch in their work, Marx's catalogue should be most helpful.

In traditional work on social problems, relevant data are defined to be descriptive, usually numeric, often aggregate information about undesirable conditions and/or conduct. These data are commonly taken to be indicators of aspects of the social world considered problematic. Troyer suggests that social factist researchers face problems of accuracy or reliability when using various kinds of archival data. Marx, similarly, cautions about the accuracy of information obtained via "whistleblowers," leaks, anonymous sources, and so on. Questions about the validity of these data, what they may be taken to mean, are usually given less attention and believed to be less problematic. An increase in the number or rate of this or that kind of crime or deviant behavior is, on its face, an undesirable change; evidence that records were falsified to enable powerful actors to realize their interests *obviously* means undesirable or dirty conduct took place. Key method and data questions are about reliability or data accuracy. Such a position, then, presupposes the moral status of the conditions and conduct in question. The conventional sociologist of social problems acts as scientific expert who helps to document, explain, and contribute to controlling these events.

For those who study social problems as definitional activities, these *same* materials are transformed into quite *different* data. Such archival and revelatory information is more in the category of an artifact of the production work that lies behind it (see Kitsuse and Cicourel, 1963). They are valued not for what they tell us about the conditions and/or conduct they seem to describe, but rather as evidence or instances of claims-making activities and definitional process. Marx's "methods" here become interesting not as available for the sociologist's use, but rather as new strategies to aid participants in claims-making work. These users do not agonize over the same kinds of accuracy questions as do those attending to social conditions, but they are nevertheless concerned to have as accurate a record of activities as possible (which is to say that they too want reliable information). Social definitional students, however, do concern themselves with what such data mean. In fact, their conclusion on this question is radically distinct from that of social factists. *All* data are products of work, and thus bear the marks and reflect the agendas, as well as foibles, mistakes, vargaries, and inconsistencies of such work. To know how we can use this information, we need to follow Aronson's advice taken from the strong programme, namely, to study the connections between knowledge and the social production context.

In this regard, those adopting a social constructionist approach may face access and accuracy problems both in archival and dirty data even greater than those who study social problems as conditions. This is because the materials required for constructionist analysis may be more difficult to find, in part because they usually are not seen by their producers as data.

Except for the reflexive in-house monitoring systems developed in some governmental agencies, we suspect the kinds of details necessary to precisely document definitional activities simply may not be recorded with the same systematic regularity and completeness that surrounds the products of this production work. This probably would be even more true in private bureaucracies less concerned with accountability. When the data are dirty and hidden, the definitional work and identities of participants are precisely what are most protected. Even when data are not dirty and hidden, we suspect few data generating and/or classification organizations have commissioned or undertaken detailed histories of their routine work, policies, personnel, and operations.

On balance, we have very little systematic knowledge about data production work. Such methodological research is precisely what *both* "factist" and "constructionist" students of social problems need in order to know what meanings may be attributed to data created from such materials. While Troyer directs attention to official government data as a source for research, and Marx urges us to sleuth for dirty data, we need also to give attention to private organizations whose routine and nonnefarious business it is to create, classify, and/or present various images of this or that kind of conduct or condition. Spector and Kitsuse (1977:7–20) have offered brief but provocative suggestions for this kind of work, yet little has been done. Spector, in particular, argues that we should study such things as The *Readers' Guide to Periodical Literature, Shepard's Law Review Citations,* and The American Psychiatric Association's *Diagnostic and Statistical Manual of Mental Disorders* as rich sources of significant definitional activities.

In their most developed form, such studies would be full-fledged analyses of the origins, development, politics, and practices of these companies and organizations; they would require detailed organizational research on data and information-producing work. In less ambitous form, the classification and information-processing systems of such organizations could be studied to review changes in categories over time or in connection with other definitional events. Troyer devotes much of his discussion of social definitional use or archival materials to such monitoring for leads on the emergence and shift of relevant social problems definitions.

The next four chapters, by Ball and Lilly, Weitz, Kitsuse, Murase and Yamamura, and Schneider, describe research stimulated by a definitional perspective. They provide an opportunity to comment specifically on some of the issues we have raised, as well as to suggest other relevant questions. In each instance, we want to emphasize the importance of definitions for organizational activities, thus reversing the more familiar argument that organization produces definition.

Richard A. Ball and J. Robert Lilly draw from their participant observation study of a "no-tell motel," a place for covert sexual assignations, to raise a question central to the definitional argument: How do ostensibly rule-breaking conditions and conduct escape collective definition as morally problematic? Ball and Lilly capture this issue succinctly in their title: "When is a 'Problem' Not a Problem?" While Marx writes about the outside researcher wanting to see inside a dirty organization, Ball and Lilly give us a view of how insiders in this motel work to maintain a definition that "nothing unusual is happening" (Emerson, 1970), and strive to control various physical and symbolic features of the setting so as to prevent any dirty data from becoming intrusively visible.

This problem relates to Howard Becker's discussion of "secret" (1963) or "potential" (1973) deviance: those situations in which a certain line of conduct has taken place but is either not perceived as an instance of this or that kind of deviance, or is simply not visible to audiences who might be expected to view it as such.

We dispose quickly of a dilemma that plagued Becker's early formulation, the "secret deviant." If social problems are, as we have argued, definitional activities, and a situation contains no such activities, then no social problem exists. A documentable condition or line of conduct may exist which may be studied in its own right, but a social problem does not.

The sociologist's warrant to recognize and document *potentially* problematic conditions is the viability of such definitions among participants, including, of course, the sociologist. Marx is concerned precisely with such dirty conduct that has not come to light. Organization members' attempts to restrict outsider access to records of such conduct speak to the common condition not of cultural dopism (cf. Garfinkel, 1967), but rather of wisdom about one's own cultural context, and sensitivity to its position relative to other cultural contexts. Erving Goffman (1959, 1963) has described social life as an on-going drama in which we spend a great deal of time and energy presenting "faces" we know ourselves not quite to possess, protecting our actual selves from the feared discredit disclosure might bring, and shifting "roles" first for one drama and audience, then for another.

Ball and Lilly's chapter contributes to our understanding of this "deflection" work by portraying how a collection of people, the motel owner, staff, and a few "wise" outsiders, cooperate to present a conventional organizational face. They demonstrate, for instance, that by cultivating sensitivities to three potentially critical outside audiences—the "morally concerned citizenry," police, and motel patrons—owner and staff prevent the motel from becoming the center of social problem activities, while other, similar establishments in the area have become so involved and have gone out of business.

Ball and Lilly's analysis details some of the complexity in these everyday actors' lay theories of trouble (cf. Emerson and Messinger, 1977) and how to avoid it. On the one hand, motel staff attend carefully to controlling *conditions.* They seem to know that, in the face of moral righteousness, an establishment dedicated specifically and solely to illicit sexual pleasure might not thrive if it *publicly* became the object of, a "problem *for,*" avowed crusaders or the police. At the same time, however, these participants have learned the power of definition. *They* know what goes on in their motel, and they know that the police and various others, perhaps even including some of the "morally concerned citizenry," know. At the same time, their work goes on unmolested, through some more or less precarious moments. The motel has operated thus for some twenty-five years!

This experience teaches these participants the importance of definition and symbolic conformity, and that they must develop a very keen sense of the social climate of opinion or supposed opinion. Ball and Lilly show that motel staff attend to the complex interaction between changes in relevant conditions (e.g., police "wars" on such establishments, whether or not X-rated movies shown on an office television can be seen from the street, naive people who might wander in and "cause trouble," and even the placement of windows, garage doors, and laundry facilities) and definitions believed likely by moral crusaders, the police, and regular patrons. It becomes clear that, while the social definitional student of social problems can focus attention only or primarlily on definitional activities, members (a category that can, of course, include the sociologist of social problems, as Marx' chapter shows) who have personal investments in maintaining certain definitions of their work and situations cannot afford to ignore what they believe to be a complex connection between the two. In any case, it is their definitions both of others' definitions as well as of "objective conditions" that provide grounds for working to keep the motel out of trouble.

While the staff and owner of the motel described by Ball and Lilly worked hard to prevent a social problem from developing, the past two decades in American society have witnessed a growing number of instances where morally tainted people have, to the surprise of some and the consternation of others, done just the opposite; namely, they have sought to create trouble. As John Kitsuse (1980) has argued, various deviants and devalued people have "come out all over" to create rather than prevent social problems. Rose Weitz, in her chapter, "From Accommodation to Rebellion: Tertiary Deviance and the Radical Redefinition of Lesbianism," details a segment of one case of this more general phenomenon. Weitz draws data from a systematic content analysis of the lesbian periodical, *The Ladder,* published between 1956 and 1972, to show the dramatic shift in how certain key participants defined lesbianism, homosexuality, the homophile movement, and themselves. She suggests that these changing definitions were a necessary condition for the rise of the lesbian and lesbian-feminist communities in the 1970s.

Weitz details how definitions of lesbianism shifted from apolitical and accommodative ones in the earliest issues of *The Ladder*, to a view of the mutual human and civil rights due lesbians in the middle 1960s, and finally, to a radical political redefinition of the lesbian and her relationship to other women and the society, beginning in the issues around 1970. A theme central to Weitz's analysis is that these changing definitions should not be seen as merely refractory to organizational changes conventionally defined as the "homophile movement" and "gay liberation." Quite to the contrary, she suggests that changes in the meanings of lesbianism, women, and society found in *The Ladder* facilitated, even enabled, these and other organizational developments. Weitz's analysis shows us one way to conceptualize and study definitional activities as analytically independent of organizational ones. She allows us to see how the availability and subsequent use of definitions have consequences for how people act, plan strategy, and develop political alliances and oppositions.

With the rise of lesbianism as a radical-feminist question and the definition of lesbianism as first and foremost a women's issue, the lesbian was defined increasingly as an example, if not the exemplar, of the "woman-identified woman"; it was a choice *by* women *for* women "in a society which only values men." In transforming lesbianism from an issue defined in terms of "homosexuality" and sexual "preference" to one on which, some argued, the entire structure of feminist philosophy turned, *The Ladder* and other cultural institutions of the lesbian community gradually gained a considerably wider audience. If lesbianism was to be a "women's issue," then certainly it would come to the attention of already established women's groups.

These new definitions probably operated on both a private, personal, as well as a more public level. For the woman who had questioned feelings about her sexuality, but had only the dominant illness rhetoric with which to make sense of those feelings, these changes in meaning could open hundreds of private closet doors. As lesbianism was considered less a bio-physiological or psychic curse with which one had to live, it became more a personal quality that, regardless of origin, should not be grounds for disenfranchisement; and finally, as a desired moral choice, women who had not done so before were able not only to consider (that is, "think about") themselves as lesbian, but also to *act* lesbian. As Weitz says, "Once lesbianism becomes defined as a sensible choice, it becomes reasonable to encourage women to choose lesbianism." Beyond the routine, private choices that this entailed, many women would also become "political lesbians," public actors who would organize to demand far-reaching social change.

One theme in Weitz's analysis of the impact of these new, positive definitions of lesbianism is that publicly presented and championed meanings can be used by people in everyday settings to transform what Mills (1959) called "personal troubles" into autobiographical instances of social issues. This relationship between "troubles" or "problems" experienced in one's daily life, on the one hand, and framing them as "social problems," on the other, is a topic we only have begun to address.

In the final two chapters of this volume, John I. Kitsuse, Anne E. Murase, and Yoshiaki Yamamura, in *"Kikokushijo:* The Emergence and Institutionalization of an Educational Problem in Japan," and Joseph W. Schneider, in "Morality, Social Problems, and Everyday Life," present data that bear on this question. Kitsuse, Murase, and Yamamura describe the origins, development, and institutional accommodations of the *"kikokushijo* problem" in Japan. The object of attention are Japanese school children whose executive and professional parents take them abroad for varying periods in pursuit of their own career development. Upon returning to Japan, these upper-middle class parents discover, much to their chagrin, that their children are educationally disadvantaged by their sojourn abroad. In the highly competitive educational system, the *kikokushijo* are conceived by school personnel to be deficient, not only academically but culturally and socially as well. While it is apparent that such treatment might create individual and possibly "personal" problems for these returning students, the constructionist perspective directed the research to the process by which the educational situation of the *kikokushijo* was transformed into a social problem.

In their investigation of this process, Kitsuse and his associates identify how a diverse "cast of characters," ranging from officials in prestigious and influential government agencies to informally organized groups of businessmen's wives, became participants in defining "the *kikokushijo* problem." Interviews with these participants produced data to show how the educational situation of the *kikokushijo,* which might have been experienced as individual cases of bureaucratic injustice, was transformed through claims-making activities against the practices of the educational system. The authors examine the ideological phrasing of those claims to suggest how the institutional accommodations they elicited express the emerging consciousness and concern about the value and costs of the "internationalization" of Japanese society.

In the closing chapter, Schneider raises the question of how people in various everyday settings use moral talk to define and, in some cases, make claims against the conduct of others. The specific case in point is cigarette smoking. Those interviewed include people strongly opposed to smoking, along with some smokers themselves. In addition to their general reactions or "loose moral talk" about smoking and smokers, anti-smoking respondents told of various specific situations, in both public places as well as their own homes, in which they were confronted by people smoking, and what they did, said, and did not do or say, in response. Smokers were asked to describe their experiences in such places and in particular their response to being asked not to smoke.

Schneider argues these data suggest that moral work, making claims against others and their conduct, is difficult, fraught with various risks that make "suffering in silence" a common experience. It appears that only in situations where aggrieved non-smokers could invoke a rhetoric or vocabulary of socially legitimate rules, e.g., some health problem or physical vulnerability, laws—city ordinances, or private regulations against smoking, a sense of one's "rights" being violated, or prerogatives of private property such as in one's home or car—were such claims likely to be made. If some representative of the rule-making authority were available, people called on them rather than making the request themselves. In one's own home, it was not simply a question of ownership determining rule enforcement. Respondents often spoke of their concern to not give offense to smoking guests, of losing friendships, and appearing too much like the "Blue Nose," self-righteous moral entrepreneur Becker (1963) has described.

Definitions can be consequential for subsequent social and political activity. If there are no such frames of meaning available, or if the participants involved cannot make a connection between such moral vocabularies and their own experience, social problems will not emerge from or be vitalized in such everyday, routine settings. While the parents of *kikokushijo* saw clearly that their complaints should be directed to educational officials, the anti-smoking respondents Schneider interviewed could only "raise" their claims-making activities to an "official" level on a situational basis, in places where someone else had made rules and in which representatives of such authority were available as enforcers. This suggests, apropos of the anti-smoking campaigns that have occurred in America (see Markle and Troyer, 1979; Troyer and Markle, 1983), that when moral rhetoric is made available through mass media and public crusades, people in everyday situations may couch their own claims against smoking in these terms. But translating "good reasons" into rules actually applied in a face-to-face interaction is perilous work. Those able to do it may distinguish themselves in others' eyes, but at the price of their reputations as "regular," "normal" people.

If this volume contributes to fruitful discussion of social problems theory, we will consider our efforts a success. The social constructionist viewpoint is still very much an open intellectual terrain. Similar to the intentions of those who began what has come to be called the "labeling" tradition in the sociology of deviance, we do not suggest this perspective on social problems addresses all questions equally well. It does, however, encourage attention to issues that traditional, condition-based and normative perspectives do not. This volume, along with a number of research reports that have appeared recently in the journal *Social Problems* and elsewhere, define and clarify a range of empirical and theoretical ideas that bear on these questions. We hope this volume stimulates more research on social problems, what they are, how they develop, and with what social consequences.

REFERENCES

Becker, Howard S.
    1963   Outsiders. New York: Free Press.
    1967   "Whose side are we on?" Social Problems 14: 239–247.
    1973   "Labeling theory reconsidered." Pp. 177–208 in H. S. Becker, Outsiders. New York:
            Free Press.
Emerson, Joan P.
    1970   "Nothing unusual is happening." Pp. 208–222 in Tomotsu Shibutani (ed.), Human
            Nature and Collective Behavior: Papers in Honor of Herbert Blumer. Englewood
            Cliffs, NJ: Prentice-Hall.
Emerson, Robert M. and Sheldon L. Messenger
    1977   "The micro-politics of trouble." Social Problems 25: 121–134.
Fuller, Richard C.
    1938   "The problem of teaching social problems." American Journal of Sociology 45:
            415–435.
Garfinkel, Harold
    1967   Studies in Ethnomethodology. Englewood Cliffs, NJ: Prentice-Hall.
Goffman, Erving
    1959   The Presentation of Self in Everyday Life. Garden City, NY: Anchor.
    1963   Stigma. Englewood Cliffs, NJ: Prentice-Hall.
Kitsuse, John I.
    1980   "Coming out all over: Deviants and the politics of social problems." Social Prob-
            lems 28: 1–13.
Kitsuse, John I. and Aaron Cicourel
    1963   "A note on the uses of official statistics." Social Problems 12: 131–139.
Markle, Gerald E. and Ronald J. Troyer
    1979   "Smoke gets in your eyes: Cigarette smoking as deviant behavior." Social Problems
            26: 611–625.
Marx, Gary T.
    1971   Muckraking Sociology: Research as Social Criticism. New York: Dutton.
Mills, C. Wright
    1959   The Sociological Imagination. New York: Oxford University Press.
Spector, Malcolm
    1981   "Beyond crime: Seven methods for controlling troublesome rascals." Pp. 127–158
            in H. L. Ross (ed.), Law and Deviance. Beverly Hills, CA: Sage.
Spector, Malcolm and John I. Kitsuse
    1977   Constructing Social Problems. Menlo Park, CA: Cummings.
Troyer, Ronald J. and Gerald E. Markle
    1983.   Cigarettes: The Battle Over Smoking. Rutgers, NJ: Rutgers University Press.

1 Science as a claims-making activity: Implications for social problems research*

Naomi Aronson
Northwestern University

SCIENCE, SOCIAL PROBLEMS, AND THE SOCIOLOGY OF KNOWLEDGE

Recent developments in the sociology of science and in the study of social problems have brought both endeavors squarely within the purview of the sociology of knowledge. Both scientific facts and social problems are being analyzed as examples of the "social construction of reality" (Berger and Luckmann, 1966). In *Constructing Social Problems*, Spector and Kitsuse (1977) lay the groundwork for a sociology of knowledge approach to social problems by distinguishing between social problems and social conditions. Similarly, advocates of the *strong programme,* the sociology of knowledge approach to science, draw a distinction between scientific problems and natural conditions by suggesting that scientific facts are socially constructed (Barnes, 1974; Bloor, 1976; Mulkay, 1979).

Critics of the social constructionist agenda raise intuitive objections to both formulations. Common sense surely suggests that scientific facts must

*I would like to thank Howard Becker, Susan Bell, Peter Conrad, Arlene Kaplan Daniels, John Kitsuse, Allan Schnaiberg, Joseph Schneider, and Malcolm Spector for their comments.

The discussion of leukemia researchers is based on a paper I presented at the 1981 meetings of the Society for the Study of Social Problems: "Social and Scientific Models of Causality in Leukemia Research 1955–1975." I would like to thank the Northwestern University Cancer Center for funding, Kathryn Talley for research assistance, and Dr. Robert Miller of the National Cancer Institute for introducing me to the fruitful topic of leukemia research.

1

be caused by the natural world much the same way social problems must be caused by the social world; in both cases, objective conditions await discovery. Although encountering similar criticisms, constructionists in the sociology of social problems and those in the sociology of science respond differently to their critics in one important respect. Spector and Kitsuse argue that established precepts of the sociology of knowledge justify the constructionist agenda for the study of social problems. In contrast, advocates of the strong programme argue that the sociology of knowledge, too long stymied by epistemological and methodological inconsistencies, must itself be justified. They see their own constructionist agenda for science studies as the key to resolving these difficulties. The strong programme is presently at the cutting edge of the sociology of knowledge. By justifying the theoretical tenets and expanding the empirical applications of the sociology of knowledge, it helps sociologists of social problems to combat intuitive objections to the constructionist approach.

The most vigorous proponents (Bloor, 1976) and opponents of the sociology of knowledge (Meynell, 1977) agree that two inconsistencies obstruct the development of the discipline. The first inconsistency is the presupposition that only some knowledge—namely, false knowledge—is socially contingent. The notion that the sociology of knowledge should study how people come to believe in incorrect ideas dates back to Marx's discussion of false consciousness in his 1845 essay "The German Ideology." So Marxists have studied why the proletariat is not uniformly socialist in its political beliefs, while liberal scholars have wondered over the propensity of their fellow intellectuals for communist ideologies. If the task of the sociology of knowledge is to explain how false ideas come to be held as true, then the sociology of knowledge in effect appoints itself the judge of what is "true" and what is "false" (i.e., socially determined) knowledge. Obviously, this is an untenable position. The second inconsistency is the alternative presupposition that all knowledge is socially contingent. This implies that the sociology of knowledge could study all ideas without worrying about whether they are "true" or "false." But, at the same time, it means that the sociology of knowledge is itself contingent, and therefore has no more explanatory power than the ideas it seeks to explain. Further, this second presupposition raises the spector of relativism; surely no sensible person can agree that any one idea is as good as another. It seems that "true" ideas must somehow transcend their social origins.

Here, then, is the impasse: Either some knowledge is socially contingent and the sociology of knowledge is untenable, or all knowledge is socially contingent and the sociology of knowledge is untenable. The strong programme sets forth a two-front strategy for eliminating the impasse. The first front is methodological, the second is substantive. First, the dilemma can be eliminated by treating all ideas—whether true or false—alike. The sociologist should not evaluate knowledge claims, but show how they are produced and then verified or rejected by the relevant communities. This method not only eliminates the paradox of the sociology of knowledge as the arbiter of truth, but also reduces the paradox of the social contingency of the sociology of knowledge to a tautology. That knowledge is socially contingent does not affect its status as knowledge; nor should the sociology of knowledge be itself exempt from sociological analysis. Second, advocates of the strong programme argue that empirical studies of the genesis of scientific ideas should be the first priority for the sociology of knowledge.[1] After all, science has long been regarded as a bastion of certainty exempt from social contingencies. If scientific facts can be shown to have their origins in the social, rather than in the natural world, then objections to the sociology of knowledge must surely be put forever to rest; if scientific reality is socially constructed, there is no reality that is not socially constructed.

The strong programme's mandate to search for the origins of scientific ideas in social interaction rather than in nature represents a drastic revision of the traditional premises of both the sociology of science and the sociology of knowledge. Sociologists of science have studied the internal organization of the scientific community and its position in the wider society, but have, until recently, rejected the notion that scientific ideas themselves could be sociologically analyzed. According to Mulkay (1979), there are three important epistemological assumptions underlying the traditional sociological view of science. The first assumption is that the natural world has an objective, orderly existence independent of the observer. The second assumption is that theoretical propositions concerning the natural world can be tested to determine whether they are consistent with observable facts. The third assumption is that, as a result of continuous testing and rejection of theories that do not fit the facts, cumulative growth of scientific knowledge occurs, through which more and more comes to be known about the underlying order of nature. Thus Mannheim (1936:116), implicitly sharing these epistemological assumptions, held that the natural sciences directly apprehended the reality of the physical world and concluded that social influences within science could only be an impediment to the discovery of truth. Similarly, Barber (1952) and Merton (1973) argued that liberal democracies, by fostering a free market of ideas and by insulating the academy from the pressures of political or religious dogma, provide the social climate most conducive to scientific progress. In sum, the traditional metaphor for science has been a search for truth in which the goal is to obtain a clear reflection of the world, as free as possible from distorting influences.

---

[1]For a recent critique of the accomplishments of the strong programme's empirical agenda, see Woolgar (1981) and the replies by Barnes (1981) and Mackenzie (1981) in the same volume.

According to the traditional view, then, scientific development occurs to the degree that social and subjective influences on knowledge are successfully neutralized.

In contrast to the traditional view, Kuhn's (1970) *The Structure of Scientific Revolutions* casts doubt on the cumulative nature of scientific progress, and argues that the fate of scientific theories depends upon social movements within the scientific community, thus opening the way for a revised view of the relationship between scientific knowledge, scientific communities, and society as a whole. The strong programme draws heavily on Kuhn's fundamentally sociological interpretation of the history of science, but is also indebted to less celebrated contributions to the recent literature on the philosophy of science. According to Mulkay (1979), the first important epistemological tenet of the revised sociological view of science is that the orderliness of the natural world is an aspect of scientists' accounts of the world, not to be confused with the nature of the world itself. The second tenet is that the facts against which theories are tested are not independent, direct observations, but are themselves imbued with underlying theoretical assumptions. Thus observation is inseparable from interpretation, and therefore interpretation in science, as in other cultural contexts, is a negotiated order resulting from processes of social interaction. According to the revised view, then, the social world is not a potential intrusion on scientific progress, but rather it is the very origin of scientific knowledge, which is a cultural artifact.

Whatever the epistemological justifications, however, the assertion that scientific knowledge is socially constructed seems to fly in the face of the certainty of scientific facts. Collins compares the difficulty in conceptualizing the process by which scientific ideas are constructed to that of visualizing how the ship gets into the bottle: "It is not easy to accept that the ship was ever just a bundle of sticks" (1975:205). But we must realize that the products of science are not the same as the processes of science; the sources on which we traditionally depend for our understanding of science systematically conceal and distort these processes. Kuhn (1970) has shown, for example, that science texts misrepresent the history of their discipline, editing out alternative directions—whether one considers them dead-ends, missed opportunities, or merely competing paradigms—so as to give the impression of the steady accumulation of facts. Others have noted that the conventions of scientific writing—such as the use of the third person voice, the formal account of procedures, and the legitimating function of citations—all have the effect of drawing the reader's attention away from the activities of scientists and focusing it on the results of their work (Gilbert, 1977; Gusfield, 1981). As a result, we picture the scientist as passively "finding" or "discovering" natural phenomena rather than interpreting or even, perhaps, creating them. In sum, retrospective accounts of scientific investigation, both original research papers by scientists and secondary studies by historians of science, sacrifice historical accuracy to the conventions of scientific discourse. In contrast to the impression of the certainty of scientific facts that retrospective accounts convey, recent ethnographic studies of scientific laboratories, which I discuss below, have begun to document the processes by which scientific facts are socially constructed.

So far I have argued that, in carrying out its mission to subject scientific ideas to sociological analysis, the strong programme is revitalizing the theoretical tenets and empirical applications of the sociology of knowledge. In doing so, it contributes to the advance of the sociology of social problems. But, as I will show in the following sections, there are two other respects in which contemporary science studies are relevant to the sociology of social problems. First, on the basis of recent ethnographic studies, I will argue that in respect to its internal relations—the interaction among scientists—science is a claims-making activity that has certain parallels to social problems. Second, on the basis of my own case studies, I will argue that in its external relations—the interaction of scientists with nonscientists—science is a claims-making activity that serves as an ongoing arena for the social construction of social problems.

SCIENCE AS A CLAIMS-MAKING ACTIVITY

Taken as a whole, the strong programme forces us to redefine the nature of scientific work. The traditional epistemological view—that science is discovery—suggests that the key interaction in scientific work is between the scientist and nature. The revised epistemological view—that science is interpretation—suggests that the key interaction is between the scientist and the scientific community's collectively negotiated cognitive order.[2] In other words, the key interaction is between the scientist and other scientists. Viewed this way, claims-making is the essence of scientific work. As individuals, or even research teams, scientists cannot make discoveries, they can only make claims to discovery. For a claim actually to count as a discovery, other scientists must accredit it by recommending that it be published in a reputable journal and by citing it in their own articles. As Brannigan (1981) has recently shown, we are quite deceived by prevailing psy-

---

[2]This does not mean, of course, as some critics have accused, that the constructionist view holds that there is no nature, or that science is merely a matter of opinion, or that reason is nothing and mob psychology all. The scientific collectivity, after all, negotiates about *something*. Although scientists are forever putting nature into conceptual boxes, nature, in Kuhn's words, "fights back." The resulting anomalies are, however, according to Kuhn (1970), only a necessary but not a sufficient condition for scientific reconceptualization.

chological models that locate scientific discovery in the mind of the individual. Psychological models equate scientific discovery with the cognitive experiences of gestalt shift and the affective experiences of insight. But no matter how personally compelling the insights of an individual researcher, only the scientific community can judge the validity of his or her contribution to the advance of knowledge. Operations on the physical world provide the basis for scientists' claims for the accreditation of their contribution to knowledge, but do not in and of themselves constitute knowledge. Thus, the main task of the scientist is to make what I call *cognitive claims* about findings to other members of the research community who have the power to accredit them, thereby conferring the status of scientific fact. In this section, I draw on the empirical findings of recent ethnographic studies of scientific laboratories to support my contention that first, science is a claims making activity and that, second, as such it has certain parallels with social problems.

The most ambitious of the recent ethnographic studies of science is Latour and Woolgar's (1979) *Laboratory Life: The Social Construction of Scientific Facts.* The authors spent two years observing a neuroendocrinology laboratory devoted to the study of releasing factors, discrete chemical substances by which the brain controls the endocrine system. Latour and Woolgar argue that, from the scientist's point of view, nature is disorderly because there are always alternative explanations for any one observation. Accordingly, scientists engage in a daily struggle to impose order on nature's "disorder" by ruling out alternative explanations. In doing so, scientists compete with each other, each attempting to convince the scientific community that his or her explanations should be retained and a rival's discarded. By following a dispute that culminated in the "discovery" of a particular substance, Thyrotropin Releasing Factor (TRF), the authors conclude that, contrary to common belief, the status of fact follows from, rather than precedes, the resolution of disagreements among scientists. In other words, "facts" are an account given by scientists to explain why they no longer consider it worthwhile to dispute a colleague's knowledge claims.

Latour and Woolgar defend their unorthodox view of science by demonstrating how all aspects of laboratory life—even those which, at first glance, seem purely technical or material—are epiphenomena of social relations among scientists. For example, apparatus in the laboratory can be viewed as, in Latour and Woolgar's terms, "reified theory," or, better fitting the present discussion, "reified claims." The products of past scientific controversies, given the existence of production and distribution networks, become part of present technical repertoire. For example, when a laboratory worker uses the nuclear magnetic resonance spectrometer to check the purity of chemical compounds, he or she is using "the outcome of some twenty years of basic physics research" (Latour and Woolgar, 1979:66). Just as arguments are transformed into apparatus, apparatus is transformed into arguments. Many of the objects of scientific work can exist as objects of scientific work—whatever their status in nature—only by virtue of the existence of appropriate instrumentation. Indeed, Latour and Woolgar argue that scientific activities are directed not toward nature, but toward an "agonistic field" consisting of operations on statements which are a matter of contention. The notion of an agonistic field blends attributes of science that have heretofore been regarded independently, either as social (e.g., competition, communication) or epistemological (e.g., fact, validity). The collective goal of scientific activity is to move claims along a spectrum of statement types from cautious, carefully qualified speculation to taken for granted fact. This is accomplished, from the viewpoint of the individual scientist, by arguing so persuasively that others are convinced that they have not been persuaded, but that the facts of nature speak for themselves and it would be foolhardy to challenge them.

An agonistic field, then, is a field of contention, much the same in science as in law, politics, or games: "The negotiations as to what counts as proof or what constitutes a good assay [chemical analysis] are no more or less disorderly than any argument between lawyers or politicians" (Latour and Woolgar, 1979:237). Latour and Woolgar compare the field of contention in the construction of a scientific fact to the game of Go. Scientists impose order on nature by making strategic moves to reduce the number of equally probable explanations of any single observation. In the game of Go, the first move may be made on any square, but successive moves are constrained by previous plays, and the game ends when there is no place left to move. In science, accepted facts, techniques and instrumentation—all results of earlier controversies—constitute the previous moves of the game. The game ends when scientists perceive alternative explanations as highly improbable. This is not just a logical concession; it is also a tactical concession, because it is based on scientists' calculations of the resources required versus the likely payoff for challenging a given claim. Thus "the set of statements considered too costly to modify constitute what is referred to as reality" (Latour and Woolgar, 1979:243). Therefore, although we speak of the resolution of scientific controversies as if it were a matter of the facts closing the case, Latour and Woolgar argue that what actually happens is that scientists close the case and then attribute their action to the existence of facts.

Other ethnographic studies of science also support my contention that science is a claims-making activity. For example, Knorr (1977), based on her observation of a laboratory studying plant proteins, argues that the individual scientist's goal is not truth, but success. Rather than describing reality, as implicit in the language of truth and hypothesis testing, scientists seize perceived opportunities for solutions and strive to "make the stuff work," an ad hoc constructive activity Knorr calls "tinkering." "What counts as success is determined by the field and the agent's position in the field" (Knorr, 1977:690). Two specific instances of the determinants of success are taken up in Collins' (1975) study of the replication of experiments in physics. In the case of a special type of laser called a "TEA laser," no matter how explicit the instructions given for duplicating the apparatus, only those scientists who worked directly with another scientist who had already built a functioning TEA laser were able to duplicate it themselves. In the case of the TEA laser, Collins concludes that there was tacit scientific knowledge that could only be transmitted through processes of enculturation. Surprisingly, in a second case, scientists attempting to detect gravitational radiation, a new and controversial procedure, were not at all concerned about replicating each other's experiments but were engaged in competition over what procedures and modifications of instrumentation were to count as competent experiments, and, by implication, how the nature of gravitational radiation was to be defined. Using Collins' data, Mulkay (1979:78, 79) observes that:

> Both the social and technical culture of science . . . provide members with flexible symbolic resources which . . . each experimenter (or research group) uses . . . to reveal the inadequacies of others' findings and to support his own claims.

As the ethnographies above suggest, Mulkay's observation can, I think, be pushed much further. The point is not just that the culture of science provides resources for the competition among scientists' claims, but that such claims making is the core of science. The work of scientists is to make what I call *cognitive claims.* These are claims concerning research findings directed toward a specialized research community for the purpose of transforming claims to certified scientific knowledge. In the case that Latour and Woolgar (1979:147) studied, scientists first made competing claims about the existence of Thyrotropin Releasing Factor (TRF); second, about what category of chemical compounds TRF belonged to; and finally, about the specific chemical structure of TRF. In the example of TRF, cognitive claims include (unsuccessful claims are in parenthesis):

1. "There is (is not) a TRF"
2. "It is (might not be/is not) a peptide."
3. "TRF is Pyro-Glu-His-Pro-NH$_2$ (OH/OMe)"

Both the audience and the content of cognitive claims is internal, that is, located within a specific research community and its specific research concerns. In the next section, however, I will show that scientists' claims-making activities are by no means confined within the scientific community, a point of special interest to the sociology of social problems.

Using the perspective of science as a claims-making activity, I want to draw some parallels between science and social problems. If, as Spector and Kitsuse suggest, there is a "natural history" of social problems, so too there may be a "natural history" of scientific problems. For example, Spector and Kitsuse (1977:143) observe that the initial stage in the construction of social problems entails efforts, in Mills' (1959) terms, "to transform private troubles into public issues." In the same fashion, a scientist faces the task of turning experimental observations into "publicly accredited factual knowledge' (Gilbert, 1976:281). Successful claims-making, in both the social and the scientific arenas, involves—at the very least—skilled documentation, the ability to command the attention of the appropriate audiences, and access to resources needed to defend claims against criticism. Indeed, Mitroff (1974) suggests that successful scientists, rather than conforming to the Mertonian norm of disinterestedness, display a tenacious attachment to their ideas—not unlike, perhaps, the zeal of a moral reformer. Finally, in both spheres, successful claims-making campaigns obliterate the evidence of their own existence; successful claims become facts that seem to exist independently of any human activity. The systematic obliteration of the role that human agency plays in the generation of "self-evident" facts has been documented for both successful scientific and social problem claims.

Latour and Woolgar (1979) traced the progressive reification of a scientific idea by showing that, as the existence of TRF became accepted as fact, the scientific literature ceased to cite the researchers who first proposed it. The conventions of scientific discourse require that claims be backed up by reference to the claimants' activities (i.e., methods) and the related activities of others (i.e., literature). In contrast, the documentation of "known facts" is considered unnecessary. Discussing the place of citation practices in the reward system of science, Hagstrom (1965) pointed out that scientific knowledge is a peculiar kind of property; the scientist can only own it by giving it away—i.e., making it publicly available to the entire scientific community. Combining Hagstrom's point with Latour and Woolgar's findings, we can view claims under contention as a liability; the scientist making the claim is held responsible for it in the sense of being accountable. We can view successful claims as an asset; the scientist is responsible in the sense of receiving credit for a contribution. Should the successful claim be rejected in the future, as often happens, the entire community rather than the individual scientist will be held accountable for the "error."[4] But if the entire community is responsible, the "error" is not "really" anybody's "fault"; therefore it appears that "no one" is responsible for what "everyone" knows.

An important exception to the convention that successful claims are

---

[3]Unless, of course, the responsible scientist is accused of fraud, which is error with malicious intent.

divorced from human agency is the practice of eponymy, naming a phenomenon after its finder, e.g., Ohm's Law. However, findings thus honored
are a miniscule proportion of the output of normal science. Further, in
memorializing the individual, the practice promotes a "great man" theory of
the history of science that further obscures the social nature of scientific
knowledge. One notable convention of the "great man" view of science is
attributing important ideas to unaccountable flashes of insight, which are
considered to be the mark of scientific genius. Latour and Woolgar (1979:169)
analyzed the following typical account of scientific genius, selected from
their interviews with laboratory researchers:

> Slovick proposed an assay but his assay did not work everywhere; people
> could not repeat it; some could, some could not. Then one day Slovick *got the
> idea* that it could be related to the selenium content of the water . . . and
> indeed Slovick's idea was right . . . [the assay] . . . worked wherever the se-
> lenium content of the water was high.

Further analysis reveals that Slovick did not simply "get an idea," a phrase
that suggests a process akin to biblical revelation. He taught in an institution
that required graduate students to study outside their own field and to
present their findings to a departmental seminar. One student presented a
paper on the relationship between the selenium content of the water and the
incidence of certain cancers in various geographical locations. Slovick applied this idea to the problem with his assay. In this example, the conventional account of genius obscures the role that social interactions and institutional arrangements play in the generation and dissemination of
scientific ideas.

Becker (1973) and Gusfield (1981) documented the obliteration of
human agency in the construction of the social problems of marijuana and
alcohol abuse, respectively. Becker showed that the 1937 federal Marijuana
Tax Act, intended to eradicate marijuana use, resulted from a carefully
conducted campaign by the Treasury Department's Bureau of Narcotics.
Although there had been no spontaneous public outcry against the drug,
during the years 1932–1937 magazines and newspapers published anti-mari-
juana literature prepared by the Bureau of Narcotics. For example, five of the
seventeen stories printed during this period repeated the story of a "youthful
addict in Florida" who "had killed his father, mother, two brothers, and a
sister" (cited by Becker, 1973:142). Stories prepared from Narcotics Bureau
information did not necessarily cite the Bureau, thus giving the impression
that scattered observers had all independently recognized the problem. In
presenting the bill to Congress, Treasury Department officials noted that
"the leading newspapers of the United States have recognized the seriousness of the problem and . . . advocated federal legislation" (cited by
Becker, 1973:143). Similarly, Gusfield found that statistics on alcohol abuse

were widely disseminated without reference to the original sources of these statistics nor to the methods by which they were derived. Although the original statistics were "guesstimates," they gained the status of "fact" by being repeated, without qualification or citation, in newspapers, television announcements, and Congressional testimony. "At each step in the process, from data to interpretation to transmission, a more factually authoritative world was made" (Gusfield, 1981:60).

Critics will protest that comparing the construction of scientific and social problem "facts" in this way is a shaky argument. After all, the fact of TRF is the result of careful scientific investigation. In contrast, the "facts" of marijuana and alcohol abuse are the result of unscientific method, allowing unsubstantiated claims to be widely disseminated. The point, however, is not the quality of the data showing the existence of TRF or of a drug problem. The point is that in successful claims-making, evidence of human actions disappears. Facts appear to arise from their objective status in the world, independent of human action. Facts are considered to be facts just because they can be divorced from particular individuals or particular circumstances; it seems that anyone who cared to look could observe them. This assumption is the same both for science and for social problems.

SCIENCE AS A CLAIMS-MAKING ACTIVITY: INTERPRETIVE CLAIMS

Although the core of scientific work is making cognitive claims to other scientists, scientists' claims-making is not confined to within the research community. For example, Latour and Woolgar (1979:72) found that almost one third of the total publications of the neuroendocrinological laboratory they studied addressed readers outside the releasing factors field. Twenty-seven percent of all papers "summarized the state of the art for scientists outside of the field." Five percent of all papers addressed lay readers of journals such as *Scientific American* or *Science Year* and physicians who keep up with recent progress in biology through journals such as *Clinician* or *Contraception*. Scientists' claims to outsiders differ from cognitive claims not only in their audience, but also in their content and purpose. When scientists make cognitive claims to fellow scientists working in a highly specialized problem area, the content of the claim refers to research findings, and the purpose of the claim is to certify scientific knowledge. In contrast, scientists' claims to outsiders refer to the broader implications of research findings for the particular concerns of the nonspecialist audience. Because the purpose of such claims is to explain expert knowledge to nonexperts, I call them *interpretive claims*. In this section, I am primarily concerned with interpretive claims to nonscientists, although scientists also make interpretive claims when they explain their own work to scientists in other specialties. First, I will show that conventional views of science disregard interpretive claims-making; at first glance, such activities appear neither as scientific work nor as claims. Second, I will argue that, contrary to the conventional view, interpretive claims are indeed claims because they legitimate science as socially necessary, and that they are indeed scientific work because such legitimation is essential to the existence of organized science. Finally, I will describe three types of interpretive claims: technical, cultural, and social problem.

At first glance, interpretive claims-making seems peripheral to the main concerns of science, and therefore not "really" scientific work. First, interpretive claims-making seems peripheral because it is a second-order activity which depends on the existence of cognitive claims-making. After all, cognitive claims-making produces scientific knowledge; if there were no scientific knowledge, there would be nothing to explain to nonscientists. Second, interpretive claims-making seems peripheral because scientists themselves view it that way. The activities which I classify as interpretive claims-making have a lower status among scientists than those I classify as cognitive claims-making. One example is the low status of applied research as compared to basic research. Another example is the wariness with which efforts to popularize science are regarded, whether such efforts are initiated by scientists or by the mass media (Goodfield, 1981). At best, efforts to popularize science are viewed as public relations; at worst, as cheap sensationalism; but never as legitimate science.

Ironically, because the popularization of science is a low status activity, only well-established scientists can afford to do it. Addressing nonscientific audiences uses time and energy that could be spent on research, writing for scientific journals, or attending professional meetings; it may even tarnish a scientist's reputation. For example, the prestigious *New England Journal of Medicine* refuses to publish studies if the authors have previously discussed their research in the mass media. Thus, interpretive claims are most likely to be made by "scientific statesmen" (Blume, 1974), eminent scientists who serve on science advisory bodies. By participating in public policy-making about science and technical issues, statesmen represent their discipline to the world at large, interacting more often with other scientific and political elites than with the rank and file members of their own profession. Scientific statesmen are generally administrators of scientific institutions. Although they must be well respected as researchers in order to obtain such positions, once they take administrative posts other scientists tend to regard them as having given up their research career, as no longer "really" scientists.[4]

---

[4]While taking up science administration symbolizes that a researcher is past his prime, taking up the study of the history of science symbolizes that he is truly over the hill. The history

Not only does it seem at first glance that interpretive claims are peripheral to science, but it also seems peculiar to call them claims. A claim is, according to the dictionary, "a demand of a right or a supposed right" or "an assertion . . . often made or . . . suspected of being made, without adequate justification" (cited in Spector and Kitsuse, 1977:78). How are scientists demanding something of lay audiences? They are certainly not asking lay audiences to certify their research findings. The audience receives information from the scientist, but is not competent to judge the technical merits of the information received. If scientists are "telling" when they impart information, how can they be "asking," as implied by the term *claim*? My answer is that, whatever the appearance, interpretive activities are always implicit claims in two respects. First, they are claims that particular scientific findings are useful, that is, relevant to the concerns of the particular audience being addressed. Second, they are claims that science is socially necessary. Whatever the findings of particular fields or particular scientists, or the concerns of particular audiences, on the whole, science is claimed to be so useful that it is essential to society. Thus, interpretive claims implicitly ask the audience to certify the social utility of research, and the content of the claim supplies the reason they should do so.

Whatever the appearance, interpretive claims are indeed claims, and they are essential, not peripheral, to the existence of organized science. Scientific communities can exist only if they are allocated a share of society's resources. Until about two centuries ago, this occurred on an ad hoc basis. Scientists either depended upon wealthy patrons to support their work or were themselves gentleman scholars who devoted their own wealth and leisure to scientific pursuits. The rapid growth of scientific knowledge in the past two hundred years is a result of the modern social organization of science, and not just of improvements in scientific theories and methods (Ben-David, 1971). First, science has been professionalized; science is now a vocation, not an avocation. Scientists devote themselves full time to their research and must be able to make a living at it. Second, the production of scientific knowledge has been industrialized (Ravetz, 1971), just as the production of most other goods and services has been industrialized in modern society. The rapid growth of scientific knowledge occurs in part because scientific work, as with textile or automobile production, is organized on a mass production basis. Modern scientific institutions can hardly be maintained by ad hoc arrangements; an ongoing commitment of resources is required.

Resources for science no longer come through individual benefactors, but from society as a whole: through private foundations, corporate contri-

of science was traditionally the province of retired scientists. With some exceptions, their work is now regarded with scorn or despair by professional historians of science.

butions, and, most importantly since World War II, government funding. In addition, science depends on society as a whole not only for material resources such as salaries, buildings, and equipment but also for moral or ideological resources. For example, able young persons are thought to be recruited into science not for the money—they might do better elsewhere—but because science is considered both intrinsically interesting and a contribution to humanity (Gustin, 1973). Corporations may sponsor research that has no prospect of immediate payoff in part because such endeavors often have profitable results in the long run, and in part because science is a worthwhile end in itself. Congressmen are willing to allocate money for research because their constituents agree, or can be convinced, that funds for science are justified. In sum, the ongoing existence of science depends, ultimately, upon the conviction among groups with authority over social resources that science is a worthwhile enterprise. Therefore, although interpretive claims-making is not a component of each and every individual scientist's work, it is necessary to the scientific community as a whole that *some* scientists engage in it.

Technical Interpretive Claims

One form of interpretive claims-making is technical advising activities. Government and industry make decisions in which understanding scientific issues is considered essential. In both the public and private sectors, scientists interpret research findings in the light of administratively defined objectives and contingencies. We are most familiar with the role of expert advisors in public policy decisions, because the issues on which scientists have been called to testify are often controversial (Nelkin, 1979; Schnaiberg, 1980). Government regulatory agencies depend on scientists to evaluate the risks posed by toxic substances in food (e.g., saccharin), in the workplace (e.g., vinyl chloride), and in the general environment (e.g., radiation from atomic testing or nuclear power plants). Congress has solicited scientists' and engineers' opinions of the effectiveness of military weapons systems. Economic policies take into account scientists' advice on energy resources or the likelihood of technological developments in various industries. Although farther removed from the limelight, scientists advise industry much as they advise government. Whether they serve as managerial consultants or laboratory researchers far removed from the executive office, industry employs scientists in the expectation that their knowledge will in one way or another advance the organization's goals.

Scientists undertake technical advising activities because there is a market for their services. However, in doing so they simultaneously maintain and expand the market for their services. Therefore the claims-making aspect of technical advising activities is most apparent when different groups of scientists give conflicting advice on the same issue. For example, Robbins and Johnston (1976) found that technical disagreements over how to measure lead in the environment and how to determine its physiological effects reflected the efforts of several competing scientific specialties to claim expert authority on the problem. In sum, technical advising activities constitute interpretive claims, because consumers of scientific knowledge have the power to certify the social utility of that knowledge and to provide material resources to certified scientists.

Cultural Interpretive Claims

A second form of interpretive claims making highlights the importance of science as a general cultural resource. While technical interpretive claims attempt to expand the total market for scientific expertise or to capture a share of that market for particular specialties, cultural interpretive claims attempt to develop ideological support for all of science as an end in itself. For example, Lewis Thomas, a prominent biomedical researcher who is president of the Sloan Kettering Cancer Center in New York City, recently argued in the Sunday *New York Times Magazine* that science education should be changed. Too many people—educators, parents, and students alike—regard science courses as preprofessional training. But science, Thomas contends, is not hard facts—"unambiguous, unalterable and end-lessly useful"—or "a search for mastery over nature"; science is an "art" which contemplates "the still imponderable puzzles of cosmology."

> An appreciation of what is happening in science today . . . ought to be a good
> in itself . . . part of the intellectual equipment of an educated person . . . .
> (Thomas 1982:93)

In addition to presenting science as "a good in itself," the cultural resource type of interpretive claim often attempts to develop ideological support for the autonomy of science. In the following example from Thomas' prize-winning *Lives of a Cell: Notes of a Biology Watcher,* he subtly and elegantly suggests that nonscientists should not try to interfere with scientists' work. He does this by comparing the wonders of science to the wonders of nature and of great works of art, all of which ultimately transcend humanity's puny attempts to predict or control them:

> Scientists at work have the look of creatures following genetic instructions . . .
> like an immense intellectual anthill. . . . In the midst of what seems . . . total
> disorder, with bits of information being scattered about . . . [seemingly] . . .
> as random and agitated as . . . bees in a disturbed . . . hive, there suddenly
> emerges, with the purity of a slow phrase of music, a single new piece of truth
> about nature. . . . It is the most powerful and productive of things human
> beings have . . . [done] . . . more effective than farming . . . or hunting or
> fishing, or building cathedrals or making money . . . . (Thomas 1974:118–119)

George Daniels, historian of American science, has called this sort of rhetoric on the part of scientists "schizophrenic" because it asserts that "utility is not to be a test of scientific work, but all knowledge will ultimately prove useful" (Daniels, 1967:1703). He traces the origin of such rhetoric to the 1870s and 1880s, when U.S. scientists found that the government funding they had obtained by promising practical results from their work had strings attached. For example, scientists working on the U.S. Geological Survey were attacked for studying paleontology and told to stick to exploring the nation's exploitable mineral wealth; they were even prevented from including "impractical" findings in government published scientific reports. Similarly, Mulkay (1976) argues that in the mid-twentieth-century American scientists attempted to justify public support for their work while circumventing government controls by arguing that science cultivates values important to the existence of a democratic society, such as impartiality, rationality, and honesty. In sum, interpretive claims which highlight the importance of science as a cultural resource generally justify both expenditures for science and the autonomy of science. In other words, society should support scientific research but not interfere with it; scientists alone should decide what projects to undertake and how to allocate resources.

Social Problem Interpretive Claims

A third form of interpretive claim, of special relevance to the sociology of social problems, asserts the existence of a social problem which a particular scientific specialty is uniquely equipped to solve. The phenomenon of the "medicalization of deviance," social problem claims-making on the part of physicians and other health professions, is a familiar one (Conrad and Schneider, 1980; Zola, 1972). But there is no equivalent accumulation of literature on the "scientization" (Cameron and Edge, 1979) of social problems. Indeed, the image of scientists as social problem "activists" is incompatible with the traditional view of the epistemology of scientific knowledge and the role of the scientist in society that I outlined in the first section of this essay. Bell (1980), however, shows that it was researchers, not practitioners, in the field of endocrinology who first claimed in the 1930s that new discoveries about hormones could be used to solve social problems by controlling human behavior. A notable alternative to the traditional view of scientists is that of Mazur, who, attempting to mediate a dispute between experts over the health risks of extremely high voltage electrical transmission lines, found that while it was possible—though difficult—to separate fact from value in the arguments raised by the adversaries, it was impossible—for political reasons—to persuade them to reconcile their differences. Mazur (1981:42) concludes that, when scientists disagree over technical issues, the dispute is often primarily "over political goals and only secondarily concerned with the veracity of scientific issues which are related to these goals," thereby suggesting that scientists do indeed act as social problem "activists."

Elsewhere I have described in detail the social problem claims of American nutrition researchers in the late nineteenth century (Aronson, 1982). From 1885 to 1900, American nutrition scientists struggled to establish their discipline at a time when resources for science were scarce but government and corporate concern over the labor movement abounded. They defined their field as the science of the physiological production and reproduction of labor power, and argued they could solve the labor problem in two ways. First, by studying human food requirements they could determine scientifically whether or not wages were adequate to supply the necessities of life. Second, by showing workers how to meet their food requirements economically they could improve workers' standard of living without forcing employers to pay higher wages. Thus, nutrition scientists argued that the problem of labor unrest was really a problem of nutrition, and proclaimed that the mission of their science was: "to teach the poor to live well on the half of what they now starve upon, to shame anarchy with universal sweet bread . . ." (Atwater, 1886) and thereby bring industrial peace.

There are three conditions under which scientists are likely to make the social problem type of interpretative claim. The first, as in the case of American nutrition research, is when a new discipline has no foothold in academe and therefore appeals to external constituencies to obtain material and political support for its work. The second condition is when public funds are at stake. In the post World War II era, scientific research has been increasingly underwritten by the government. Associated with this has been the call for a national science policy that will consider both social and scientific benefits in the allocation of research funds. Recently, the economic policies of the Reagan administration have intensified long standing concerns about the financial dependence of science on government. According to Senator Daniel Patrick Moynihan of New York, who is intimately familiar with the contingencies of both research and politics:

> Universities must now expect a long, for practical purposes permanent, regimen of pressure from the Federal Government to pursue this or that national purpose, often at variance with either the interest or the inclination of the universities themselves. (quoted in Freedman, 1982)

Rather than altering their research to fit government priorities, enterprising scientists will attempt to show that their existing research agendas are in the national interest. Enterprising scientists are likely to claim either that their work contributes to the solution of a recognized social problem, or that it will solve a previously unrecognized problem. A third condition under which social problem claims-making is likely to occur is when scientists are confronted by social movements to restrict their research, as in the case of public furor over recombinent DNA research. In the wake of this uproar, leading molecular biologists, whose specialty is the cutting edge of genetic research, have called upon their colleagues to take an active role in lobbying legislatures and educating the general public about the importance of their work. In the words of Nobel laureate David Baltimore, "the new biology has become the new politics" (cited in Fudenberg and Melnick, 1978:xi).

Finally, I want to emphasize that the three conditions I have noted above are likely to promote all three forms of interpretive claims, not just the social problem type. In their efforts to obtain public funding while maintaining professional autonomy, scientists will recount their technical accomplishments, will show how their endeavors enhance cultural values that are an end in and of themselves, and will point to social problems that they are uniquely capable of solving. However, I think that because the underlying theme of all three types of interpretive claims is the social utility of science, there is a tendency for the first two forms to be transformed into or subsumed by the social problem form. That is because almost anything that improves the human condition can, if the claimant chooses to pursue the tactic, be asserted to solve a social problem of some sort. In addition, while it is most likely that scientists will pursue the social problem tactic when attempting to obtain public funds, there is no reason why the same appeal cannot be made to private foundations or corporations. Indeed, American nutrition researchers made their claim that nutrition was a social problem to both the U.S. Department of Agriculture and the Carnegie Institution of Washington, a private foundation. The claim, however, was a far more important factor in obtaining federal funding than in obtaining foundation support.

An example from a recent book, *Science and the Cure of Diseases* by Efraim Racker, Albert Einstein Professor of Biochemistry and Molecular and Cellular Biology at Cornell University, shows how easily all forms of interpretive claims are transformed into the social problem type. The book was written in response to the 1976 Senate Health Subcommittee hearings that criticized the National Institutes of Health for wasting taxpayers' money on basic research instead of making targeted attempts to cure important diseases such as cancer, diabetes, and heart conditions. The author suggests that, if scientists face inadequate funding and growing restrictions on research, they have only themselves to blame for failing to communicate with the public. The format of the book, "letters to members of Congress," shows scientists how to go about remedying the problem. First, Racker makes the technical type of interpretive claim to Congress by recounting how past discoveries had unanticipated consequences for medical progress and by showing how some ongoing studies, which seem peripheral to major health problems, might actually have novel applications for medicine. Racker (1979:78) then makes claims for science as a cultural resource by "pleading" for "special treatment of science and scientists," because science is a valued end in itself; indeed, he believes, it is "the salvation of mankind." Racker concludes with a broadly defined social problem interpretive claim on behalf of science:

> The solutions to most problems—physical, economical, and psychological problems of crime and war; hate, discrimination, and oppression—are dependent on our understanding of their causes. History tells us that for over thousands of years we have made little progress in solving basic social problems. On the other hand, look at the extraordinary progress made in medicine during the past hundred years because of advances in biology. . . . The solutions to most problems besetting the human race will more likely come from scientific progress . . . than from political revolution. (Racker, 1979:94)

In order to show that social problem interpretive claims arise from the cognitive claims of particular groups of scientists, and not just from the general need of science as a whole to demonstrate its social utility, I will describe the conflicting cognitive and social problem interpretive claims made by three different groups of U.S. leukemia researchers from 1955 to 1975.

COGNITIVE AND SOCIAL PROBLEM INTERPRETIVE CLAIMS IN SCIENCE: THE CASE OF U.S. LEUKEMIA RESEARCH 1955–1975

From 1955 to 1975, leukemia research was a forum to air fundamental disagreements about the nature of cancer, as both a biological and social problem. The key questions were: What causes cancer? What should be done about it, especially by the government? Scientists' answers to the first question constitute cognitive claims; their answers to the second constitute social problem interpretive claims. I will restrict myself to describing the conflicting cognitive and social problem interpretive claims made by U.S. leukemia researchers. In conclusion, I will enumerate the sorts of questions that my case suggests for the sociological investigation of scientists' social problem claims-making. In other words, my purpose here is to show *that* scientists' cognitive claims give rise to social problem interpretive claims; the agenda for the sociology of social problems is to show *how* this happens and the conditions determining the fate of scientists' social problem interpretive claims.

Leukemia accounts for only five percent of all cancer deaths in the United States (Cairns 1979: 20–23), but investment in research on the disease has surpassed its relative importance as a public health problem. From 1955–1975, prominent oncologists regarded leukemia as "a window to the whole neoplastic problem" (Dameshek 1968:501), for two reasons. First, it was an easy type of cancer to study. Blood samples were easier to obtain and involved less risk to the patient than analyses of solid tumor specimens; the short latency period (about five years as opposed to twenty or more years for other human cancers), and rapid course of the disease, made it more accessible than other cancers to both clinical and experimental observation. Second and most important, was the identification of leukemia viruses in mammals, leading some researchers to believe that not only would a human leukemia virus be found, but that all human cancers would ultimately be shown to be caused by viruses. The viral hypothesis influenced all scientists working on cancer at the time, even those who rejected it.

By reviewing scientific publications, National Cancer Institute documents, and transcripts of congressional testimony, and by interviewing prominent leukemia researchers, I identified three major approaches to the study of human leukemia: environmental, genetic, and viral. Scientists representing each approach to leukemia made different cognitive and interpretive claims. The most fundamental point of disagreement was cognitive: the exact mechanism of leukemogenesis. To this day, the scientific evidence on the etiology of human leukemia remains inconclusive. The scientific groups also differed in their interpretive claims: how they explained the causes, prevention, and cure of leukemia to medical practitioners, national policy makers, and lay audiences. Based on its own definition of biological cause (cognitive claim), each group made a different recommendation (social problem interpretive claim) for government intervention to solve the social problem of leukemia and, by implication, all other cancers.

The earliest approach to leukemia was environmental; until the mid-1950s, scientists believed that all leukemia was caused by radiation (Cronkite, 1980). The environmentally oriented investigators were mostly epidemiologists and biostatisticians. At first, they studied people who had been exposed to radiation on the job or through medical treatment; later, they conducted long term follow up studies on the victims of Hiroshima and Nagasaki through the Atomic Bomb Casualty Commission (ABCC). At least one early investigator, E. P. Cronkite (1961), a noted hematologist, observed that some chemicals, particularly benzene, might induce leukemia, and suggested that any carcinogen which could be carried to the blood should be regarded as a potential leukemogen. However, chemical leukemogens were largely ignored until the 1970s, when labor unions pressed for federal standards on occupational exposure to benzene.[5]

Surprisingly, few environmentally oriented leukemia researchers have

---

[5]This draws our attention to how social problem claims affect the research agendas of scientists. But in this paper, I am interested in how the research agendas of scientists might lead them to make social problem claims.

ever claimed to policy makers or the general public that leukemia is an environmentally caused cancer. Most agree that, first, known leukemogens seem to account for only a very small proportion of all leukemia cases, and second, that almost all industrialized regions show about the same rate of leukemia—implying that the environment makes no difference (Heath, 1975). They have, however, used their epidemiological data to refute the viral hypothesis and to argue that the government was spending too much money looking for a human leukemia virus while underfunding other potential solutions to the cancer problem.

However, a small, but vocal, minority of scientists have claimed that leukemia is an environmental cancer. E. B. Lewis, a California Institute of Technology biologist who, two decades ago, devised a method for calculating the risk of leukemia which the U.S. population faced from atomic testing, argues that leukemia, rather than being independent of environmental factors, in fact reflects the background rate of environmental carcinogenesis. He suggests (Lewis, 1973) that since the latency period of leukemia is so short, it is an ideal early warning signal of the presence of environmental hazards. Although most leukemia investigators think that the total number of leukemia cases is too small for his idea to be practical (Graham, 1980), Lewis argues that, if leukemia deaths were closely monitored, areas showing an excess could immediately be investigated for the presence of environmental carcinogens, and corrective measures taken. Finally, some environmentally oriented leukemia investigators have charged that evidence demonstrating the leukemogenic effects of radiation and chemicals has been suppressed by both the government and private industry (Boffey, 1970; Sterling, 1980).

The viral approach dominated research on leukemia during the 1960s. Scientists had identified leukemia viruses in several animal species as early as 1908, but little progress was made in viral oncology until 1950, when the development of the electron microscope and new tissue culture techniques markedly facilitated work in the area (Berenblum, 1967:97). No one had been able to induce leukemia in a healthy animal by innoculating it with a virus from a diseased one until 1951, when Ludwik Gross, a surgeon turned experimentalist working at the Bronx Veterans Administration Hospital, found that the desired effect could be achieved in newborn mice. (Scientists now realize that the undeveloped immune system of newborns makes them especially susceptible to the virus.) Gross (1961) suggested that radiation might induce leukemia by triggering a latent virus. There was enormous scientific interest in the viral hypothesis, because it presented a general biocellular theory which could explain the mode of action of a wide variety of specific carcinogenic substances. Further, the recent conquest of polio encouraged optimism over the possibility of vaccine against leukemia (Upton, 1980).

Some leading viral researchers claimed to Congress, to federal policy makers, to influential individuals, and to the general public that a vaccine against leukemia, and perhaps other cancers, was a realistic possibility. For this reason, and because it seemed a promising line of research from the perspective of basic biology, viral oncology ascended to a unique institutional status within the U.S. National Cancer Institute, thus giving the federal imprimatur to the viral definition of cancer as a social problem. The Virology Research Resources Program, begun in 1961, "undertook immediately to provide essential materials and services to all scientists working in this field" (National Advisory Cancer Council, 1962:9). In 1964, the Special Virus Leukemia Program was established with the specific objective of "identification of a human leukemia virus and the subsequent development of a vaccine or other control methods" (U.S. House of Representatives, 1966:337). The program was expanded to include solid tumor research shortly thereafter. According to *Science,* the "very expensive, very targeted Virus Cancer Program made a lot of people very mad" (Culliton, 1974:143); a federally appointed review panel, known as the Zinder Committee, concluded that the main problem was that the Virus Cancer Program was a "closed shop," awarding contracts to a small circle of scientists. Viral research never resulted in a vaccine against a human cancer—which now seems too simplistic an objective—but it did result in significant progress in understanding the basic biology of cell replication.

Genetically oriented leukemia researchers, like the environmentally oriented investigators, argued that epidemiological evidence offered little support for the theory that leukemia was an infectious disease caused by a virus. Based on studies of human populations at excessive risk of leukemia, including survivors of Hiroshima and Nagasaki, Robert Miller, Chief of Clinical Epidemiology at the National Cancer Institute, argued that genetic damage was the most likely mechanism of leukemogenesis (Miller, 1967). Former director of the National Cancer Institute, Arthur Upton (1980), suggests that genetically oriented researchers were less successful than the viral researchers in advancing their scientific goals within the National Cancer Institute during the 1960s because their interpretive claims were less persuasive: "It was a pessimistic hypothesis . . . there is not much you can do about your genes . . . ." Genetically oriented researchers did not actually claim that leukemia was inherited. Rather, they proposed studying the incidence of certain cancers in genetically abnormal populations in order to get a better understanding of the process of cell mutation, which they believed to be the biological mechanism of carcinogenesis (Miller, 1980).

I have shown that the three groups of leukemia researchers differed in their cognitive claims concerning the biological cause of leukemia, and their social problem interpretive claims concerning how the public health problem of leukemia, and other cancers, should be solved. Each group defined the problem, and proposed a solution, in terms of its own special skills. Thus, the genetic approach emphasized the contribution that specially trained clinicians could make to solving the problems of the cause, cure, and prevention of cancer. In contrast, the environmental approach emphasized the role of epidemiologists and biostatisticians who studied long range trends among large populations. The viral approach emphasized laboratory experiments by virologists. The cognitive and social problem interpretive claims of each group are summarized in Table 1. Note the contradictory claims arising from the environmental approach, reflecting the fact that these scientists disagreed over whether leukemia was an environmental cancer.

Today, the three approaches to leukemia are no longer regarded as so divergent theoretically as they once seemed. Viral research has evolved from a simplistic search for the leukemia virus to a deeper understanding of the processes of cell reproduction. Evidence is accumulating that carcinogens "initiate" a process of cell mutation which, given the presence of other "promoting" factors, results in cancer (Cairns, 1979). Since many environmental carcinogens are known to be mutagens (substances that cause mutations) as well, the genetic approach now overlaps to some degree with the environmental perspective (Knudson, 1977). Recent reflection on the original laboratory work on viral leukemogenesis identifies the presence of at least four contributing components in the experimental protocol: (a) the virus; (b) x-radiation; (c) inbred species of mice highly susceptible to leukemia; and (d) the immunological deficiency of the newborn mice (Gross, 1977; Haran-Ghera and Peled, 1979; Rapp and Reed, 1977). In the words of former National Cancer Institute Director Arthur C. Upton (1980), "The most sophisticated and scientific approach would be to see cancer as multicausal." Nevertheless, each of the three groups I have discussed interpreted the available evidence in the light of its own scientific concerns and defined the leukemia problem in terms of a single cause.

That divergent definitions of cause are held by specialized groups of scientists is unremarkable. First, it is the nature of a scientific specialty to interpret evidence in terms of its own narrow concerns (Campbell, 1969; Kuhn, 1970). Second, philosophers argue that cause cannot be defined without reference to human intentions and actions:

> A cause is an event or state of things which it is in our power to produce or prevent, and by producing or preventing which we can produce or prevent that whose cause it is said to be. (Collingwood, 1976:180)

Put simply, an event has a cause when there is something someone can do about it, either to make the event happen or to keep it from happening. Any given individual will define the cause of an event as that means by which he or she can intervene in the outcome. Thus, for virologists, the virus was the

Table 1
Summary of Cognitive and Social Problem Interpretive Claims made by
U.S. Leukemia Researchers 1955–1975

Research Orientation	Cognitive Claims	Social Problem Interpretive Claims
Viral	Viruses induce leukemia in laboratory animals. There is a human leukemia virus. Many, perhaps most, human cancers are caused by viruses.	Cancer is a scientific problem, it can be solved through technical innovation and medical intervention. Virologists are best able to solve the problem. Therefore: 1. The National Cancer Institute should give high priority to viral research in order to develop vaccines against leukemia and other cancers.
Genetic	Groups prone to develop leukemia have genetic features which suggest that genetic damage plays a role in leukemogenesis. If human leukemia is of viral origin, it should display the epidemiological patterns typical of infectious diseases, but it does not.	Cancer seems to be a genetic problem, but we are not sure. Physicians trained in clinical epidemiology are best able to generate the research questions that will provide a solution in the future. Therefore: 1. More physicians should be trained to be alert to possible relationships between cancer and genetic problems in order to generate further hypotheses about how genetic damage might cause leukemia and other cancers. 2. The National Cancer Institute should spend less money on viral research, and more on other types of investigations. 3. Exposure to agents known to produce genetic damage and/or leukemia—such as radiation—should be prevented.
Environmental	Radiation causes leukemia. Certain chemicals cause leukemia. Any carcinogen that can be carried to the blood may cause leukemia.	Cancer is an environmental problem. Epidemiologists can show which cancers are of environmental origin, which are not, and what agents cause cancer. Then public

cause of leukemia. For environmentally oriented researchers, radiation and chemicals and unknown factors were the cause of leukemia. For genetically oriented researchers, chromosomal aberrations were the cause of leukemia.

The question which the case of leukemia research suggests for the sociology of social problems is: How is it that some scientific groups are more successful than others in influencing the public definition and solution of particular social problems? Clearly, the virologists were more suc-

Table 1 (*Cont.*)

Research Orientation	Cognitive Claims	Social Problem Interpretive Claims
		health measures, including regulatory legislation, can be taken to prevent cancer. Therefore:
		1. Since known leukemogens account for only a small portion of leukemia cases, leukemia cannot be considered an environmental cancer.
		2. Since leukemia reflects the background level of environmental carcinogens, it can be used as an early warning system to monitor environmental hazards.
		3. Although leukemia may reflect the background level of environmental carcinogens, there are too few cases of leukemia to warrant using it as an early warning system.
		4. Leukemia appears not to be an environmental cancer only because evidence that low level radiation and certain chemicals cause leukemia has been suppressed.
		5. Since neither the viral nor the genetic hypothesis has been substantiated, we need to look for environmental factors in leukemia and other cancers.
		6. Even if we don't know the exact biological causes of leukemia and other cancers, we should still take steps to remove from the environment substances that epidemiological studies show to be associated with increased risk of leukemia and other cancers.

cessful in their social problem interpretive claims-making than the other two groups of leukemia researchers, although we must not underestimate the effectiveness of the counter claims made by the nonvirological researchers. In order to explain the success of the virologists, we need to examine the characteristics of the competing groups, the characteristics of the social environment within which they were competing, and the strategies that each group evolved to advance its claims.

In respect to the competing groups, we would ask such questions as: With what specialties were group members affiliated? What was the institutional location of these specialties? How cohesive was each group in its professional affiliations, scientific views, and policy recommendations? What sorts of segmentations existed within each group, and what was the significance of those segmentations? What research developments were occurring within each of the specialties? In which specialties was research progressing rapidly, in which was it declining? What interdisciplinary relations did each group have with scientific specialties not engaged in leukemia research? How might such interdisciplinary relations impinge upon federal science policy? What role did members of each group play in science policy making?

In respect to the social environment, we would ask such questions as: What were the general political and economic trends of the period? What public and private agencies were concerned about cancer? What social movements existed that might influence, favorably or unfavorably, the fate of leukemia researchers' claims?

In respect to the leukemia researchers' strategies, we would ask such questions as: What nonscientific groups were mobilized in support of each scientific group's claims? What claims were made in order to mobilize nonscientists' support? Did scientists make different claims to different groups of nonscientists? What resources did these nonscientific groups have access to, and what did they contribute in support of the scientists' claims?

CONCLUSION: IMPLICATIONS FOR SOCIAL PROBLEMS RESEARCH

The sociology of social problems can draw on new developments in the sociology of science in two ways. First, theoretical and empirical studies of the social construction of scientific knowledge help to advance the constructionist agenda for the sociology of social problems. Second, considering science as a claims-making activity draws our attention to science as an arena for the construction of social problems. The main work of science is to produce specialized knowledge, but in the process some scientists will invariably produce social problem claims. Sociologists of social problems will be interested in social problem claims that scientists make, the conditions under which they make such claims, and the factors determining the ultimate fate of scientists' social problem claims.

REFERENCES

Aronson, Naomi
     1982   "Nutrition as a social problem: A case study of entrepreneurial strategy in science."
               Social Problems, 29:474–487.

Atwater, Wilbur O.
1886   Letter to Edward Atkinson, November 6, Box 6, Wilbur O. Atwater papers, Olin
        Library, Wesleyan University, Middletown, CT.
Barber, Bernard
1952   Science and the Social Order. New York: The Free Press.
Barnes, Barry
1974   Scientific Knowledge and Sociological Theory. London: Routledge and Kegan Paul.
1981   "On the 'hows' and 'whys' of cultural change" (response to Woolgar). Social
        Studies of Science, 11:481–98.
Becker, Howard S.
1973   Outsiders. New York: The Free Press. Originally published in 1963.
Bell, Susan E.
1980   The Synthetic Compound Diethylstilbestrol (DES) 1938–1941: The Social Construc-
        tion of a Medical Treatment. Unpublished doctoral dissertation, Brandeis University.
Ben-David, Joseph
1971   The Scientist's Role in Society. Englewood Cliffs, NJ: Prentice Hall.
Berenblum, Isaac
1967   Cancer Research Today. Oxford, England: Pergamon Press.
Berger, Peter L. and Thomas Luckmann
1966   The Social Construction of Reality. New York: Anchor Books.
Bloor, David
1976   Knowledge and Social Imagery. London: Routledge and Kegan Paul.
Blume, Stuart S.
1974   Toward a Political Sociology of Science. New York: The Free Press.
Boffey, Philip M.
1970   "Goffman and Tamplin: Harrassment charges against AEC, Livermore." Science
        169:838–43.
Brannigan, Augustine
1981   The Social Basis of Scientific Discoveries. Cambridge, England: Cambridge Univer-
        sity Press.
Cairns, John
1979   Cancer: Science and Society. San Francisco, CA: W.H. Freeman and Company.
Cameron, Ian and David Edge
1979   Scientific Issues and Their Social Uses: An Introduction to the Concept of Scien-
        tism. Woburn, MA: Butterworths.
Campbell, Donald T.
1969   "Ethnocentrism of the disciplines and the fish-scale model of omniscience." In
        Muzafer Sherif and Carolyn W. Sherif (eds.), Interdisciplinary Relations in the
        Social Sciences. Chicago, IL: Aldine.
Collingwood, R. G.
1976   "Three senses of the word 'cause'." In Myles Brand (ed.), The Nature of Causation.
        Urbana, IL: University of Illinois Press.
Collins, Harry M.
1975   "The seven sexes: A study in the sociology of a phenomenon, or the replication of
        an experiment in physics." Sociology 9:205–24.
Conrad, Peter and Joseph Schneider
1980   Deviance and Medicalization: From Badness to Sickness. St. Louis, MO: C. V.
        Mosby.
Cronkite, Eugene P.
1961   "Evidence for radiation and chemicals as leukemogenic agents." Archives of En-
        vironmental Health 3:297–303.
1980   Author's interview, August.

28   ARONSON

Culliton, Barbara J.
    1974   "Virus cancer program: Review panel stands by criticism." Science 184:143–5.
Dameshek, William
    1968   "Conference summary." In C. J. D. Zarofonetis (ed.), Proceedings of the Interna-
            tional Conference on Leukemia-Lymphoma. Philadelphia, PA: Lea & Febiger.
Daniels, George H.
    1967   "The pure-science ideal and democratic culture." Science 156:1699–1703.
Freedman, Samuel G.
    1982   "Punch a time clock? Not for scholars, thank you". The New York Times, Sunday,
            March 28:10E.
Fudenberg, Daniel and Vijaya L. Melnick
    1978   Biomedical Scientists and Public Policy. New York: Plenum Press.
Gilbert, G. Nigel
    1976   "The transformation of research findings into scientific knowledge." Social Studies
            of Science 6:281–306.
    1977   "Referencing as persuasion." Social Studies of Science 7:113–22.
Goodfield, June
    1981   Reflections on Science and the Media. Washington, DC: American Association for
            the Advancement of Science.
Graham, Saxon
    1980   Author's interview, July.
Gross, Ludwik
    1961   Oncogenic Viruses. New York: Pergamon Press.
    1977   "The development of the concept of viral etiology of leukemia and related neo-
            plastic diseases, present status and prospects for the future." In P. Bentvelsen, J.
            Hilgers, and David S. Yohn (eds.), Advances Comparative Leukemia Research.
            Amsterdam, Holland: Elsevier.
Gusfield, Joseph R.
    1981   The Culture of Public Problems. Chicago, IL: University of Chicago Press.
Gustin, Bernard H.
    1973   "Charisma, recognition and motivation of scientists." American Journal of So-
            ciology 78:1119–34.
Hagstrom, Warren O.
    1965   The Scientific Community. New York: Basic Books.
Haran-Ghera, Nechama and Alpha Peled
    1979   "Induction of leukemia in mice by irradiation and radiation virus variants." Ad-
            vances in Cancer Research 30:45–87.
Heath, Clark W., Jr.
    1975   "The epidemiology of leukemia." Chapter 12 in David Schottenfeld (ed.), Cancer
            Epidemiology and Prevention: Current Concepts. Springfield, IL: Charles C.
            Thomas.
Knorr, Karin D.
    1977   "Producing and reproducing knowledge: Descriptive or constructive?" Social Sci-
            ence Information 16:669–96.
Knudson, Alfred G.
    1977   "Genetic and Environmental Interactions in the Origin of Human Cancer." In J. J.
            Mulvihil, R. W. Miller, and J. F. Fraumeni, Jr. (eds.), Progress in Cancer Research
            and Thearpy. Volume 3: Genetics of Human Cancer. New York: Raven Press.
Kuhn, Thomas S.
    1970   The Structure of Scientific Revolutions. Chicago, IL: University of Chicago Press.
            Originally published in 1962.

Latour, Bruno and Steve Woolgar
    1979   Laboratory Life: The Social Construction of Scientific Facts. Beverly Hills, CA: Sage.
Lewis, E. B.
    1973   "Leukemia and the somatic risks of chemical mutagens." Environmental Health Perspectives 6:185–90.
Mackenzie, Donald
    1981   "Interests, positivism and history." Social Studies of Science 11:498–504.
Mannheim, Karl
    1936   Ideology and Utopia. New York: Harcourt, Brace and World.
Mazur, Allan
    1981   The Dynamics of Technical Controversy. Washington, DC: Communications Press.
Merton, Robert K.
    1973   "The normative structure of science." Pp. 267–78 in Robert K. Merton, The So-
    (1942) ciology of Science, Norman W. Storer (ed.), Chicago, IL: University of Chicago Press.
Meynell, Hugo
    1977   "On the limits of the sociology of knowledge." Social Studies of Science 7:489–500.
Miller, Robert W.
    1967   "Persons at exceptionally high risk of leukemia." Cancer Research 27:2420–2423.
    1980   Author's Interview, February.
Mills, C. Wright
    1959   The Sociological Imagination. New York: Oxford University Press.
Mitroff, Ian
    1974   The Subjective Side of Science. Amsterdam, Holland: Elsevier.
Mulkay, Michael J.
    1976   "Norms and ideology in science." Social Science Information 15:637–656.
    1979   Science and the Sociology of Knowledge. London, England: George Allen & Unwin.
National Advisory Cancer Council
    1962   Progress Against Cancer 1961. Public Health Service Publication No. 914. Washington, DC: U.S. Government Printing Office.
Nelkin, Dorothy (ed.)
    1979   Controversy: Politics of Technical Decisions. Beverly Hills, CA: Sage.
Racker, Efraim
    1979   Science and the Cure of Diseases. Princeton, NJ: Princeton University Press.
Rapp, Fred and Cathy Reed
    1977   "The viral etiology of cancer: A realistic approach." Cancer 40:419–29.
Ravetz, Jerome R.
    1971   Scientific Knowledge and Its Social Problems. New York: Oxford University Press.
Robbins, David and Ron Johnston
    1976   "The role of cognitive and occupational differentiation in scientific controversies." Social Studies of Science 6:349–68.
Schnaiberg, Allan
    1980   The Environment: From Surplus to Scarcity. New York: Oxford University Press.
Spector, Malcolm and John I. Kitsuse
    1977   Constructing Social Problems. Menlo Park, CA: Cummings.
Sterling, Theodor D.
    1980   "The health effects of low-dose radiation on atomic workers: A case study of employer-directed research." International Journal of Health Services 10:37–46.
Thomas, Lewis
    1974   The Lives of a Cell: Notes of a Biology Watcher. New York: Bantam Books.
    1982   "The art of teaching science." New York Times Magazine, March 14: 89–93.

Upton, Arthur C.
　　1980　　Author's Interview, August.
U.S. House of Representatives
　　1966　　"Report on special virus leukemia program." Hearings Before a Subcommittee of
　　　　　　the Committee on Appropriations. Departments of Labor and Health, Education
　　　　　　and Welfare Appropriations, Part 4:338–41.
Woolgar, Steve
　　1981　　"Interests and explanation in the social study of science." Social Studies of Science
　　　　　　11:365–94.
Zola, Irving
　　1972　　"Medicine as an institution of social control." Sociological Review 20:487–504.

2 On the side: Practical action and social constructivism in social problems theory

Joseph R. Gusfield
University of California, San Diego

It is almost a cliche to point out that language carries meanings at more than one level. The instrumental language of routine, daily life is alive with symbolism, metaphor and *double entendre,* as are the grand theories of philosophy, history, and sociology. That area traditionally labelled "sociology of knowledge" has created an awareness of the political overtones and undertones which seemingly "neutral" writings bear (Mannheim, 1949; Schwartz, 1981, Ch. 1). The study of the "domain assumptions," "root metaphors," and "images of man" has preoccupied many analysts of sociological theory (Friedrichs, 1970; Gouldner, 1970; Nisbet, 1976; Pepper, 1966: Rieff, 1959; Stoll, 1975). Most recently, the documents of scientific reports have also been drawn into the analysis of thought as analysable through the devices of rhetoric, linguistics, and literary criticism (Gusfield, 1981; White, 1976). What these analyses lead me to maintain is that sociological perspectives do more than draw a map for understanding; they also carry in the language and connotations of their viewpoints images which convey moral and ethical attitudes. They tell us not only what *is,* but how it *ought* to be.

In this chapter, I shall discuss these aspects of social problems theory. I want to understand what and how sociological perspectives toward social problems pre-figure the relationship between the observer—the sociologist—and the "man of action"—the partisan, the policy maker, the personnel in social problems fields. My subject is not what sociologists say they are doing, but what the language and logic of their perspectives and their research tell us they do. What are the practical and political imputations of

31

social problems theory, the attitudes toward social problems conveyed? What are readers being taught to know, to feel, and to do? I recognize that these may be levels of meaning which the proponent has not knowingly intended.

More particularly I want to assess these pedogogical implications in the social constructivist approach to social problems. This is a perspective now gaining in credence and use among American sociologists. It represents a view with which I feel myself and my own work deeply identified. (Gusfield, 1963, 1976, 1981). To make the analysis clearer and more pointed, I shall refer to the specific case of alcohol problems and their study.

SOCIOLOGY: SUPPORT AND NEGATION

In the 1930s and 1940s, sociology carried an enlightenment message of progressive rationalism. The dominant, influential sociologists of the period, the ones that undergraduates would read and that graduate students would study, projected an image of a rational and technical world in conflict with the vested interests and outmoded traditions of the past. The sense that technological change and institutional professionalism were harbingers of a new and better world was an underlying theme in the work of such widely read sociologists as William Fielding Ogburn and Robert and Helen Lynd. In his classic work, *Social Change* (1922) Ogburn laid down the perspective which dominated his later works and his widely adopted text with Meyer Nimkoff (Ogburn and Nimkoff, 1940, 1946, 1950, 1958). The Lynds' community studies *Middletown* (1929) and *Middletown in Transition* (1937) were the outstanding sociological research works of their time.

Ogburn's hypothesis of a cultural lag between changes in the material aspects of life and changes in the nonmaterial culture was, in one form or another, the leading explanatory perspective among pre–World War II sociologists. Here is his statement of the idea:

> The thesis is that the various parts of modern culture are not changing at the same rate, some parts are changing much more rapidly than others; and that since there is a correlation and interdependence of parts, a rapid change in one part of our culture *requires* readjustments through other changes in the various correlated parts of culture. (Ogburn, 1922: 200–201; emphasis added)

The key term expressing the "social problem" is "maladjustment," as later in the above paragraph:

> The extent of this lag will vary according to the nature of the cultural material, but may exist for a considerable number of years, during which time there may be said to be a *maladjustment*. It is desirable to reduce the period of malad-

justment to make the cultural adjustments as quickly as possible. (Ogburn, 1922: 201; emphasis added)

The Lynds followed this formula in understanding Middletown in 1925 and again in 1935 (Lynd and Lynd, 1929, 1937), although more diffusively and with greater detail. Like Ogburn, they saw technological and material change as the independent variable, and nonmaterial culture—the dominant values and institutions—as dependent. Ogburn, using Veblen's term, referred to the "vested interests" as a major source of inertia and resistance to change, but for both Ogburn and the Lynds it seemed clear that it was nonmaterial culture that lagged and technology that led. An alternative formulation might have been that nonmaterial culture stood firm while technology overran. The scene was changing and the agent was "required to change, to adjust."

    The Lynds, in concretizing this general view of the origin of social problems, provide us with a clear sense of who is applauded and who is decried. They conclude *Middletown* with the following, in the final paragraph:

> When the "problem" has become so urgent that the community has felt compelled to seek and apply a "remedy," this remedy has tended to be a logical extension of *old* to the *new* situation, or an emotional defense of the earlier situation. . . . The foregoing pages suggest the possible utility of a deeper-cutting procedure that would involve a reexamination of the institutions themselves. (Lynd and Lynd, 1929: 501–502; emphasis added).

The Lynds' treatment of Middletown schools in 1935 illustrates how the theoretical perspective puts the sociologist on the side of institutional change and how he or she becomes the defender of the new and the critic of the established. They describe the clash between the developing profession of teaching and the views and interests of community elites. Much of this conflict emerged over the new professional ideals and techniques developed in the graduate school university centers, especially Columbia Teachers College. The description creates a drama of underdogs and their masters:

> In such a period, it is natural for Middletown to attempt to resolve conflicts by grasping fixedly the points in its educational system which seem to offer the readiest means of measuring success and the greatest assurance of stability. And in the struggle between quantitative administrative efficiency and qualitative educational goals in an era of strain like the present, the *big guns* are all on the side of the heavily concentrated controls behind the former. (Lynd and Lynd, 1937: 240–241; emphasis added)

What has this sociology to offer to its audience of students, readers, and policy-seekers? My brief examination of the logic and the imagery of these two leading works of pre-war sociology suggests the following:

      1.   The sociologist presents an interpretation of social problems which "reduces" or redefines them as manifestations of latent or less-recognized processes and/or conditions.

      2. In the emergence of social problems, the sociologist defines some elements as "necessary"—independent variables—while others can only "adjust." Social problems are solvable by change in existing institutions. It is "Middletown in Transition" and not "Middletown's Search for Continuity."

      3. The rhetoric of the argument, the perspective seen as a system of persuasion, adds up to a defense of the new, the modern, and a criticism of the past. It provides solace and support for the cosmopolitan in struggle with the local, for the professional against political or amateur criteria, of the technological and utilitarian against the emotional and symbolic aspects of culture.

Sociology was able to provide an enlightened source for understanding and redesigning social organization. It sounded a call of scientific support to permit new techniques to flourish within more congenial frameworks. I can imagine the Middletown teacher, trained at Columbia, who found Ogburn's *Social Change* a vindication of his or her own fight with the local school board. When the Lynds described Middletown as "caught between past and future" (1937: 510) that teacher knew to which tense he or she belonged.

For the individual student, the lay public, or the professional practitioner, sociology, like other academic disciplines, carries its moral message and becomes, because of this, the support or the negation of preexistent attitudes, opinions, or procedures. In the late nineteenth and early twentieth century in Europe, physics was the site for political radicals on university campuses. It carried a moral message of a new and brighter world through science, and was enveloped in conflict with the evil forces of organized religion and the vested interests of monopoly enterprise (Feuer, 1969). In the 1920s in the United States, ministers' sons and daughters found both the emancipating air of cultural relativism and the supportive doctrine of tolerance and concern for the welfare of immigrants and the urban poor. That same sense of help and sympathy for the downtrodden lingered on in the implications of labelling theory for getting across the viewpoint of the "heroic" deviants and the "villainous" labellers. (I think this is apparent in Becker's work on deviance and, even though critical, in Gouldner's assessment. Becker, 1967; Gouldner, 1968).

THE GENERATIONAL GAP: THE ALCOHOL PROBLEM

But there is often a generational gap in the relations between sociology and its audiences, a gap composed of the differing images of the subject matter held by the two. Armed with yesterday's sociology, as conveyed by past education or by the popular media, the consumer seeks the support he or she expected and is dismayed to discover that the product is not what was anticipated by the label on the package. In the 1960s, sociology was often the site of political radicals but it was also their disappointment. They carried the flag not "for sociological ideas" but against them. They found their banner-waving inspirations in the humanities in works such as those of Herbert Marcuse or Theodore Roszak, with an image of C. Wright Mills as the noble sociological dissenter, tilting at the entrenched windmills of a sociological establishment that (allegedly) persecuted such critics. In his work, Mills was part of that older tradition with which sociology had been identified—the populist radicalism of agrarian sentiment that carried the underlying message of distrust of authorities and the explanation of economic injustice as a product of unequal political and economic power (Mills, 1957).

This attitude of the 1960s towards sociology was not too far off the mark. Certainly, the dominating viewpoints in political sociology were reacting against the sociology of the pre–World War II period. Emphasizing the attacks on civil liberties as the dominating intellectual issues of the 1950s, they consciously attacked the identification of progress with lower-income and working classes (Stouffer, 1955; Lipset, 1960). American sociologists of the 1930s and 1940s, of whom Lynd is the prime example, maintained a sense of the "common man" as victim of social injustice and the market mentality of laissez-faire capitalism. The political sociology of the 1950s, reflecting both the trauma of Nazi Germany and the more local McCarthyism, found a new focus for progress in the educated middle class, where freedom of speech, association, and dissent gave greater support to intellectuals. By the 1960s, social problems theory was less supportive and comforting to critics of American society than a reader of the 1930s and 1940s sociologists might have expected.

I am especially aware of this gap between student expectations and academic responses in the field of alcohol studies. For some years, Jacqueline Wiseman and I have given a joint undergraduate seminar on Alcohol and Society. Much of our energy has gone in the effort, often fruitless, of dispelling what we see as the fallacies about alcohol which the students bring with them. Involved in their struggles against a public they see as moralistic toward people who suffer from alcohol problems, they expect a strong endorsement of the disease model of alcoholism and a set of facts which supports a view of the deviant as someone caught in circumstances beyond his or her control or responsibility. They hope to be shored up in their liberal battle with a conservative society. They mirror the paradigm of Ogburn and the Lynds, seeing in sociology the source of the new and the knowledgeable.

Their expectations are not without justification. In the two decades following the repeal of Prohibition, the universities became the seat of a new orientation toward the problem of alcohol. It differed radically from the condemnation of drinking and the call for willpower and law as measures of reform. Defining the social problem of drinking as that pertaining to a deviant minority—the alcoholic—they removed from the alcohol issue the moral and religious character it had acquired over the previous century. Defining the alcoholic as a victim of a disease served to place him into the waiting rooms of medicine and alleviated him from being an object of moral disapproval. It was of a piece with a general liberal position in which sufferers—the poor, the mentally disturbed, the handicapped, and the alcoholic—have a claim on public attention and help (Gusfield, 1982). In the struggle between the enlightened who recognize the medical status of the alcoholic, and the unenlightened who do not, sociology is looked to for confirmation as it has in the past and for the strategies which will diminish the extent of "the problem."

> A small group of the thoughtful people had a brilliant idea. Drinking and the associated problems had been around a long time, and neither legislation nor . . . the fear of disease or hellfire had been effective in preventing or ameliorating them. Were we not in the age of science? Could not the power of science at last be brought to bear on these problems? (Keller, 1976: 20)

But our message is not very supportive. We cast great doubt on the "reality" of the disease concept of alcoholism, the increasing severity and extent of alcohol problems, the expanding character of teenage alcoholism, and the actual or potential effectiveness of treatment. We attack the veracity of those public images which have moved students to an interest in the field. What we are about is an analysis of how it is that public agencies and lay persons have come to define a set of phenomena as alcohol problems, and how it is that they have come to emphasize and point attention to a class of deviant drinkers called "alcoholics." Many students respond by ignoring such wisdom and continuing to wax emotional over the plight of the stigmatized alcoholic and the deepening problem of alcohol in American society. Armed with a sense of mission, they are led into the discipline from which they expect that mission to be enhanced; to be told that they are right. They hope that the real world is indeed a world of social problems that have a definite causal source and that in the rational approach of social science they can find resolutions. Instead they are exposed to the academic analysis of how it is that alcoholism has come to be *the* problem of alcohol use in public arenas; how it is that the label is applied, and what alternative conceptions of "alcohol problems" are possible. Looked to by our students for solutions to problems, we respond by reconstituting the field and making the beginning of the problem itself the subject of study.

The Constructivist Approach to Social Problems and to Alcohol
  Studies

In reconstituting the public problem of alcohol, Professor Wiseman and myself were engaging in just that shift of subject matter which so frequently differentiates one theoretical approach from another in the social sciences. In this matter of the use of words and ideas there is much to be learned from literary critics whose primary "business" this is. R. S. Crane, one of the leading figures of the New Criticism movement of the 1950s, has stated the idea well. In analyzing two seemingly opposed interpretations of the Shakespearean tragedies, he remarks that they are really reconcilable rather than opposed. Each is actually attending to different subject matter in Shakespeare—one, being attentive to "poetry," is concerned with form and technique, with the words. The other, being attentive to "drama," is concerned with the conceptions of character and development.

> The real subject-matter of any critic can never be accurately defined by noting merely that he is talking about such things as . . . Shakespearean tragedy or Macbeth. His real subject matter is not any of those things in itself. . . . Rather it is simply that aspect, or those aspects, of his indicated subject upon which our attention is focused by the semantic and logical constitution of his discourse; it is what, in short, he has thus *taken* his subject matter to be. (Crane, 1974: 149)

Our teaching of alcohol problems exemplified the shifting of the subject matter of our inquiry. It is also an illustration of the general change in the subject of social problems which is explicit in the recent emergence of constructivist social theory.

The constructivist approach in the study of social problems is an aspect of the great impetus toward a reconstituted sociology which has been one of the dominant theoretical movements in the realm of ideas during the past decade. It has gone by many names and in many directions: ethnomethodology, phenomenology, various kinds of structuralism, cognitive sociology, hermeneutics, symbolic interaction. What all of these have in common is that they focus on the processes of interpretation by which a subject matter is constructed by its users (Giddens, 1976; Collins, 1981). Given social problems, the sociologist's concern is not the problem but how and why such phenomena have come to be a social problem. In what is perhaps the major statement of this viewpoint toward social problems, Spector and Kitsuse's *Constructing Social Problems,* the authors put the matter clearly: "The process by which members of a group or societies define a putative condition as a problem—is the distinctive subject matter of the sociology of social problems." (Kitsuse and Spector, 1973; also see Spector and Kitsuse, 1977)

From this perspective, what is the activity of the sociologist? The study of social problems is focussed on the process by which a set of conditions becomes defined as a "social problem" among members of a society, and the resulting claims which arise. The "reality" of the conditions, the lay theories which emerge to account for them, or alternative conditions, are not within the scope of constructivist perspectives. Not the problem but the problem-making process is the central concern of the sociologist. "The central problem for a theory of social problems is to account for the emergence, nature and maintenance of claims-making and responding activities" (Spector and Kitsuse, 1977: 76).

What these views are about may be described as a shift in attention from object to subject. Ogburn and the Lynds looked to sociology for an accurate portrayal and analysis of the changing environmental scene. The problems of their concern operated to push ("require" is Ogburn's word; "compelled" is that of the Lynds) the subjects, the actors, to respond. There are external conditions which sociology can describe and explain and about which applied sociologists can develop policies and solutions.

What both symbolic interaction, through labelling theory, and social constructivism have been about is a refocus on the agent, the actor, the subject. The subject becomes an active agent who, through his or her actions, selects and interpretes conditions. The "social problem" is not an external entity, lying in the road to be discovered by passersby. It is shaped in the activities of people. The external conditions of problems should not be the subject matter of sociologists. Instead, their subject matter is found in the actions and the language through which conditions become interpreted as "social problems." "The notion that social problems are a kind of *condition* must be abandoned in favor of a conception of them as a kind of *activity*" (Spector and Kitsuse, 1977: 73).

In using quotation marks around *social problems* in the above paragraph and below, I have indicated its ambiguous status as factual, objective reality. I have suggested its fictive character as an interpreted rather than a factual condition. It is this view which I call that of the sociologist as outsider; as a student of people going about the action of creating and defining "social problems."

The Normative Perspective Toward Social Problems

An opposite point of view, as Spector and Kitsuse recognize, is the more conventional sociological approach, best stated by Robert Merton in his and Robert Nisbet's edited *Contemporary Social Problems* (Merton and Nisbet, 1976, Introduction). Here social problems are discovered where there is a discrepancy between an objective set of conditions and a subjective sense of what ought to be. Merton leaves little ambiguity about what he considers included in the role of the sociologist studying social problems. While he grants that analysis of the subjective side of the coin has importance, he is unwilling to leave the definition of conditions as a social problem entirely in the hands (or minds) of the lay audience. One of the major functions of the sociologist, as he posits it, is to make the lay audience aware of conditions that are discrepant with their norms or values:

> It is therefore a function of sociologist to study not only manifest social prob-lems—those widely identified in the society—but also latent social prob-lems—the conditions that are also at odds with current interests and values but are not generally recognized as being so. (Merton and Nisbet, 1976: 13)

> A major function of the sociologist, then, is to make latent social functions manifest. By discovering unwanted consequences of institutionalized arrange-ments, *the sociologist inevitably becomes a social critic* . . . . (Merton and Nisbet, 1976: 14; emphasis added)

This is the classic role of the sociologist in public affairs. He or she brings to public analysis and discussion a recognition of conditions which violate the public sense of what ought to be, whether or not that public is so aware. The sociologist provides an understanding of how these conditions have come to be, what consequences they have and how they might be ameliorated or abolished. In this formulation, the problem possesses a reality independent of the audience. It is an object of appropriate scientific study. The work of the sociologist provides a depiction of institutions, environments, or nor-mative systems about which the instructed may strike an attitude. Such a perspective might well have disputed popular thought about alcohol, but would have given our students a new version of the reality of alcohol prob-lems to which they could have attached their affect.

The implications of the normative approach for social actions can be exemplified through an analysis of the excellent article by Robert Straus on "Alcoholism and Problem Drinking" in the Nisbet and Merton book on social problems (Straus, 1976). The article is a factual and theoretical back-ground to the problem of alcholism and other drinking problems. It conveys to the neophyte the then most recent data and theoretical conclusions "in the field." As such, its subject matter is the set of conditions constituting the problem of the use of alcohol: "Individuals suffering from various forms of alcoholism and also others who encounter problems with alcohol" (Straus, 1976: 193).

The narrative of the Straus article begins with a section entitled "Identi-fying the Problem of Alcohol." It is an account of the magnitude of problem drinkers and alcoholics, and the detrimental consequences of excessive alcohol use. It establishes the legitimacy of studying alcohol use and abuse as problems. It provides material for an argument to convince possible doubters of the reality of an alcohol problem.

Following the short designation of the existence of the problem, Straus proceeds to examine physiological, psychological, and social effects of alcohol, to describe alcoholism and problem-drinking and discuss causal theories explaining them. Several specific problems—alcohol and youth, alcohol and the auto, and family and work relations are examined, and the factual bases, or lack of such, for popularly held beliefs are discussed. The article ends with a discussion of social responses, such as treatment programs, Alcoholics Anonymous, laws, and movements in public opinion.

In reporting on studies and data, the article serves two functions relevant to this discussion of the "messages" of social problems theories:

1. *It conveys the existence and gravity of the alcohol problem.* It presents a body of descriptive and analytic "fact" which the reader can point to and which provides a "convincing argument" to attest to the problem of alcohol. It summarizes the thought and findings of experts about a reality-alcohol problem.

2. *It provides a corrective to popular beliefs* about that subject matter, indicating where such beliefs are misleading or where fact is absent. Thus, the author tells us that alcoholism among youth is not as great as believed, that there is no definitive "alcoholic personality," but also that the annual cost of alcohol problems has been estimated at 25 billion dollars.

This is the stance of the expert—telling us that a situation exists. Whether or not we are aware of it, the condition is productive of detriments, that he or she (the author) has some special knowledge of it and his or her knowledge is superior to popular beliefs. He or she gives readers a knowledge about the subject matter which arms them with fact and theory for convincing others.

THE CONSTRUCTIVIST RESPONSE

The constructivist position can be seen as one reaction against the interventionist approach of sociologists, for whom like Merton professional expertise is offered to public affairs as a source for the solution to and definition of social problems. Viewing social problems as objective conditions, independent of the theories and factual beliefs among lay citizens, the sociologist can bring factual and theoretical knowledge to bear on social policy, to tell the public about the conditions, to suggest policy solutions. From the constructivist standpoint, the object of study is not a set of conditions; it is the activities of people who perceive conditions as problems. The sociologist cannot appear as expert on the problem but on the problem makers.

The constructivist argument places its emphasis on the activity through which a set of conditions seen from the constructivist viewpoint are accounts by the audience itself, by those who define the conditions and the processes as being "problems" (Mauss, 1975; Scott, 1969; Freidson, 1970, Gusfield, 1981; Conrad and Schneider, 1980; Cicourel, 1968; Douglas, 1967).

The subject matter is the "claims-making activity" (Spector and Kitsuse, 1977: Ch. 5) in which groups define phenomena as problems. In this formulation, what is the expected role of the sociologist and what becomes of the mission about the problem, the moral tone or "starch" which is so redolent in the conventional sociology of social problems?

Labelling theory was the logical precursor to social constructivism. In shifting attention from exclusive attempts to explain the deviant to explanations of those who create the labels, Lemert, Becker, and others began the process of examining the claims maker as well as those about whom claims were made.

> . . . "outsiders", from the point of view of the person who is labelled deviant, may be the people who make the rules he had been found guilty of breaking . . . To what extent and under what circumstances do people attempt to force their rules on others who do not subscribe to them? (Becker, 1963: 15–16)

Becker's own work on marihuana use and that of others on drug addiction (Schur, 1965) produced just this revision of social problems approaches; it made the claims makers, the official agencies, themselves the subject matter of the study of social problems.

> The chapters in this book do not so much treat "social problems" as they do areas in which people-citizens, politicians, professional experts, cultural critics, social scientists, and other interested parties—define many kinds of social problems as arising. (Becker, 1966: 7)

Who is the audience for this approach, and what use can they make of the factual and theoretical materials? The normative approach presents facts and theories about a condition; facts and theories which others can use to make claims for their expertise, their mandate to lead and make policy and to persuade others. To make "social problems" *putative* and to turn attention toward the study of the claims makers and their activities is to remove that claim to authoritative knowledge and that sense of mission which comes from knowing a body of fact and theory which others lack. In her analysis of labelling theory, Rains points out that there is a great difference in talking about "reactions that *impute* mental illness" and "reactions *to* mental illness" (Rains, 1975; emphasis added). The latter creates a sense of authority which the former lacks. It downgrades factual authority to place quotation marks around a supposed condition.

In this sense, the constructivist approach does not provide scientific support for claims makers. Instead, it studies them, some of whom may be past or present students of these constructivist sociologists. Spector and Kitsuse recognize the implications of their orientation:

> The definitional approach, then, pursued to its logical conclusion, requires that the sociologist, as a participant in the politics of defining social problems, be denied the special status of one who stands outside the process as objective observer or scientist (1977: 70).

Whether or not the sociologist will be accorded any special status as expert is an empirical not a logical question, maintain Spector and Kitsuse. Logically, however, sociologists cannot make a claim to any special knowledge or information from which to define a condition as "social problem." Empirically, neither can their students use sociological teachings to bolster a claim to knowledge or expertise. The subject matter of social problems seen as claims-making is the very claims makers who look to us for support. To paraphrase a famous popular "sociologist": We have met the problem and it is us.

The Alcoholism Movement

I want to elucidate the intellectual issue by examining some recent work in alcohol studies and its implications.

I had originally titled this chapter, "Why I Am Always Introduced as an Expert on Alcoholism But Am Not." While I have been involved in all phases of the social study of alcohol use off and on for the past thirty years, my research has primarily dealt with legal and political activities in relation to alcohol use. My claim to sociological knowledge about that condition labelled "alcoholism" is peripheral to my vision. Yet both academic and lay people persist in "seeing" the problems of alcohol as the problem of *alcoholism;* the special inability of certain deviant people who cannot control the consumption of alcohol as can most "normal" people. Alcohol problems are perceived as synonymous with alcoholism. What Robin Room calls "the governing image" in alcohol studies for the past four decades has been that of the alcoholic (Room, 1979; Beauchamp, 1980).

That image is, however, decidedly *not* a foregone, natural, or logical development. It is the product of recent times, of what is now called the Alcoholism Movement. This movement emerged after Repeal (1933) in the endeavors of groups including Alcoholics Anonymous, academic research units, and treatment professionals to change the moralistic attitude toward drunkards to a view of them as victims of a disease who could be helped by peers and/or by professional healers (Room, 1979; Gusfield, 1982; Schneider, 1978; Beauchamp, 1980).

Recent work in one or another instance of the constructivist *genre* has greatly expanded our sense of the historical and interpretive character of drinking problems. In the late 1960s, MacAndrews and Edgrton cast much doubt on the supposed physiological effects of alcohol as the creator of drunkenness by pointing to the variety of situational definitions of drunkenness in many of its cultural variations (MacAndrew and Edgerton, 1969). In the past few years, Levine's work and Schneider's have demonstrated that both alcoholism and drinking problems are matters of history, culture, and social structure (Levine, 1978; Schneider, 1978; Conrad and Schneider, 1980). Explaining casualties or drunken behavior as an effect of alcohol or of a permanent condition called "alcoholism" has a history. It is a matter of how a "putative set of conditions" achieve a validity as causal; how the theory of a problem has come to be accepted. Such constructivist perspectives have gained considerable importance in alcohol studies in the past few years (Robinson, 1976; Gusfield, 1975, 1976; Beauchamp, 1980).

It is not that new perspectives and "facts" have developed about an object "alcoholism." This has of course continued, as in the effort to redefine the class of deviants as "problem drinkers," including but by no means equivalent to the classic Skid Row depiction of the alcoholic (Cahalan, 1970; Cahalan and Room, 1974). What is different in interpretive sociologies is that they take as subject matter the very conditions of "alcoholism" or of "drinking problems" which conventional social problems approaches assume (Straus, 1976). What is studied are not the conditions but how such conditions have emerged from interpretive procedures and collective action (Blumer, 1971; Gusfield, 1981).

Chauncey's recent work on teenage alcoholism is a clear illustration of the approach applied to alcohol studies (Chauncey, 1982). His interest from the start was in the activities and events by which the public came to believe that there was a special problem of alcoholism among teenagers, that it was increasing, that it called for special programs, and that it accounted for other phenomena seen as peculiarly related to adolescents. His analysis led him to describe the political and organizational process of government agencies, and the exigencies of mass communication by which the problem was generated. In the process, he projected a decidedly negative attitude toward much of the assumed factual base for the problem of teenage alcoholism, but that was not necessary to his focus (Blane, 1977). Whether or not the conditions are seen as true or false, they are seen as matters of interpretation, open to choice and not to logical development of scientific method applied to social issues. Those who seek a social technology on which to base a practice or a policy cannot avoid disappointment with social constructivism.

Cognoscenti and Populi
There are significant consequences to this change in the direction of subject matter. The conventional perspective, outlined in Merton's discussion

above, leads the sociologist to the stance of social critic. The interpretive perspective becomes the critic of the social problems professionals and their lay constituencies. It is difficult for me, given a considerable knowledge of the field and a perspective focused on modes of interpretation, not to find almost every proposition about alcohol stated in popular communication or by alcohol professionals to be either false, or so much a matter of choice among alternative interpretations as to lose the ring of certainty with which it is projected at the public or at clients e.g., "fifty percent of all automobile deaths are attributable to drunken drivers" (Gusfield, 1981).

For the professional practitioner in the alcohol field—the counselor of alcoholics, the probation officer working with public drunkenness or drinking drivers, the government official—and for the partisan of a movement, alcohol problems are matters of public conflict. There are people to be persuaded to viewpoints helpful to the practice or the movement. There is resistance to the aims and aspirations of professionals and partisans. The stigma against the alcoholic, the resistance of "problem drinkers" and "alcoholics" to treatment, of judges, attorneys, and police toward law enforcement of the alcohol industry to further constraints, are all barriers to be overcome. The expertise of the expert is a weapon in that war against doubters and enemies.

The sense of mission about the solution to exigent problems has been a significant ingredient in the actions of practitioners and partisans. It has been built on a belief in the certainty that the problem actually exists, that it is of major proportions, and that the work of the program or the movement can help in resolving it. It involves a theory and a body of presumed fact, both of which are assured. Such theories and facts are not neutral matters; a point of view held in an academic seminar. They constitute vital sources for a sense of professional esteem, client respect, and the abllity to maintain legitimate occupational place. They constitute the source of belief that a knowledge base has been buttressed by the methods and expertise of scientific and technical professionals (Gusfield, 1982).

The sociologist as normative critic of that abstraction "society," or some group within it, provides a basis for that missionary zeal with which the practical person operates in the swirl of hostile opposition; it imbues him or her with a commitment involving a real set of conditions, to be contrasted with opposing theories and propositions. The academic world of social problems research may provide new and contrasting theories and facts to challenge and upset the professionals and the partisans, but does so only in establishing a new mission, a new vantage point from which to organize politics or policy or carry out the day-to-day action of agencies and movement. The facts and theories of the social scientists support the claims to authority made by claims makers. The cognoscenti and the populace are in the relation of leader and follower, teacher and student, guru and disciple. They act together against the public that waits to be persuaded of their criticism. The history of sociology in fields of juvenile delinquency and race relations are two examples. The role of the Yale (later Rutgers) School of Alcohol Studies is another (Keller, 1976). People working often against opposition could refer to books, articles, experts, and instruction which offered pronouncements about the conditions producing juvenile crime, racial differentiations, or alcohol problems. The dominant views of sociologists have supported the separate treatment of juveniles, equality between races, and treatment of alcoholics. The views were publically proferred as matters of professional knowledge, not solely as those of laymen. The practitioner could build on them.

A constructivist approach, however, drives a wedge between the elite in the know—the cognoscenti—and the practical people who attempt to achieve programmatic and personal victories. The sense of reflecting a natural, science-validated view of real conditions is undermined by a focus which brackets out the reality of the conditions around which the problem exists. It takes the affective starch—the driving sense of mission—out of social problems by viewing them as matters of partisan or professional *choice* rather than conclusions forced upon us by the *nature* of things. It removes the science that validates argument and sustains certainty, and leaves professionals and partisans facing the existential void alone and the political conflict unarmed.

The distinction between the two perspectives is a bit like that of explanations for protest movements. Those protesting explain their actions by the external conditions to which their protest is a just and normative response. Those dubious about the justice or wisdom of the protest look to the "outside agitators" who have "stirred up trouble" among satisfied groups by creating the awareness of a problem.

Rains has pointed out the effect of constructivist and labelling perspectives in challenging the existence of "deviance" as part of an external and real condition: "Kitsuse's rider notwithstanding, terms like 'putative' and 'imputation' have in fact come increasingly to mean 'questionable' and 'unwarranted'" (Rains, 1975: 6).

The gap here, between cognoscenti and populace, is the gap between the skeptic and the believer. What the practitioner and the partisan see as true phenomena, the cognoscenti see as public relations, political choice, social movement, or some other form which reduces its value as a basis for partisanship or occupational authority. In this sense the would-be disciples, seeking confirmation and support, are instead demeaned. In the conventional approach it is "society," "the power structure," "the institution" that is the rhetorical villain.

The relation between elite and would-be follower sounds much like Gibbon's classic analysis of religious toleration in ancient Rome: "To the people, all religions were equally true; to the philosophers all were equally false and to the magistrates all were equally useful."

SOCIOLOGY: ENGAGÉ AND DETACHÉ

What is emerging, I suggest, is a sociology not *engagé* but *detaché;* a sociology whose ironic skepticism about the factual basis of social problems places the sociologist in an Olympian position. Not action but understanding is the aspiration of interpretive sociologies. The sociologist as one of the cognoscenti assumes towards the problems and its proponents an attitude, if not hostile, at least skeptical, satirical, and doubting. In studying claims-making, the sociologist disputes, implicitly, the claim of sociology to effect a rational base to social problems policy; to be itself a maker of claims for public action. Asked whose side are we on, the answer is: "On the side."

Yet this development is one that I welcome. It seems to me to be a useful corrective to a period in which social science has promised far more than it has been able to achieve in the field of public problems. Witness the dead end of normative criminological theory and the rehabilitative rhetoric that it gave birth to. In alcohol studies, the message of destigmatizing and treatment has not proven adequate either to understanding or to action. In focusing our attention on the subjective component, on the ways in which the definition of problems is a matter of choice and values, of cognition and morality, the constructivist perspective recognized the inherent limits of science as a method in the solution of human conflicts and goals. The 1930s and 1940s sociologists embraced technology as a necessary and even valued source of progress. In the 1950s and 1960s social technologies—professional action and public programs—seemed the cutting edge through which sociology might engage the public welfare. We are less sanguine about social technologies and technicians in the 1970s and 1980s.

THE MORAL MESSAGE OF CONSTRUCTIVISM

But even a rhetoric of detachment contains a moral message, and hence a mission, though diluted. Sociology has been a foundation for the social problems concerns, through its search for a technology of human relations and for social criticism based on it. That is, it has shored up belief in the efficacy of public action and the benefit of public agencies and social problems professionals to implement it. The sociology of detachment moves us away from that supportive stance.

Here it is that I find the sociologist reemerging as critic. But now it is not the society or societal arrangements that constitute the object of scorn and the target for change. *It is the social problems industry itself that emerges as the object of critique.* In scrutinizing the definition of problems and claims of professional problems professions, the sociologist becomes the critic of the effort of public agencies and associations to make legitimate claims to solve social problems as technical problems, as the domain of the professional. Most of the sociological literature of constructive perspectives cited here has borne precisely that message. The critique of psychiatry and the medical model in Goffman, Szasz, and Scheff is only one example (Goffman, 1961; Scheff, 1966; Szasz, 1961). Scott's study of agencies for the blind is another (Scott, 1969). My own recent analysis of the drinking–driving arena is further illustrative (Gusfield, 1981).

As others have also recognized, the labelling perspective was especially utilized in studying official public agencies, including medical institutions (Rains, 1975). Lemert's major research on deviance was done on alcohol use and on mental disturbance; Becker's on marihuana use and drug "addiction;" Goffman's on institutions for the mentally disturbed; Kitsuse's on attributions of homosexuality. These problems have been at the foreground in the medicalization literature (Conrad and Schneider, 1980). The "victimless crimes" have constituted the major source for empirical insight and study in studies of deviance in recent decades.

In the general development of a welfare politics, sociology has been a source of knowledge and mission for what I have elsewhere called "the troubled-persons industries" (Gusfield, 1982). These include agencies and their staffs who are employed to help groups perceived as deviant or handicapped. They include many forms of counselling, treatment, and/or research connected with such conditions as mental illness, sexual problems, alcoholism, juvenile delinquency, deafness, blindness, child abuse, and the gamut of often changing forms of stigmatized attributes. Such professionals who make up the employees are drawn from social work, guidance and counselling, psychiatry, clinical psychology, sociology, recreation, and general social science and humanistic education. They are the professions or industries spawned by the definition of problems as social or public problems, demanding the intervention of professional services.

In challenging the factual status of the social problems as part of an independent reality, those of us using the constructionist approach undercut the normative thrust of the social problems professions. The critics of medicalization come to be the champions of the deviants against the arbitrariness, partiality, and authoritative claims of the professional experts whose mandate rests on belief in the factual existence of the conditions they attempt to alleviate. When these are placed in doubt the agents are dispossessed.

In the alcohol studies field, for example, by examining the constructed definition of alcohol problems this perspective has produced a new approach which is inherently a critique of the alcohol treatment agencies (Beauchamp, 1980; Robinson, 1976; Gusfield, 1976, 1983). Thus much of my own work in the field has, in its policy orientations, been a critique of the emphasis of alcohol studies on the individual as "causal agent" and on treatment and/or persuasion as major policies. In analyzing the definitional processes that produce the disease concept of alcoholism and the dominance of alcoholism as *the* problem of alcohol, this work is one aspect in the rise of the prevention approach in current alcohol discussion. That approach seeks for policies involving alcohol situations redefined as *events* rather than as characteristics of *persons*. It looks to law, to economic policies, to politics, and to policies less related to drinking as ways of influencing drinking events. It becomes a description which robs the existing agencies and industries of their authority by placing in doubt their claims to represent as necessary fact what is a selected definition of a problem.

An enlightenment orientation toward social science has been a major presupposition of conventional sociology. The hope has been that public policy could be made to rest on a body of politically neutral theory and fact, validated by scientific method and beyond the disputes of moral and political sides. In rejecting the deterministic view of human beings implicit in the method of physical science, interpretive sociologies emphasize a humanistic view of the subject whose own activity helps construct the stimuli as well as the responses. In doing so, such sociologies insist on the limits of scientific method and emphasize the inescapable place of moral and political choice in human actions.

The enlightenment tradition has itself been a major source of the sociologist's own sense of mission; the conviction that what he or she did was useful and valuable. An egalitarian society cannot accept an aristocratic belief in the value of aesthetic experiences and artistic products as beneficial or worthwhile irrespective of distributive rewards. A sociology that makes no pretense to instruct or lead the public, that provides no scientific rationale for the authority of practitioners, is neither likely to be sought after by a State and its agencies nor by political critics. If we search for analogies, perhaps our best choices lie in the self-awareness which literature, philosophy, and history have made their raison d'être. It lies in a humanistic self-awareness of the moral and spiritual aspects of public action, in the inescapability of politics.

Such a sociology cannot offer the society a technology, a method for discovering or solving public problems, nor a science, a body of knowledge whose indisputable character resolves moral and political conflict. Its social value lies in widening our understandings of self and others and in revealing the many alternatives from which to make choices and interpret events. Its aesthetic value lies in the joy of knowledge and interpretation that is neither science or art, but yet is both.

REFERENCES

Beauchamp, Dan
  1980   Beyond Alcoholism. Philadelphia, PA: Temple University Press.
Becker, Howard S.
  1963   Outsiders. Glencoe, IL: The Free Press.
  1966   (ed.) Social Problems: A Modern Approach. New York: John Wiley & Sons.
  1967   "Whose side are we on?" Social Problems, 14 (winter): 239–427.
Blane, H. T. and L. E. Hewitt
  1977   "Alcohol in use: Analysis of literature, 1960–1957." Report prepared for NIAAA.
          MTIS Report No. PB–268–698. Springfield, VA: National Technical Information
          Service.
Blumer, Herbert
  1971   "Social problems as collective behavior." Social Problems, 18 (winter): 298–306.
Cahalan, Don
  1970   Problem Drinkers: A National Survey. San Francisco, CA: Jossey-Bass.
Cahalan, Don and Robin Room
  1974   Problem-Drinking Among American Men. New Brunswick, NJ: Rutgers Center of
          Alcohol Studies.
Chauncey, Robert
  1982   Teen-Age Alcoholism. Unpublished manuscript.
Cicourel, Aaron
  1968   The Social Organization of Juvenile Justice. New York: John Wiley & Sons.
Collins, Randall
  1981   "On the micro-foundations of macro-sociology." American Journal of Sociology, 86
          (March).
Conrad, Peter and Joseph Schneider
  1980   Deviance and Medicalization. St. Louis, MO: C. V. Mosby Co.
Crane, R. S.
  1974   "The languages of criticism and the structure of poetry." Pp. 146–155 in N. J.
          Handy and M. Westbrook (eds.) Twentieth Century Criticism. New York: The Free
          Press.
Douglas, Jack D.
  1967   The Social Meanings of Suicide. Princeton, NJ: Princeton University Press.
Feuer, Lewis
  1969   The Conflict of Generations. New York: Basic Books.
Freidson, Eliot
  1970   The Profession of Medicine. New York: Dodd, Mead Co.
Friedrichs, Robert W.
  1970   A Sociology of Sociology. New York: The Free Press.
Giddens, Anthony
  1976   New Rules of Sociological Method. New York: Basic Books.
  1979   Central Problems in Social Theory. Berkeley, CA: University of California Press.
Goffman, Erving
  1961   Asylums. New York: Doubleday & Co.
Gouldner, Alvin
  1968   "The sociologist as partisan: Sociology and the welfare state." The American So-
          ciologist, 3 (May): 103–116.
  1970   The Coming Crisis of Western Sociology. New York: Basic Books.

Gusfield, Joseph
    1963   Symbolic Crusade: Status Politics and the American Temperance Movement. Ur-
            bana, IL: University of Illinois Press.
    1975   "Categories of ownership and responsibility in social issues: Alcohol abuse and
            automobile use." Journal of Drug Issues, 5 (fall): 285–303.
    1976   "The prevention of drinking problems." Pp. 267–292 in W. Filstead, J. J. Rossi and
            Mark Keller (eds.) Alcohol and Alcohol Problems: New Knowledge. Cambridge,
            MA: Ballinger.
    1981   The Culture of Public Problems: Drinking-Driving and the Symbolic Order. Chicago,
            IL: University of Chicago Press.
    1982   "Deviance in the welfare state: The alcoholism profession and the entitlements of
            stigma." Pp. 1–20 in Michael Lewis (ed.) Research in Social Problems and Public
            Policy Vol. 2, Greenwich, CT: JAI Press.
    1983   "Prevention: Rise, decline and renaissance." In Alcohol, Science, and Society. New
            Brunswick, NJ: Rutgers Center of Alcohol Studies.
Keller, Mark
    1976   "Problems with alcohol: An historical perspective." Pp. 5–28 in W. Filstead, J. J.
            Rossi, and Mark Keller (eds.) Alcohol and Alcohol Problems: New Knowledge.
            Cambridge, MA: Ballinger.
Kitsuse, John and Aaron Cicourel
    1963   "A note on the use of official statistics." Social Problems 11: 131–139.
Kitsuse, John and Malcolm Spector
    1973   "Toward a sociology of social problems." Social Problems 20 (spring): 407–-441.
Levine, Harry G.
    1978   "The discovery of addiction." Journal of Studies on Alcohol 39 (January): 143–174.
Lipset, Seymour Martin
    1960   Political Man. Garden City, NY: Doubleday.
Lynd, Robert and Helen Lynd
    1929   Middletown. New York: Harcourt, Brace and Company.
    1937   Middletown in Transition. New York: Harcourt, Brace and Company.
MacAndrew, Craig and Robert Edgerton
    1969   Drunken Comportment. Chicago, IL: Aldine Press.
Mannheim, Karl
    1949   Ideology and Utopia. New York: Harcourt, Brace and Company.
Mauss, Armand
    1975   Social Problems as Social Movements. New York: Lippincott.
Merton, Robert and Robert Nisbet
    1976   Contemporary Social Problems. New York: Harcourt, Brace, Jovanovich.
Mills, C. Wright
    1957   The Power Elite. New York: Oxford University Press.
Nisbet, Robert
    1976   Sociology as an Art Form. New York: Oxford University Press.
Ogburn, William F.
    1922   Social Change. New York: Viking Press.
Ogburn, William F. and Meyer Nimkoff
    1940   Sociology. Boston, MA: Houghton, Mifflin Company.
    1946   Sociology. New impression. Boston, MA: Houghton, Mifflin Company.
    1950   Sociology. Second edition. Boston, MA: Houghton, Mifflin Company.
    1958   Sociology. 3d ed. Boston, MA: Houghton, Mifflin Company.
Pepper, Stephen
    1966   World Hypotheses. Berkeley, CA: Univeristy of California Press.

Rains, Prudence
    1975   "Imputations of deviance: A retrospective essay on the labelling perspective."
            Social Problems 23 (October): 1–11.
Rieff, Philip
    1959   Freud: The Mind of the Moralist. New York: Viking Press.
Robinson, David
    1976   From Drinking to Alcoholism. New York: John Wiley and Sons.
Room, Robin
    1979   "Governing Images of Alcohol and Drug Problems." Ph.D. dissertation, Department
            of Sociology, University of California, Berkeley.
Scheff, Thomas
    1966   Being Mentally Ill. Chicago, IL: Aldine Press.
Schneider, Joseph
    1978   "Deviant drinking as disease: Alcoholism as a social accomplishment." Social
            Problems 25 (April): 361–372.
Schur, Edwin
    1965   Crimes Without Victims. Englewood Cliffs, NJ: Prentice Hall.
Schwartz, Barry
    1981   Vertical Classification. Chicago, IL: University of Chicago Press.
Scott, Robert
    1969   The Making of Blind Men. New York: Russell Sage Foundation.
Spector, Malcolm and John Kitsuse
    1977   Constructing Social Problems. Menlo Park, CA: Cummings.
Stoll, Clarice
    1975   "Images of man and social control." In R. Akers and R. Hawkins (eds.) Law and
            Social Control. Englewood Cliffs, NJ: Prentice Hall.
Stouffer, Sanuel
    1955   Communism, Conformity and Civil Liberties. New York: Doubleday.
Straus, Robert
    1976   "Alcoholism and problem drinking." Pp. 181–218 in R. Merton and R. Nisbet (eds.)
            in Contemporary Social Problems. New York: Harcourt, Brace, Jovanovich.
Szasz, Thomas
    1961   The Myth of Mental Illness. New York: Harper and Row.
White, Hayden
    1976   "The fiction of factual representation." In Angus Fletcher (ed.) The Literature of
            Fact. New York: Columbia University Press.

3 Better read than dead: Notes on using archival materials in social problems and deviance research*

Ronald J. Troyer
Drake University

(the) sociologist has erred in the past by ignoring historical data. (Lipset, 1968:22)

most of what passes for sociological research in this country is not informed by much in the way of historical perspective. (Erikson, 1970:331)

These kinds of assessments are generally acknowledged as all too accurate characterizations of sociological scholarship.[1] Numerous explanations for this situation have been offered. Erikson (1970), for example, cites an intellectual division of labor, whereby the past is seen as the province of history and the present the sociological domain. Others have cited the ahistorical character of sociological theories (Zaret, 1978) or pointed out that the methodologies popular among sociologists "do not easily allow for historical analysis" (Williamson et al., 1977). Whatever the reasons, this shortcoming "severely handicaps our ability to answer two questions: (a) How and why

---

*I would like to thank John I. Kitsuse, Armand L. Mauss, Gerald E. Markle, Joseph W. Schneider, and Malcolm Spector for helpful comments on an earlier version of this paper.
[1]Some notable exceptions include *Wayward Puritans* by Kai T. Erikson (1966), *Symbolic Crusade* by Joseph Gusfield (1963), *Theft, Law and Society* by Jerome Hall (1952), *The Child Savers* by Anthony Platt (1969), "A sociological analysis of the law of vagrancy" by William Chambliss (1964), and "Rediscovering delinquency: social history, political ideology and the sociology of law" by John Hagan and Jeffery Leon (1977).

have social forms come to assume their present shape? and (b) What shapes are they likely to assume in the future?" (Williamson et al., 1977).

Whether attempting to answer such questions or focusing on other issues, scholars are beginning to address the uses and role of history in sociological concerns. Stinchcombe (1978) has written a monograph arguing for the use of historical materials in doing social theory, and Burke (1980) has suggested that the distinction between social history and historical sociology should become irrelevant. Accompanying these theoretical treatises has been the publication of empirical social problems and deviance studies using historical materials (see, for example, Hagan and Leon, 1977; Schlossman, 1977; Monkkonen, 1975; Rothman, 1971, 1980; Lane, 1979; Alix, 1978; and Fox, 1978).

Although the number of historical studies is growing, most sociologists are unaware of the kinds of historical data available and how to locate, evaluate, and use it within a sociological framework. This chapter attempts to help alleviate this condition by showing that archival collections are a potentially rich source of data for social problems and deviance research. Specifically, this essay will identify sources of national, state, and local archival data, describe the kind of information contained in each source, and then suggest, in a very general and preliminary way, how the sociologist might design a research project using these materials.

THEORY AND HISTORY: A VITAL CONNECTION

Most of the recent historiographic research in social problems and deviance has been produced by historians. Although often utilizing sociological concepts, these studies generally do not clearly specify theoretical and methodological frameworks. However, as Pisciotta (1981:116, 127) notes, "a simple numerical increase in historiographic research will not . . . optimally increase our understanding . . . unless historical researchers identify their a priori assumptions, methodology, and theoretical perspective."

Anyone who has followed the developments in the social problems and deviance literature the past few years is well aware of two divergent perspectives concerning the proper subject matter for the sociological approach. Ritzer (1975) has called these the social factist and social definitionist paradigms. The former, in the Durkheimian tradition, takes as its basic subject matter the social fact, including such phenomena as groups, societies, social systems, norms, values, and so forth. This approach treats these "social facts" as if they were real and external to the individual. These ideas fit nicely with quantitative techniques which are used by social factists to discover the causes of things that are assumed to exist in reality. In studying social problems, for example, the social factist usually describes the extent and nature of the condition assumed to exist, and asks, "What are the causes of this problem (condition)?" In recent social problems theory, the social factist position has been most precisely formulated by Manis (1976), who defines social problems as conditions detrimental to human well-being.

The social factist focus on causal relations has led to an emphasis on quantitative analysis of data produced specifically for research.[2] However, in using historical materials, the researcher must rely on types of data pertaining to past populations produced by others for varied purposes. As a result, the data often fall short of the requirements for traditional quantitative causal analysis.[3] The major exceptions to this general assessment are the manuscript rolls of the federal census (Murphey, 1973). These materials present some opportunities but have been under utilized by sociologists.

The social definition paradigm, according to Ritzer, begins with the assumption that social reality is *not* a static set of coercive social facts, but that man is an active creator of his own reality. Blumer (1962:189), for example, writes that "the organization of a human society is the framework inside which social action takes place and is not the determinant of that action." These assumptions produce a very different approach to studying the social world. For example, if we are active creators of our social reality, the focus becomes the process by which that reality is constructed, created, and maintained. In studying social problems and deviance, the social definitionist examines the processes by which people or a society have come to define a condition as undesirable. Spector and Kitsuse (1977) have emphasized this approach with their definition of social problems as "the activities of individuals or groups making assertions of grievances and claims with respect to some putative conditions."

As Hindus (1979) has noted, a majority of the historical social problems and deviance studies fit into this tradition, because the researcher can avoid the "hidden," that is, not officially reported, deviance problem. Since the basic research question of this approach is a how question, that is, how has something come to be seen as a social problem or deviant, the concern is not whether the materials accurately reflect the incidence of crime, mental illness, or whatever. Instead, this perspective views historical data as the products of interested actors playing important roles in the definitional processes under scrutiny (Kitsuse and Cicourel, 1963). Rather than looking for

---

[2]Stinchcombe (1978) has argued that historical materials can be used in causal analysis through the "deep analogies" approach. Although intriguing and suggestive, Stinchombe has not solved sampling and historical accuracy problems (Graff, 1980).

[3]Several scholars (for example, Monkkonen, 1975; Lane, 1979) have attempted hypothesis testing studies using historical materials. Although admiring their efforts, reviewers (Hindus, 1979; Smith, 1980) have emphasized that the limitations of the data make such studies suggestive rather than definitive.

unbiased records, social definitionists assume historical materials represent the interested views of the person or group that produce them.

It is the contention of this paper that both social problems and deviance approaches can profitably use archival materials. After covering a few basics, this paper will attempt to show how this can be done.

ARCHIVAL BASICS

Before identifying some specific data it is necessary to cover some introductory information, definitions, and address a few basic issues. First, the archives section of the library is a place where public records or historical documents are preserved. Public documents include records of government agencies and other organizations or institutions. Many archives also contain private records, usually of individuals, which have been donated by families. Public records are generally available to researchers,[4] while permission from the donor or their representative may be required for access to private collections.

The above points to a related distinction that must be kept in mind when using archival materials. Official materials are those records created by a person as a member of an organization, both governmental and private. "Personal materials" refers to what is written by an individual as a private citizen. The most noteworthy examples of the latter are diaries, although articles in newspapers or journals might be included here. The sociologist will be most interested in the official materials, although personal records could be used to supplement public records.

Another important distinction to keep in mind is the difference between primary and secondary sources. Primary sources are original accounts produced by eyewitnesses, including all official proceedings, personal memiors, autobiographies, and so forth. Secondary sources are mediated accounts constructed with information gathered from others, including eyewitnesses. They are descriptive and, sometimes, interpretive. The goal for the researcher should be to get primary sources whenever possible. The interpretations offered in secondary sources, however, may provide data valuable for sociological analysis. Erikson (1966) and Gusfield (1963) have demonstrated the fruitfullness of using both types of materials.

---

[4]This statement describes the situation for documents already deposited in archival collections. If the researcher is seeking records still controlled by an agency or institution, access may be more restricted. Access to court records, especially juvenile court records, may be gained only by obtaining a court order. Although this sounds imposing, it is not that difficult for academic researchers.

However, it is essential that the researcher keep in mind the distinction between the two sources, and their different nature.

In working with archival materials, it is necessary to recognize the assets and limitations of this type of data. Major advantages include the potential for longitudinal studies, low cost, and nonreactivity (Webb et al., 1966). While there have been relatively few longitudinal studies in sociology, archival records offer some real opportunities. The census materials are one of the best sources, but other kinds of longitudinal records are also available (some of these will be identified below). Data collection costs are minimal, since all that is needed is time to pull materials off the library shelf or to read microfilm. In addition, there is little possibility for the researcher to influence the data, that is, change the nature of the response by his or her presence.

These advantages should make archival records attractive to many sociological researchers. However, anyone embarking on such an endeavor must also be aware of the concomitant disadvantages. One difficulty concerns the representativeness of the records, usually because of selective deposit and selective survival (Webb et al., 1966). For example, one often finds that the records the researcher is interested in are available only for a few years. The question then arises as to what generalizations can be drawn on the basis of a limited time frame.

A major problem is determining the accuracy of the records. Since new data cannot be obtained, the researcher may have to rely on internal analysis such as dividing the data into subclasses and making cross-checks (Webb et al., 1966). Occasionally, it is possible to determine accuracy by finding other documents containing the same data.

These limitations mean that the researcher must view historical materials cautiously. Erikson (1966) has suggested that sociologists need to approach the data more like historians, being skeptical and thoughtful, recognizing that written history reflects the "talent and temper of the mind that produced it." Few historians are skeptical enough to endorse T. E. Lawrences's comment (Garnett, 1938:559) that "The documents are liars," but would embrace Brooks' (1969) warning that researchers must first determine by whom, where, and under what circumstances the document was produced, before studying its content. Some scholars even argue that these and other data problems are solvable, permitting rigorous hypothesis testing (Bogue and Clubb, 1977). The sociologist is well advised to remember Williamson's et al. (1977:263) comment that "The central methodological question a researcher ponders when he or she works with historical data is: How much faith can I place in the evidence? To what extent can I believe the data?"[5]

---

[5]The issue discussed in this paragraph is more of a problem for the social factist than

An equally important methodological issue concerns the context for the production of the documents and data. How does the sociologist ". . . deal with the variable social processes that were the occasion for the construction of categories in the census, the taking of counts, the recording of events, the invention of new measures, the formulation of new social concerns, and so forth?" (Kitsuse, 1981). It may not be possible to always address this matter satisfactorily, but at least two strategies seem desirable. First, as I try to demonstrate below, it is possible to gather some data on these variable social processes. Congressional debates and hearings, for example, provide insights into the forces influencing the construction of census categories. The general difficulty here is that, often, the evidence available is not as extensive as desired. A second way of addressing this issue is to consult histories of the period in question to gain a general picture of the times. An historian's concern usually focuses on presenting a definitive account of a slice of time as it represents a unique set of events. The goal is to "discover how it came to be and what it contributed to the later events of that society" (Gusfield, 1963:58). This is where the sociologist begins. For him or her, the question is what can be learned from this slice of time that is generalizable to a wider social process. Consequently, it is necessary to read history in order to understand the context of the time and help sharpen the focus.[6]

Prior to beginning the research, the scholar also needs to do some other preliminary work, such as studying the history and operation of the administrative agency or organization that has produced the records, developing and sharpening the questions to be investigated. Unless this background work is completed and the research goal developed in the context of this information, there will be a great deal of floundering in archival collections.

Finally, and perhaps most importantly, the researcher *must* find a good archivist. Archives generally do not have card catalogs which tell where and how to locate materials. That information can be obtained only from a professional archivist.[7] The researcher must be sure to carefully and clearly

---

the social definitionist. The social factist assumes there is a reality and wishes to work with measures of that reality. The social definitionist, by contrast, assumes the social world is created. The concern, therefore, is with the construction of the reality the author of the document is presenting, rather than its congruence with "reality."

[6]This is not an argument that the sociologist should accept the historian's interpretation. This, in fact, may be the focus for investigation. The point is that the sociologist needs to be familiar with descriptive and interpretive accounts of the period in question.

[7]My experience has been that archivists are very happy to help. This part of the library is not frequently used by the public except by persons conducting genealogical research. Consequently, the professional archivist is usually pleased to see a serious scholar.

explain what his or her interest is. Only then will the skills of the archivist be fully utilized.

ARCHIVAL MATERIALS

To give the social problems and deviance scholar some ideas about the types of data available and how they might be used, I will identify and briefly discuss some of the nineteenth century[8] documents a typical archival collection contains.[9] The discussion is organized according to origin of the data, with United States government materials considered first, state materials reviewed next, and city and county documents surveyed last. In each case, the quality of the data will be assessed and some general suggestions offered on how social factists and social definitionists might use the documents. These general suggestions will be illustrated with a more detailed discussion on using the materials to study mental illness.

United States Government Materials
At the federal level, the primary source of data on social problems and deviance is the United States decennial census. The census data are available in two forms: microfilm of the manuscript census rolls, and published compiliations. The manuscript rolls provide raw data, with entries for each family (1840 and previous censuses) or each individual (1850 and after). This information is presented in aggregate form in numerous general summary and special report publications. For the nineteenth century, these publications are listed with a subject index in *Catalog of United States Census Publications, 1790–1945* (Dubester, 1950).

Table 1 shows when the census schedules with questions of likely interest to the social problems and deviance scholar were administered. As the table illustrates, much more data is available for the second half of the nineteenth century than the first half. However, the 1800–1840 censuses

---

[8]The discussion will be limited to nineteenth century materials simply because this makes the topic manageable. It should be noted that there are many relevant early twentieth century documents available on most of the topics discussed here.

[9]Most of the material for this paper was gathered at the Archives of Western Michigan University. Some universities will have more materials, especially those located in state capitals, while others will have fewer materials. Types of documents available will also vary with some collections sparse on local records. The point is that there is a vast amount of data available that has been ignored by sociologists.
There are several sources that identify archival collections and their location. Among the more useful are *A Guide to Manuscripts and Archives in the United States* (1961) edited by Philip M. Hamer, and the *National Union Catalog of Manuscript Collections* (1962–), compiled by the Library of Congress.

Table 1

Administration of Nineteenth Century United States Census Schedules Containing Information for Social Problems and Deviance Scholars

Census Schedule	Year Administered									
	1800	1810	1820	1830	1840	1850	1860	1870	1880	1890
General Population	X	X	X	X	X	X	X	X	X	X
Mortality (includes suicide and homicide)						X	X	X	X	X
Social Statistics (includes crime and pauperism)						X	X	X	X	X
Supplemental Schedules crime, pauperism and benevolence									X	X
mentally and physically defective									X	X

59

provide more information than the table indicates, since a number of pertinent questions were included on the general population schedule. To illustrate, beginning in 1820 questions about "foreigners," an item relevant to studies of ethnicity and minority groups, were asked. The 1830 schedule added queries on the deaf, dumb, and blind with new items on insanity, idiocy, and literacy appearing in 1840.

As Table 1 indicates, the 1850 and later censuses collected much more information. In fact the 1850, 1860, and 1870 censuses were carried out under virtually the same law and procedures, with only minor changes from year to year. Not only do these general population schedules contain sections titled "Deaf and dumb, blind, insane, idiotic, pauper, or convict," but special mortality and social statistics schedules also provide useful information. During these years, the social statistics included items on the number of criminals convicted within the year and number in prison on June 1, subdivided, in each case, by native and foreign birth, with similar items for paupers. The mortality schedules called for demographic characteristics of every person dying during the year (suicides and murders included) as well as the cause of death.

One of the rules for census workers during the 1850, 1860, and 1870 censuses was that when they came to an asylum, house of refuge, or poorhouse, they had to list each inmate's name on a separate line of the general population schedule and fill in all the standard columns. As a result, basic demographic information such as age, sex, color, country or state of birth, and occupation is available for each resident of the institution.

The 1880 and 1890 censuses provide even more information, since a number of supplemental schedules were administered. This point is illustrated in Table 2, which presents a summary of the information contained in the 1880 census. Clearly, the supplemental social statistics schedules on defective, dependent, and delinquent classes, idiots, deaf mutes, blind, insane, homeless children, prison inhabitants, and pauper and indigent inhabitants of institutions should provide a wealth of data for the student of social problems and deviance.

Table 2 also lists state census summaries. During the nineteenth century these summaries were published by a number of states, not the federal government.[10] They are identified in the table because they report the aggregate totals for each census schedule item by county and the entire state. Consequently, this document provides vital information for comparative studies between states, as well as between counties within states.

To illustrate how these data can be used, I will briefly examine some of

---

[10]Usually a state official is required by law to gather the statistics from the United States census and publish them. In Michigan, for example, this duty was assigned to the Secretary of State.

Table 2
Information in 1880 United States Census Pertaining
to Social Problems and Deviance

Census Schedule	Information Contained*
General Population	Name of person, relationship to head of family, color, age, sex, marital status, occupation, health (blind, idiotic, insane, maimed or crippled), education (attended school during past year, cannot read, cannot write), place of birth, place of birth of father, place of birth of mother.
Social Statistics	
Defective, dependent, and delinquent class	Residence when at home (city, county), name, paying patient, form of disease, hospital or asylum, (length, date of discharge), epileptic, suicidal, homicidal.
Idiots	Cause, in training schools, insane.
Deaf Mutes	Cause, in training schools, insane.
Blind	Cause, in training schools, insane.
Homeless Children	Name, residence when at home, (city or town, county or state), father deceased, mother deceased, abandoned by parents, born in the institutions, year admitted, illegitimate, ever arrested, if yes, what offense, ever convicted or sentenced, been rescued from criminal surroundings, idiot, blind, deaf-mute.
Pauper and Indigent Inhabitants in Institutions, poor houses or asylums, or boarded at public expense in private houses	Residence when at home (city or town, county or state), name, how supported (city, county, state, cost of institution), able-bodied, intemperate, epileptic, ever convicted of crime, disabled, date of admission, husband, wife, mother, father, sons-daughters (how many), brothers-sisters (how many), blind, dumb, insane, idiotic.
Mortality	Name, age at death, reason, occupation, place of birth, place of birth of father, place of birth of mother.
State Census Summaries	Contains aggregate totals for all of the above for the state organized by counties, sex, and so forth.

*The items in this column represent the exact wording used on the census schedules.

the materials on insanity. Here the census rolls should be a virtual gold mine for the social factist researcher, since many of the questions measure variables often used by these sociologists. Furthermore, most of the microfilm is of such good quality that the data can be coded directly from the census form.

Using insanity as an example and working only with the 1870 general population schedule, I gathered the information contained in Tables 3 and 4. For those familiar with the sociology of mental illness, Table 3 provides some interesting comparisons to the distributions reported in current social problems and deviance textbooks. As an illustration of a very suggestive preliminary finding in Table 3, note that thirty and one-tenth percent of the

Table 3
Kalamazoo, Michigan Asylum Inmates by Age, Sex, and Place of Birth
According to 1870 Census*

	Males			Females		
Age	Michigan	Other state	Foreign	Michigan	Other state	Foreign
under 30	18	19	10	17	11	10
30–39	3	18	20	8	34	12
40–49	1	17	11	4	20	12
50–59	1	7	5	. . .	15	3
60+	. . .	4	2	. . .	5	3
Total	25	65	48	29	85	40

*Since these data are presented for illustrative purposes only, percentages were not computed.

inmates at the Kalamazoo Asylum were foreign born, a figure approximately twice the percentage of foreign born in Western Michigan and the entire state in the 1870s. Furthermore, only eighteen and one-half percent of the inmates were born in Michigan, the location of the asylum. How do these figures compare to those of other states? What is the national pattern? These are only some of the findings and questions that could be pursued.[11]

Table 4 provides information useful for comparison to more recent findings relating mental illness and institutionalization to lower class status. If one assumes that farmers fall into the lower class (perhaps a questionable assumption), it becomes clear that the Kalamazoo Asylum was an institution populated by those at the lower portion of the socioeconomic order, a finding that appears to support Rothman's (1971) thesis concerning the role such institutions played in the nineteenth century.

Certainly, the above is a crude and preliminary analysis of the data. Furthermore, only a portion of the data contained in the general population schedule has been discussed. Much more information is available on the statistics and other schedules, and needs to be analyzed before generalizations can be made. However, the intent here is suggestive, with the hope that those studying problems and deviance will begin to use these materials.

The major limitation of these census materials for the social factist scholar concerns their accuracy. While it is doubtful that any census has ever been entirely accurate (even the 1980 census has been challenged in court),

[11]There is some disagreement among historians about the relationship between mental illness in the nineteenth century and foreign birth. Rothman (1971) claims that the foreign born comprised a disporportionate share of the insane asylum inmates, while Fox (1978) has argued that this may not be correct. The point is that some additional studies are needed to resolve the issue.

Table 4
Occupation of Kalamazoo Asylum Male* Inmates According to 1870 Census

Occupation	Frequency	Occupation	Frequency
Farmer	55	Cooper	1
Laborer	12	Driver	1
Farm Laborer	7	Gardener	1
Clerk	6	Policeman	1
Student	6	Peddler	1
Carpenter	3	Porter, stone	1
Merchant	3	Priest	1
Physician	2	Saddler	1
Brick mason	2	Sailor	1
Soldier	2	Sea Captain	1
Agent, mining Co.	1	Stoneworker	1
Blacksmith	1	Tailor	1
Boilermaker	1	Teamster	1
Butcher	1	None	11
Cabinet maker	1	Missing or unable	
Chain maker	1	to read entry	9
		Total	138

*Only the occupations for males are listed, because the census worker usually did not make an entry for female inmates.

the compilations of the early nineteenth century social statistics are especially suspect. The 1840 materials, for example, appear to contain many errors. Not only do the figures appear to be highly inaccurate when compared to other sources (Wright and Hunt, 1900:37; Holt, 1929:13) but internal comparison points up serious discrepancies (Wright and Hunt, 1900:37). Congress responded to these criticisms by establishing a census board charged with the task of rectifying the problems. This board's recommendations led to improved procedures for the 1850, 1860, and 1870 censuses. Although some problems remained, as the Superintendent of the 1870 census acknowledged (Walker, 1872), comparisons for these three censuses are feasible and more legitimate, since roughly the same procedures and forms were used.

The 1880 and 1890 counts were conducted under new legislation designed to correct the problems with previous censuses. These improvements probably did not produce error-free results, but the point is that these data can be used with much greater confidence, especially if the materials are used in conjunction with state and local records. Lane (1979), for example, has demonstrated this possibility with his study of violent deaths in nineteenth and twentieth century Philadelphia.

These data accuracy problems are much less significant for the social definitionist scholar because very different questions are being asked. From this framework, the crucial issue is explaining the social definition of insanity, pauperism, crime, and so forth, as social problems. The kinds of research questions pursued include: Why did the nineteenth century censuses begin including items on social problems and deviance? (For example, why did the 1840 census include questions on insanity for the first time?) What terms are used at various times? (The 1890 schedule asked about the number of Negroes, mulattoes, quadroons, and octoroons.) What questions are asked repeatedly, from one census to the next, about a given "problem"? (Beginning in 1840, items on insanity appeared on each census schedule.) What new problems or kinds of deviance are asked about? (The 1880 census included an item on illegitimacy for the first time.) And what types of problems are no longer covered? (The 1870 census queried about "constitutional relations," an item dropped in subsequent enumerations.)

To illustrate how one might proceed, I tried to gain some insight into why the 1840 schedule included social problems items, especially the insanity question. One census historian has attributed the new items to the "humanitarian movements' . . . stimulation of social consciousness" during the Jacksonian period (Holt, 1929:11), but little evidence is provided to support this interpretation. Others have attributed the new items to President Polk's suggestion to Congress that the census be extended to obtain statistics on the "interests entrusted to and influenced by legislation" (Wright and Hunt, 1900:36). I looked into the Congressional proceedings for the 1840 census[12] and found there were a number of unsuccessful attempts to add various items to the schedule. There was nothing, however, pertaining to the specific question of insanity. Further research, for example, locating Senate and House journals, might yield more data, although one of the problems for this early nineteenth century period is that records, even of Congressional debates, are not always complete.

Another source did yield some insight. In his introduction to the 1880 census *Compendium* (xxix), the Superintendent of the Census (Francis A. Walker) cited four reasons for collecting information on these "unfortunate classes:" to enable the intelligent direction of philanthropic efforts; discover the underlying scientific causal laws; provide the state with information on the proportion of its citizens incapacitated for military service; and determine the burden these classes place on productive labor. Certainly, additional analysis of Congressional Proceedings for the various censuses might shed light on the relative importance of these factors.

The major difficulty for the social definitionist is that few archival

---

[12]Congressional proceedings for the nineteenth century are contained in the following documents: *Debates and Proceedings in the Congress of the United States, 1789–1824.* (42 vols. Washington, DC: Government Printing Office); *Register of Debates in Congress, Containing the Debates and Proceedings, 1825–1837.* (29 vols. Washington, DC: Gales and Seaton, editors and publishers); *Congressional Globe, Containing the Debates and Proceedings, 1833–1873.* (109 vols. Washington, DC: F. O. Blair, et al., editors and publishers); *Congressional Record, Containing the Debates and Proceedings, 1873–.* (Washington, DC: Government Printing Office).

collections have all of the early nineteenth century Congressional materials (the problem I encountered above). As a consequence, it may be necessary to visit several archival collections.

State Materials

As Table 5 demonstrates, there is a vast quantity of data contained in the materials either produced by or collected by the state. For purposes of brevity, the detailed listing of the demographic information collected was not included for each source. Since the materials and the data contained in Table 5 are far too numerous for detailed discussion of each one, I will make some general research suggestions and offer a brief remark about the source. To illustrate the use of these documents, this section will conclude with a discussion of the way one scholar has handled these data in the study of mental illness.

The first type of document listed, Attorney General reports, is somewhat disappointing in that there are few statistics or evaluative comments. The kinds of statistical data on crime the social factist needs is usually summarized on a few pages, with the rest of the reports devoted to technical legal questions, court decisions, lists of county prosecutors, judges, and so forth. The social definitionist might use these summary statistics to examine the activities of prosecutors in defining certain matters as criminal behavior. For example, a preliminary perusal revealed a number of nineteenth century prosecutions for adultery and using profanity in public. By noting the trend over the years, changing definitions of deviant behavior and the emergence or decline of particular classifications and categories can be identified.

The Bureau of Labor reports were a very pleasant surprise. By state law, the commissioner was required to include a report on state penal institutions. Therefore, these documents provide a wealth of statistical information on prisons and inmates suitable for numerous social factist studies. In addition, many of the reports contain written statements on prisons, the crime problem, causes of crime, and so forth. Analysis of these documents would permit a social definitionist to gain insights into the official definition of the crime problem, purposes of prisons, and determination of penal goals or claims made about the effects of penal sanctions.

For some reason, these Bureau of Labor reports seem to concentrate on special topics. As Table 5 shows, there are extensive sections in certain reports on convict labor, child labor, pauperism, and even suicide. Besides presenting numerous statistics, these documents include written statements from officials and citizens concerning the nature of the problem and often prescribing solutions. These written comments, of course, are a resource for the social definitionist.[13]

---

[13]A perusal of the 1887 Report of convict labor led to the discovery of a comment by a W. T. McGarrigle, former superintendent of the Chicago police, mindful of a labeling theory analy-

Table 5
Information in State Archival Records on Social Problems and Deviance

Document	Type of information	Dates of records in Michigan
Primary Sources		
Attorney General (annual reports)	Summary statistics on offenses charged, number prosecuted, number convicted, written summaries of important cases in the state, actions of the state Supreme Court, and letters written by prosecutors to Attorney General.	1896–1920
Bureau of Labor (annual reports)	Statistical data on penal institutions and prisoners (occupation, offense committed, prior commitments, age), discussions of contracts with business (wages paid to inmates, etc.), and letters from prison superintendents.	1884–1920
	The 1887 annual report deals with the controversy over convict labor, includes a wealth of statistics, interviews, and so forth. This report also has letters from superintendents of prisons in other states summarizing practices at their institutions.	
	The 1887 annual report has 72 pages on child labor (statistics and letters).	
	The 1894 annual report includes statistics on pauperism in Michigan going back to 1871.	
	The 1901 report includes materials on suicides (names, dates, marital status, means used, and reason for suicide).	
Legislature (journals and investigatory reports)	Statistical data on nature of the problem, institutions, and inmates. Also contain statements from officials, interested groups, inmates, and politicians on the problem.	
Prisons and Reformatories (annual reports)	Mass of statistical data on prisoners, staff, and institutional operation, letters, and summary statements by superintendents and other prison personnel.	1859*

At first glance, the state legislative journals and investigatory reports appear to contain statistical information important to social factists. Caution, however, is in order, since, as Rothman notes (1971:303), these documents are the product of political pressures. But this is just what the social definitionist is looking for. Statements in these documents show how various interests defined the problem and the solution they prescribed.

---

sis. Mr. McGarrigle noted that the released convict was often unable to find a job because people knew him and he was harassed by police because they felt he was a "criminal." As a consequence, McGarrigle suggested that released persons often associated with criminals and turned to further crimes.

Table 5 (*Cont.*)

Document	Type of information	Dates of records in Michigan
Secretary of State: Vital Statistics (annual reports)	Statistical data on deaths including violent deaths by month, region, county, nature (accident, battle, homicide, suicide, and execution) with detailed data on suicide (data, marital status, sex, color, occupation, and means used), illegitimacy (birthplace of mother, age of mother, etc.), and mixed marriages.	1868–1920
Reports of Sheriffs Relating to Jails (annual reports)	Summary statistics of persons detained in jail (offenses charged with, length of stay, etc.), and a brief statement from sheriff on condition of jail.	1872*
State Census	Used U.S. general population schedule (statistical data on foreign birth, illiteracy, deaf, dumb, blind, and insane).	1874
Superintendent of Public Instruction (annual reports)	Statistical data on inmates (especially educational statistics), and written materials from reformatory staff on the nature of their work and goals of the institution.	1859–present
Secondary Sources *Michigan History* (journal)	Articles by state and local historians on problems such as temperance, prisons, care of insane, capital punishment, crime, and women's rights. Description and location of state archival records.	
Michigan Pioneer and Historical Collections	Includes articles on asylums for the insane, death penalty debates, temperance, reformatory progress, and philosophy of imprisonment.	

*The data identified are the first year covered by the report, since I was unable to determine when these reports ceased.

An excellent supplement to the Bureau of Labor reports is provided in the annual reports issued by each prison and reformatory.[14] Again there is material here for both the social factist (many statistics on the inmates) and social definitionist (discussion of crime problems and penal efforts).[15]

---

[14]It was standard practice for states to require all institutions to submit annual reports, usually to the legislature. Unfortunately, I was unsuccessful in the effort to locate the Michigan Asylum reports.

[15]The researcher must keep in mind that the superintendents of these institutions had a clear vested interest in the image presented by these reports. This, of course, is the very thing the social definitionist wants to analyze.

The Secretary of State's Office documents include two very useful reports, vital statistics and sheriff's reports. Vital Statistics reports offer social factists a wealth of information on suicide, violent deaths, illegitimacy, and mixed marriages. The Sheriff's reports not only contain annual statistics on persons detained, charges, and so forth, but evaluate statements about jail conditions and the crime problems in each county.

A number of states took their own interdecennial census during the latter half of the nineteenth century. In 1885, for example, at least 11 states and several territories gathered information from their citizens.[16] Many of these states simply used the United States census general population schedule, which included items on illiteracy, foreign birth, deaf, dumb, blind, and insanity. The results of these counts were published and are generally available within the state conducting the enumeration. Although these data are available only in aggregate form, they constitute an additional measure for the social factist. By comparing the state enumeration methods with United States census procedures, it might also be possible to gain some insight into errors and biases of the respective measures.

The Superintendent of Public Instruction's annual reports also contain useful information for the social problems and deviance scholar. Each report, after 1859, includes a section on schools in reformatories providing statistics, statements of teachers, and an evaluation of the educational process:[17] again, good material for both the social factist and social definitionist.

In addition to these primary source materials, secondary sources are also important for archival researchers. In most states, historical societies began publishing journals during the nineteenth century. In Michigan, the journals *Michigan History* and *Michigan Pioneer and Historical Collections* contain articles written by local and state historians on such relevant topics as crime, asylums for the insane, capital punishment debates, temperance, and women's rights. Many of these articles were written by close observers and participants during the time the issue was being debated, providing useful information for social definitional studies.

The journal *Michigan History* also includes several articles describing the nature and location of state archival records. For example, the location of state prison reports, parole records, state prison inspector reports, and the report of an investigation of the Michigan Asylum for the Insane at

---

[16]According to Wright and Hunt (1900), these states were Florida, Nebraska, Colorado, Massachusetts, Rhode Island, Kansas, Oregon, New Jersey, Wisconsin, Iowa, Minnesota, and Michigan. The District of Columbia and the territories of New Mexico and Dakota also conducted counts.

[17]Again, caution is in order. For example, the reader will find the optimistic claims about student "progress" and rehabilitation suspect. Perhaps most importantly, these reports do provide a discription of how the education system within prisons was designed and statements of the goals established.

Kalamazoo, 1891, is identified in one volume. In other words, this should be a useful source for locating additional documents.

One of the characteristics of these state history journals is a major emphasis on persons. There are many articles on public officials, war heroes, and leading citizens. While the sociologist, and particularly the social factist, is often inclined to dismiss such material, it seems to offer the opportunity for a study of elites. Certainly additional materials are needed, but these journals do provide some important data.

To illustrate in more detail how these state materials might be used, I will briefly examine two recent works by a social historian. Rothman (1971, 1980) has published several volumes discussing the emergence and operation of insane asylums (as well as other institutions), in which state materials were a primary source of data. Specifically, Rothman has drawn on the annual institutional reports, legislative investigatory reports, the writings of the superintendents of these institutions, and other materials. His work constitutes a broad historical study (much of the volumes being descriptive in nature) placed in the framework of a social control argument; that is, these institutions represented the elites' attempt to control the unruly elements of society.[18]

In many ways, Rothman's work illustrates the valuable contributions that broad historical works make to an understanding of the nineteenth century. His discussion of the emergence of the institution in the context of Jacksonian democracy is valuable, and the suggestion that asylums became warehouses for the lower classes and immigrants is provocative. Yet the sociologist will not be convinced, because the argument is not supported with systematic analysis of the materials. Rothman's use of the writings of superintendents and the annual reports illustrates the problem. While numerous quotations and even statistics from these sources are cited, there is no evidence that a systematic structured content analysis was conducted. For example, how frequently are various themes mentioned in the superintendents' statements? How many of the superintendents discuss these themes? Is there a change in these themes over time? Furthermore, a comparative analysis is needed to systematically test some of Rothman's ideas. Did these institutions really become warehouses for immigrants? What proportion of inmates were immigrants in the early years compared to later years? How does this change (if there is a change) compare to the proportionate change in the general population?

These issues are not adequately addressed by Rothman, but the so-

---

[18]Fox (1978) focuses on California, specifically the San Francisco area, and takes issue with Rothman's social control thesis. Instead of elites imposing control on the lower classes, Fox argues that lower class families and the community cooperated with the elites, reaping some real benefits from the institutionalization of those designated as insane.

ciologist will be interested in just such questions. The social factist has been especially trained to analyze the data in a manner permitting answers to these questions. Furthermore, the sociologist, of whatever theoretical persuasion, can put these questions within theoretical frameworks suggesting broader generalization.

While the above discussion notes a few of the limitations associated with state archival records, some additional comments are in order. One of the problems for the social factist scholar is the lack of consistency over time. The kind of data reported seemed to change every time the head of the respective department changed. For example, one head of the Bureau of Labor prepared reports with extensive data on prison labor, while the next chief administrator limited convict work data to only a few pages. This fluctuation creates data gaps for longitudinal studies.

Other problems for the social factist include questions of accuracy and completeness. As with the United States census, the data were often collected by local officials who could easily have done shoddy work or may have been more interested in protecting self interests than submitting an objective report. Additionally, it seems likely that geographically remote and less populated portions of the state were not enumerated completely. A partial remedy for these problems is cross-checking the figures with other sources. As indicated in Table 5, for example, the Bureau of Labor reports can be compared to the annual reports submitted by the superintendents of state prisons. There are two difficulties with such a procedure. First, while different state offices published the reports, they could easily have used the same source for the statistics. Second, not everything can be cross-checked.

More practical difficulties for the researcher involve finding the documents. A frustrating problem in some archival collections is that not all of the records have been cataloged. Some may even be stored in boxes "somewhere in the southwest corner." Locating the relevant records is both time consuming and frustrating. Additionally, the researcher may discover that the pertinent records are scattered in several libraries instead of being housed in one central location. This requires travel time and maintaining cordial relationships with two or more archives' staffs.

These limitations also present difficulties for the social definitionist. Selective survival and consistency over time do present problems, although the latter may become a phenomenon to be analyzed. For example, analyzing the changes in the type of information reported over time clearly shows changing definitions of problems. Similarly, the self-serving nature of the annual institutional reports is exactly what is of central concern to the social definitionist. The question is not whether these reports are objective statements, but what claims are being made? What is the definition of the problem and prescription for solution offered in these documents? A content analysis of these materials should yield answers to these questions.

City and County Materials

City and county materials constitute the third category of archival documents available for social problems and deviance scholars. Few sociologists have used these sources, perhaps because the records' representativeness of a larger population is difficult to determine, but they certainly hold promise for case studies. Table 6 and the following discussion attempt to provide support for this assessment.

The first source listed in Table 6, the City Directory, has been used for social mobility studies, but its relevance to the social problems and deviance area may not be readily apparent. The possibility is to gather the names of those labeled as deviant from the census materials, poorhouse records, or other sources and trace them back over the years in the city directory. Their movement, ethnicity, occupation, and other characteristics could be determined in this manner.

Monkkonen (1975) has made such linkages in a study of criminal

Table 6
Information in City and County Archival Records on Social Problems
and Deviance

Documents	Type of Information	Dates Available
Primary Sources		
City Directory	Names (alphabetized), occupation, address	1867–present
Court Records	Legal documents pertaining to cases. Criminal cases—bill of information, warrants, court testimony, age of defendant, and age of victim. Chancery cases—divorce matters (complaints, depositions, and testimony).	1880–1920
Newspapers	Items on various "problems" in the community	1837–present
Poorhouse Records	Name, age, sex, residence (before admission), nationality, date of receiving into poorhouse, on whose order received, date of discharge, cause of pauperism, time in poorhouse (weeks and days), cause of discharge, blind, mute, epileptic, idiotic, insane, and remarks	1885–1912
Secondary Source		
Local histories	Background of institutions such as jails, poorhouses, asylums for insane, and so forth.	

defendants and paupers admitted to the poorhouse in Columbus, Ohio. Using the city directory, the 1870 manuscript census, and court and poorhouse records, he was able to answer questions about social origins and socioeconomic status, occupations, age, and family setting. This imaginative linkage produced results challenging many of the ideas about the existence of distinct pauper and criminal classes.

The relevance of court records is readily apparent, although they are not always as fruitful as the researcher might wish. In the court records identified in Table 6, the case files were often incomplete (several files were found where information on the disposition of the case was missing) and there was inconsistency from case to case with reference to the information contained. This certainly was not true for other researchers such as Erikson (1966) and Fox (1978), indicating that court records hold great potential for social problems and deviance scholars.

Fox (1978) has conducted a study that in many ways illustrates the social factist use of court records. Drawing upon the data contained in San Francisco Superior Court records, Fox focused on the civil commitment process. Although an historian, he pursued some very sociological questions (1978:4): "What types of people were officially judged insane? What brought them to the attention of the court, and what behavior did the court cite as evidence of insanity? What familial and professional groups, which instititional agencies lay behind the commitment system?" While Fox's approach is often limited to percentage calculation and tabular analysis, a sociologist trained in the social factist tradition should be able to explore relationships with more sophisticated analytic techniques.

The social definitionist can also use court records. Perhaps most obviously, these materials reveal the definitions of deviant behavior prevailing at the time. As an illustration of this point, examination of one chancery court divorce case revealed that the husband's first charge against his wife in the bill of particulars was that on a specific day she had told him to "shut his damned mouth!" A content analysis of divorce case testimony could yield fruitful results.

There are many additional possibilities for the social definitionist in the criminal case records. By examining the kinds of charges brought or persons prosecuted, various insights into the deviance defining process can be gained. To illustrate, when I examined the criminal court cases in Kent County, Michigan for 1880, there was no prosecution for liquor related cases. However, the records for 1897 reveal that 24.7 percent of all cases brought before the court concerned charges of "keeping saloon open" or liquor law violations. Furthermore, most of the cases resulted from complaints brought by two gentlemen named Hale and Hickox. The prosecuting attorneys were named Rogers and Wolcott. Many of the defendants, though certainly not all, had ethnic names such as Melbocher, Damsky, Vellema, Vander Putta, Wichtman, and Hammerschmidt. This preliminary analysis seems to provide evidence for Gusfield's (1963) argument that the temperance movement represented a status battle of native-born Protestants against other groups such as immigrants.

Among the richest of local materials are old newspapers. Some information of interest to social factists is available from this source, since newspapers often publish official reports from prosecutors and police. However, the original report, if available, would be a much better source for the social factist.

Newspapers provide much more of interest and relevance to those using the social definitional approach. Since one of the major points of focus for this scholar is the claims-making process, newspapers of any time period become important because they are a forum for such activities. Schwartz and Leitko (1977) have described newspapers as "thermometers" for rise of social problems and illustrated how the researcher can measure this phenomenon.

As a very simple illustration of this point, an index of items appearing in the *Kalamazoo Daily Telegraph* during the 1870s was consulted.[19] The social problems that received the most attention during these years were insanity (including the local asylum[20]), crime,[21] poverty, and paupers. Other problems discussed included drunkenness, nudity, vandalism, prostitution, cruelty to animals, adultery, tramps, fast driving on the streets at night, and young boys breaking laws. Certainly it may not be the case that this newspaper always reflected what the majority of the community's citizens felt, but it does provide one indicator of what behavior was defined as problematic or deviant. By noting the changes over time and conducting further analysis, much can be learned about the natural history of social problems.

The last category of primary source materials is the Kalamazoo Poorhouse records covering 1885 to 1912. The items listed in Table 6 are the exact terms used on the record keeping form. Examination of these records reveals that they are usually complete for each inmate. Consequently, for the interested researcher, the variables are already there, the answers only need to be copied. Note that information for both the social factists (age, sex, dates) and social definitionists (attributions regarding cause of pauperism) is included here.[22]

---

[19]Most nineteenth century newspapers have not been indexed. In this case, I benefited from the work of John Houdek, a local historian.

[20]These newspaper articles indicate community pride and support for the local asylum. After a Chicago newspaper attacked the institution, the local paper editorialized against such "libelous" attacks, and several citizens wrote letters to the editor defending the asylum.

[21]Einstadter (1979) has examined one nineteenth century newspaper's coverage of crime, suggesting that coverage of this problem in a specific manner played an important role in community building.

[22]Resisting analysis of the cause of pauperism entries required a herculean effort. Several that made an imprint on my mind are "licentiousness" and "indolence."

Finally, a secondary source that must be checked out in any research on community institutions is the local histories. These provide background information on the history of institutions such as poorhouses, jails, and asylums for the insane. As with state histories, these publications tend to focus on leading citizens of the community. As noted in the discussion of state materials, it appears such volumes would be valuable in the study of community elites.

Since most of the general limitations and advantages associated with these local archival materials are similar to those for the state documents, just a few specific difficulties will be addressed here. Perhaps the major difficulty is the problem of generalizing on the basis of local records. It is simply quite hazardous. A more practical problem is that local records are seldom as well organized as other documents such as state reports.[23] Usually the materials are not indexed, which means much more research time.

CONCLUSION

The above discussion must not be seen as providing an exhaustive list of archival materials. The intent here is illustrative, showing what is available in one university library. The hope is that this paper has stirred some interest and alerted scholars to new possibilities.

One final suggestion when undertaking historical research is to realize that the three categories of materials discussed here are quite arbitrary. Almost every study will require data from all three types of sources. The best studies (for example, Monkkonen, 1975; Fox, 1978; and Lane, 1979) have imaginatively employed a diversity of materials. Approaching the documents with a flexible research strategy is clearly a prerequisite.

This chapter has attempted to demonstrate that, irrespective of theoretical orientation, data relevant for sociological studies of social problems and deviance are contained in archival collections. Such historical materials offer the opportunity to develop and refine theories by comparing social processes at several points in time. Ignoring these and similar materials means that much of sociology will continue to be ahistorical, with short-lived relevance.

This chapter argues that sociologists do not always have to "produce" new data. In today's environment, surveys and fieldwork are becoming more

---

[23]I recently discovered something that suggests this general statement may need qualification. In the course of doing some other research in Des Moines, Iowa, I encountered a volume put together by workers in the New Deal Work Projects Administration which lists and gives the location of the archival records in the local county. If similar volumes were compiled in other areas, these will prove to be major assets.

costly, while financial support is decreasing. But there is no reason to despair. Not only are many of the same research skills applicable to historical materials, but the data, available at relatively low cost, are right under our noses. Remember, many of the great sociologists worked with historical materials. Surely, the meaningfulness of our scholarly efforts will be enhanced by such endeavors.

Certainly historical materials have limitations. Problems of representativeness and accuracy are perhaps the most serious. At the same time, it is difficult to see that the problems are more severe than those associated with the data sociologists have been using (see Phillips, 1971). Furthermore, many of the data limitations may be overcome if the same effort devoted to analysis of other data is given to historical materials.

REFERENCES

Alix, Ernest Kahlar
    1978   Ransom Kidnapping in America, 1874–1974: The Creation of a Capital Crime. Carbondale, IL: Southern Illinois Press.

Bogue, Allan G. and Jerome M. Clubb
    1977   "History, quantification and the social sciences." American Behavioral Scientist 21: 167–186.

Brooks, Philip C.
    1969   Research in Archives: The Use of Unpublished Primary Sources. Chicago, IL: University of Chicago Press.

Blumer, Herbert
    1962   "Society as symbolic interaction." Pp. 179–92 in Arnold Rose (ed.), Human Behavior and Social Processes. Boston, MA: Houghton Mifflin.

Burke, Peter
    1980   Sociology and History. London: Allen and Unwin.

Chambliss, William J.
    1964   "A sociological analysis of the law of vagrancy." Social Problems 12: 67–77.

Dubester, Henry J.
    1950   Catalog of United States Census Publications 1790–1945. U.S. Department of Commerce. Washington, DC: Government Printing Office.

Einstadter, Werner J.
    1979   "Crime news in the old west: social control in a northwestern town, 1887–1888." Urban Life 8:317–334.

Erikson, Kai T.
    1970   "Sociology and the historical perspective." The American Sociologist 5:331–338.
    1966   Wayward Puritans. New York: John Wiley and Sons.

Fox, Richard W.
    1978   So Far Disordered in Mind: Insanity in California, 1879–1930. Berkeley, CA: University of California Press.

Garnett, David (ed.)
    1938   The Letters of T. E. Lawrence. London, England: Jonathan Cape.

Graff, Henry J.
    1980   "Review of Theoretical Methods in Social History by Arthur L. Stinchcombe." American Journal of Sociology 88:1442–1446.

Gusfield, Joseph R.
    1963   Symbolic Crusade: Status Politics and the American Temperance Movement. Ur-
            bana, IL: University of Illinois Press.
Hagan, John and Jeffery Leon
    1977   "Rediscovering delinquency: social history, political ideology and the sociology of
            law." American Sociological Review 42:587–598.
Hall, Jerome
    1952   Theft, Law, and Society. 2nd edition. Indianapolis, IN: Bobbs-Merrill.
Hamer, Philip M. (ed.)
    1961   A Guide to Manuscripts and Archives in the United States. New Haven, CT: Yale
            University Press.
Hindus, Michael S.
    1979   "The history of crime: not robbed of its potential, but still on probation." Pp. 217–
            241 in Sheldon L. Messinger and Egon Bittner (eds.), Criminology Review Year-
            book, Volume 1. Beverly Hills, CA: Sage Publications.
Holt, W. Stull
    1929   The Bureau of the Census: Its History, Activities and Organization. Washington, DC:
            The Brookings Institution.
Iowa Historical Records Survey
    1942   Inventory of the County Archives of Iowa-Polk County, No. 77. Des Moines, IA:
            Division of Community Service Program, Work Projects Administration.
Kitsuse, John I.
    1981   Personal Correspondence. January 22.
Kitsuse, John I. and Aaron V. Cicourel
    1963   "A note on the uses of official statistics." Social Problems 11:131–139.
Lane, Roger
    1979   Violent Death in the City: Suicide, Accident, and Murder in Nineteenth-Century
            Philadelphia. Cambridge, MA: Harvard University Press.
Library of Congress
    1962   National Union Catalog of Manuscript Collections. Washington, DC: Library of
            Congress.
Lipset, Seymour Martin
    1968   "History and sociology: Some methodological considerations." Pp. 20–58 in
            Seymour Martin Lipset and Richard Hofstadter (eds.), Sociology and History: Meth-
            ods. New York: Basic Books.
Manis, Jerome G.
    1976   Analyzing Social Problems. New York: Praeger.
Monkkonen, Eric H.
    1975   The Dangerous Class: Crime and Poverty in Columbus, Ohio, 1860–1885.
            Cambridge, MA: Harvard University Press.
Murphey, Murray G.
    1973   Our Knowledge of the Historical Past. Indianapolis, IN: Bobbs-Merrill.
Phillips, Derek L.
    1971   Knowledge From What: Theories and Methods in Social Research. Chicago, IL:
            Rand McNally and Company.
Pisciotta, Alexander W.
    1981   "Theoretical perspectives for historical analyses: A selective review of the juvenile
            justice literature." Criminology 19:115–129.
Platt, Anthony
    1969   The Child Savers. Chicago, IL: Chicago University Press.

Ritzer, George
    1975   Sociology: A Multiple Paradigm Science. Boston, MA: Allyn and Bacon.
Rothman, David J.
    1980   Conscience and Convenience: The Asylum and its Alternatives in Progressive
            America. Boston, MA: Little, Brown and Company.
    1971   The Discovery of the Asylum. Boston, MA: Little, Brown and Company.
Schlossman, Steven L.
    1977   Love and the American Delinquent: The Theory and Practice of "Progressive"
            Juvenile Justice, 1825–1920. Chicago, IL: University of Chicago Press.
Schwartz, T. P. and Thomas Leitko
    1977   "The rise of social problems: Newspapers as 'thermometers'." Pp. 427–36 in Ar-
            mand L. Mauss and Julie Camile Wolfe (eds.), This Land of Promises. Philadelphia,
            PA: J. B. Lippincott.
Smith, Tom W.
    1980   "Review of Violent Death in the City: Suicide, Accident, and Murder in Nineteenth-
            Century Philadelphia by Roger Lane." American Journal of Sociology 86:441–443.
Spector,Malcolm and John I. Kitsuse
    1977   Constructing Social Problems. Menlo Park, CA: Cummings Publishing Company.
Stinchcombe, Arthur L.
    1978   Theoretical Methods in Social History. New York: Academic Press.
Walker, Francis A.
    1883   "Introduction." Pp. xv–xxxvii in Compendium of the Tenth Census. Department of
            Interior. Washington, DC: Government Printing Office.
    1872   "Report of the Superintendent of Census to the Secretary of Interior." Pp. ix–xlix in
            Ninth Census of the United States, Vol. I. Department of Interior, Washington, DC:
            Government Printing Office.
Webb, Eugene J., Donald T. Campbell, Richard D. Schwartz and Lee Sechrest
    1966   Unobtrusive Measures: Nonreactive Research in the Social Sciences. Chicago, IL:
            Rand McNally and Company.
Williamson, John B., David A. Karp and John Dalphin
    1977   The Research Craft: An Introduction to Social Science Methods. Boston, MA: Little,
            Brown and Company.
Wright, Carroll D. and William C. Hunt
    1900   The History and Growth of the United States Census. Washington, DC: Government
            Printing Office.
Zaret, David
    1978   "Sociological theory and historical scholarship." The American Sociologist
            13:114–121.

4 Notes on the discovery, collection, and assessment of hidden and dirty data*

Gary T. Marx
Massachusetts Institute of Technology

What do ABSCAM, the Santa Barbara Oil Spill, Serpico, and the Freedom of Information Act have in common? Or what do blackmailers, police, priests, journalists, and some social problems researchers have in common? (Perhaps we'd better not answer that.) In the first case, aside from what they may communicate about the pathos of the last decade, each represents a means of collecting hidden and dirty data. These means are *experiments, accidents, whistle blowing,* and *coercive institutionalized discovery practices.* In the second case, we have actors who routinely deal with discovering secret and dirty data.

Issues of discovering and protecting secrets confront everyone in daily life. But they are highlighted for certain occupations such as public or private investigators (including detectives, inspectors general, Congressional investigators, auditors and spies), journalists, social reformers and sometimes social researchers. They have particular saliency for the social problems researcher who may seek data which insiders wish to keep secret.

As a result of research on substantive topics such as agents provocateurs, informants, undercover work, frame-ups, cover-ups, and muckraking, I have become interested in what can be called the "hidden and dirty data problem."

What follows is an essay on dirty data research. It offers neither an explanation, nor fresh empirical data. Instead its purpose is to call attention

*I am appreciative of comments offered by Robert Perrucci, Diane Vaughan, and Ron Westrum.

Table 1
Types of Data

A. Nonsecretive and nondiscrediting data:
   Routinely available information.
B. Secretive and nondiscrediting data:
   Strategic and fraternal secrets, privacy.
C. Nonsecretive and discrediting data:
   a. sanction immunity,
   b. normative dissensus,
   c. selective exposure,
   d. making good on a threat for credibility,
   e. discovered dirty data.
D. Secretive and discrediting data:
   Hidden and dirty data.

to this data gathering problem, suggest some of the issues it raises and a framework for approaching them, and speculate on what may be involved. I self-consciously raise a number of questions which I do not begin to answer adequately. This is a necessary first step in the generation of the more systematic empirical inquiry and theoretical development that is needed. In what follows, I define dirty data; consider some factors contributing to an apparent increase in the ease of discovering it; contrast some basic discovery mechanisms; and consider some of the implications of dirty data for the study and understanding of society.

By hidden and dirty data, I mean just that. We can locate it more precisely by combining two variables into a typology (Table 1). The first variable involves information which is publicly available, unprotected, and open, at one end of the continuum, and information which is secret, private, closed, or protected at the other. If we bring this together with the second variable, which is a continuum with nondiscrediting information at one pole and highly discrediting information at the other, we have the typology of Table 1.

Hidden and dirty data lie (no pun intended) in Type D: It is information which is kept secret and whose revelation would be discrediting or costly in terms of various types of sanctioning.

The data can be dirty in different ways. But in all cases, it runs contrary to widely (if not necessarily universally) shared standards and images of what a person or group should be. Of course, all persons and organizations have minor discrediting elements and show a gap between ideal standards, public presentations, and private reality (e.g., Hughes, 1971; Goffman, 1963).[1] But by dirty data, I have something rather more formidable in mind

---

[1] In noting its occupational ubiquity, Hughes observes, "It is hard to imagine an occupation in which one does not appear, in certain repeated contingencies, to be practically compelled to play a role of which he thinks he ought to be a little ashamed morally" (1971:343).

than soft-core discrepancies. Dirty data at the organizational level ought to be of particular concern to the social problems researcher. Issues of hidden and dirty data are likely to be involved to the extent that the study of social problems confronts behavior that is illegal, the failure of an agency or individual to meet responsibilities, cover-ups, and the use of illegal or immoral means.

While Hughes' (1971) concepts of "dirty work" and "guilty knowledge" may at times overlap with dirty data, they are distinct. Neither of the former have to be hidden, and they may be central to the legitimate license and mandate of an occupation or organization. Worker designations of selected tasks as "dirty work" may be a means of sustaining a heroic or moral definition of their occupation (e.g., Emerson and Pollner, 1976). Society needs dirty workers. Certain occupations must engage the profane and are empowered to violate standards that apply to others. However, because of the protected opportunity structure they face, such workers often generate dirty data.

Discrediting or dirty data and secrecy tend to go together. They can, of course, be independent and even inversely linked. Secrecy is a basic social process contributing to group boundaries (Simmel, 1950; Tefft, 1980). A mandate to use it can easily lead to its unintended expansion (e.g., Lowry, 1972). In the form of privacy, it represents an important societal value (Shils, 1966; Warren and Laslett, 1980). Organizations protect dirty as well as clean data. As Type B implies, this protection need not serve nefarious ends. Furthermore, all that is dirty is certainly not kept secret, as in the very interesting cases in Type C, where efforts to protect discrediting information are not taken.[2] But such subtleties aside, a major issue for the social prob-

---

There is of course an important element of cultural relativism with respect to specifics. Thus kickbacks in the U.S. are hidden and illegal, while in some non-Western countries they are simply seen as a regular part of business overhead. In this chapter we assume that the researcher and target of the research share the same definition of what constitutes dirty data (or at least share the view that the broader culture will see the behavior in question as dirty).

[2]Among factors that confound the expected dirty data–secrecy relationship: (a) people whose power comes from the ability to coerce or threaten others must occasionally make good on the threat, and this must be publicized to the relevant target; (b) situations where persons have adequate power that precludes their having to worry much about covering up dirty deeds (the ruthless dictator); (c) situations that call for selective exposure of the action in order to attract clients or coconspirators (e.g., vice operatives need to let customers know about their services); (d) situations where generators of dirty data have immunity from sanctioning. This may be because they help police, as with informants or because of strict rules of evidence. The distinction between procedural and substantive guilt (Skolnick, 1966) is relevant here. For example, police often know who the fences, gamblers, and prostitutes are, but arrests leading to prosecution are rare, partly because it is hard to collect legally admissable evidence; (e) situations of normative dissensus. What is seen as discrediting by one group may not be seen that way by another group. Counter culture groups or rebellious personalities may not hide, and may even flaunt, as a matter of principle and politics, behavior or facts about self that outsiders

lems researcher is how to pierce the secrecy that so often surrounds the subject matter.

Commentaries on field research of course often consider the difficulties in obtaining valid and reliable data (e.g., Douglas, 1976; Van Maanen, 1979). They assume that individuals and organizations present a veil of secrecy masking what is really going on. The researcher must find a way to lift or slip through, over, or under the veil. Both self and group boundaries are partially maintained by controlling information given to others and outsiders.

Well known barriers to data collecting are concern for privacy, suspiciousness of, or reticence towards, outsiders asking questions, a lack of reciprocity in the researcher–researched relationship, a desire to keep information from rivals or competitors, and a wish to put forward one's best face or group image. This is the case even when the data sought are not particularly discrediting. The problems are compounded, however, when we seek data that are in some way "dirty," as with some social problems, political sociology, and criminology research.

In these cases, data gathering is even more difficult. The vested interest in maintaining secrecy may be much stronger because illegal or immoral actions are involved and the costs of public disclosure very high. We may be dealing with people who are specialists at maintaining secrecy and deception. They may be part of organizations that routinely mislead or obscure. The issue can go beyond the withholding of information to offering what, in the intelligence trade, is called "misinformation" and "disinformation." Well kept secrets or deception may prevent the researcher from even knowing what to look for, questions of restricted access aside. How can the researcher hope to gather dirty data when the will and resources to block this are so strong?

Perhaps the most common response has simply been to stay away from such topics (the founding of the Society for the Study of Social Problems [SSSP] was a reaction against this). Like a river, researchers follow the path of least resistance. Or, perhaps better, like immigrants, we tend to go where, if we are not necessarily welcomed, we are at least tolerated. Often, of course, this is at the bidding (or at least with the resources) of the very elites who sit atop mountains of dirty data.

Yet, if it is valid to describe our attraction to more easily gathered "clean" data as a central tendency, such a characterization misses the considerable variation around the mean. While not the norm, nor a thriving industry, we do not lack for research of an investigative, muckraking, or

---

see as discrediting. Kitsuse (1980:3) considers the last decade's increase in the willingness of many of such persons to ". . . declare their presence openly and without apology to claim the rights of citizenship."

scandal producing nature. The amount of such research has increased significantly in the last two decades, and it is possible that, human subjects limitations aside, such research will become more prevalent and prominent.

FACTORS CONTRIBUTING TO INCREASED ACCESSIBILITY

Whether or not the relative amount of dirty data in our society has been increasing or decreasing is an interesting, and probably unanswerable, question.[3] However, there can be little doubt that accessibility to dirty data has increased in recent decades.[4] A not insignificant number of journalists, social reformers, and researchers have been able to gather information on highly discrediting phenomena which, according to a conspiracy perspective on the dirty data problem, we should be unable to study (one is reminded of the mathematical proof that airplanes cannot fly). The record might be read to suggest that there is an abundance of riches here. The streets may not be paved with gold, but they are often lined with partly visible muck. Instead of a paucity of information, we may suffer from a kind of dirty data overload. Rather than a lack of access, the problem may be in deciding, in a context of abundance, just which dirty data should be focused on. What factors bear upon the increased accessibility of such data?

New resources and changing standards partly account for it. Public interest groups and foundations offer support and audiences for such data. Technical changes such as computer advances in the storing, retrieval, and analysis of data, new devices for unobtrusive data gathering,[5] and better

---

[3]How data is labeled to an important extent depends on the point of view of the observer. Expectations and standards have changed, making general historical conparisons difficult. Good measures on the actual amount of dirty data and the ease of discovery are lacking. This question involves highly debatable beliefs about the idea of progress and the state of morality. With increased complexity and expanded efforts at intervention (especially on the part of government), the potential for things to go wrong, and hence the possiblity for leaks or whistleblowing, may be increased.

[4]Accessibility and the sheer amount of dirty data may of course be inversely linked. Judged from the sunshine theory of social control, openness should serve to reduce illegal and questionable actions. The conditions under which it does this, rather than simply generating clever forms of neutralization or displacement, is an important question.

Just as high accessibility may reduce the amount, the amount may have been a prior factor in affecting the degree of accessibility. Thus the increased access to dirty data of recent years might be interpreted as a response to pressures for reform that have emerged in light of a vast increase in dirty data (beyond the fact that there is more dirty data available for discovery). The ratio of discovered to hidden dirty data (Types C and D of Table 1) in different conditions and settings is an issue well worthy of study.

[5]For example, new or improved forms of bugging (in some cases using lasers), wire taps, videotaping and still photography, remote camera systems, periscopic prisms, one-way mirrors, various infrared, sensor, and tracking devices, truth serum, polygraphs, voice print and stress analysis, pen registers, ultraviolet radiation, and aircraft and satellite surveillance.

measurement techniques and means of communication have greatly increased the capacity for such research. We are measuring more and better than ever before. Not surprisingly, some of what is measured has discrediting implications.[6]

New laws and procedures such as the Freedom of Information Act,[7] the Buckley Amendment requiring access to one's own records, the many state and local "sunshine laws" requiring open meetings, recent legislation (e.g., Civil Service Reform Act of 1979) and judicial decisions protecting whistle blowing, toll free lines for anonymously reporting government fraud, ombudsmen programs and more formalized procedures for filing grievances, new forms of public disclosure and reporting requirements offer a cornucopia of data. Entrepreneurs such as former CIA agent William Walter Buchanan may bring this material to our library microfiche machines. Buchanan summarizes, indexes, and reproduces for sale on a subscription basis recently declassified documents. A majority of large universities and research libraries subscribe, as does the U.S.S.R.

New organizations concerned with dirty data discovery have appeared, such as the University of Missouri's Center for Investigative Reporters and Editors, the Freedom of Information Clearing House, and an investigative organization made up of journalists, former congressional investigators, and lawyers put together by Watergate prosecutor Terry Lenzner.[8] A concern of many public interest groups is encouraging data collection on topics such as auto safety and energy.

There is an emerging dirty data methodology and increased sophistication in using it. Books, articles, and how-to manuals abound. Radical caucuses within academic disciplines and professional associations have con-

---

[6]To be sure, as the recent report (1979) of the Privacy Study Commission makes clear, the new data collection is a mixed blessing with an ominous doubledged sword potential. On balance, its negative aspects may far outweigh the positive. But it is not about to go away. We should seek to limit abuses while maximizing implications for an open society.

[7]The FOIA was passed in 1966. Following Watergate, it was amended and new protections were added against misuse of the classification system (e.g., using a "national security" classification to cover illegal behavior). I don't wish to suggest that the agencies subject to the FOIA are cheerfully conforming to the letter and spirit of the law. Beyond lobbying efforts to weaken the law, institutionalized evasion practices (and cover-ups) are certainly present. Downes' (1967) law of countercontrol certainly applies to the new openness efforts. But implementation issues aside, the FOIA is of tremendous symbolic and practical importance to researchers. It offers statutory recognition to the right of freedom of access. It involves the concept that the First Amendment includes the right to have *access* to ideas and information, as well as the right to communicate. A government agency which wishes to withhold information now has the burden of proving that it is entitled to do so.

[8]Lenzner (1980:104) observes, "Lawyers are not well trained in obtaining facts . . . Reporters have a unique capability for getting people to talk to them." Sociologists have much to learn from both: from journalists, how to better discover what happened at particular times and places; from lawyers, how to use court records, procedures, and resources.

tributed to it, as have college courses such as those on investigative journalism. The cohort of journalists, lawyers, and social researchers receiving its professional socialization during the 1960s through the mid-1970s has played an important role in such research.

Persons ready to work in the dirty data fields found a ready market for their crop. Career options, rewards, and publishing outlets were available. It is significant that "60 Minutes" was one of the most profitable and highly rated television programs in the 1970s. Even if one were to question whether accessibility has increased, the case for the increased ability to publish such data seems clear (though whether the publication of dirty data materials has increased proportionately or only absolutely, as the total amount of published material has increased, can not be determined without sampling and content analysis).

Righteous indignation, which once went into concern over gambling, prostitution, liquor, radicals, and ethnic groups has found new targets such as consumer rip-offs, corruption, and environmental spoliation, where discovery and documentation may play a greater role. With improvement in many of the social, economic, and political aspects of American life, procedural issues may be taken more seriously. In fine Tocquevillian fashion, with improvement has come higher aspirations. The size of the gap between ideals and reality which the general public is willing to tolerate has been steadily reduced in the twentieth century. This may receive expression in efforts to make it easier to discover dirty data.

Of course, one can argue that the availability of dirty data is illusory, diversionary, and lulling. Following Marcuse, it could be argued that the belief in a free and open society masks what is really happening. The real dirt stays hidden, while the masses are tittilated with what used to be *confidential Magazine* (and now *People*) revelations, or an occasional sacrificial goat like Agnew. In the cycle of infinite regress, which generates continual uncertainty for spies, seeming discoveries may be designed to throw you off, being faked or unrepresentative. It could be argued that the continued exposure of dirty data, rather than being shocking, becomes boring, and may indirectly perpetuate a corrupt system through generating public cynicism and lowering expectations. As Sherman (1978) observes, scandal as a mechanism for social change is limited. The high media visibility given to some data might also offer a distorted picture of how much discovery is actually going on. The costs of discovery and publication can be very high. At the extreme there is death, as with investigative reporters Don Bowles in Arizona and Paul Jacobs in California (the former was murdered and the latter died from exposure to radiation). There may be imprisonment, as with reporters who fail to reveal their sources when a judge demands it, or the loss of income (e.g., impounding of the royalties of former CIA employee Frank Snepp after the publication of his book *Decent Interval* in 1977).

Accessibility is also relative and tentative. While the U.S. may be more

Table 2
Methods of Obtaining Hidden and Dirty Data

Deception	Coercion	Volition	Uncontrollable Contingencies
experiments, infiltration, covert surveillance, or information gathering	institutionalized discovery practices— (grand jury, Freedom of Information Act, discovery motions, record keeping requirements), manipulation (hypnosis, chemicals, ESP)	whistleblowers, leaks, gossip, informants, open field work, archives, personal documents	accidents, mistakes, victims, coincidences, traces, fall-out, residues, remnants

open than most countries, it could be appreciably more open in terms of adherence to laws currently in existence, as well as in terms of new laws and procedures designed to insure an even greater degree of openness. There are also counter trends, such as increased organizational sophistication regarding protective measures (codes, paper shredders, debugging devices, and other electronic surveillence, lie detectors, and nondisclosure agreements). The Reagan administration's efforts to restrict the FOIA suggest the fragility of recent advances.

However, regardless of its broader meaning or whether ease of discovery and publication has increased, it is clear that dirty data exists and researchers sometimes make use of it. What is involved in the discovery (or failure to discover) such data? Let us consider four broad ways that dirty data is discovered: uncontrollable contingencies, volitition, deception, and coercion. (These methods are given in detail in Table 2.) In doing this we will look beyond the current changes considered above, to more enduring characteristics of American society, social structure, interaction, and personality which are conducive to disclosure and discovery.

Uncontrollable Contingencies

The complexities and interdependencies of modern life, which too often thwart efforts at rational planning and intervention for the public good, may also thwart conspiracies. Former spy and novelist John Le Carre, in speaking about intelligence operations, finds it "difficult to dramatize the persistent quality of human incompetence. I don't believe that it's ever possible to operate such a clear conspiracy (as in his novel *The Spy Who Came in From the Cold*) where all the pieces fit together."[9] While this may overstate the

---

[9]Judge Burt W. Griffin, an attorney for the Warren Commission, argues that given American civil liberties and the requirement of proof beyond a reasonable doubt for criminal conviction, that ". . . it is virtually impossible to prosecute or uncover a well-conceived and well executed conspiracy." However, the occasional successful prosecution of a sophisticated conspiracy ". . . almost always results from accidental discoveries" (Blakey and Billings, 1981:397–398).

case, there is an element of indeterminacy in human actions which often works in favor of disclosure. Folklore and literary treatments such as Cervantes's "murder will out" and Shakespeare's "by indirections find directions out" capture elements of this.

Those involved with dirty data may face exposure or suspicion due to factors beyond their control. Failures, accidents, mistakes, coincidences, victims, fall-out, remnants, and residues can all offer indications of dirty data close at hand. Strictly speaking, these offer an opportunity rather than a strategy, for data collection. The strategic elements emerge in the varying degrees of skill required to ferret them out. The event is also distinct from data collected about it which, of necessity, must be selective.

Some uncontrollable contingencies are "merely personal." Thus we learn that Richard Pryor, as a result of a fire in his home, was probably using cocaine, or that the late Governor Rockefeller, when he died in the company of a young assistant, may have been having an affair. But others are keys to organizational deviance and problems. The death of Dorothy Hunt in a plane crash, with thousands of dollars, tells us about Watergate hush money; miscarriages and infertility in Oregon and upstate New York reveal hazards of pesticides and industrial waste; the oil spill in Santa Barbara points to collusive relationships between the oil industry, academics, and government (Molotch and Lester, 1974); the mishap at Three Mile Island shows the failure of equipment and regulatory policies; the fire at the Las Vegas MGM Grand Hotel exposes fire and building code violations; the deterioration of a new building at the University of Massachusetts tells us about fraud in the awarding of construction contracts.

Traces or residue elements are separate from accidents and mistakes, and perhaps surer sources, in that for certain types of infractions they will always be present.[10] The difficulty is, of course, knowing how to identify and interpret them. Some trace elements are manifest and available to anyone: a missing person, signs of forced entry, missing documents, gaps on a tape, or red dye on money, clothing, or skin (from a cannister slipped between currency that exploded shortly after a bank robbery). Other trace elements are latent: powder that can be seen only under ultraviolet light, fingerprints, electronic impulses, inadequacies of counterfeit money, or documents. These require special skills to discover. Many electronic surveillance devices emit signals which can be read. Most complex illegal undertakings will leave physical clues, whether fingerprints or the paper trail of laundered money. Some investigators have received notoriety for literally sifting through the garbage, looking for telltale signs. Instructional manuals and

---

[10]Webb et al. (1966:35) observes that "physical evidence is probably the social scientist's least used source of data, yet because of its ubiquity, it holds flexible and broad gauged potential." As attention to environmental issues increase, it becomes even more important.

training materials are another trace element. Thus, the Supreme Court in the Miranda decision drew upon such material as evidence of police violations of Constitutional protections.

Trace elements involving victims are likely to become publicly known to the extent that (a) the gap between victimization and its discovery is short (b) the victim is personally identifiable, (c) the victim is aware of the victimization, and (d) does not fear retaliation for telling others about it. There is a parallel here to the ease of discovering victim as against victimless crimes. The former are much more likely to be known about.

Trace elements, of course, need not be physical. One clue to possible dirty data lies in an organization's internal rules and policies, external laws concerning it, and professional codes of ethics. As Durkheim suggested, their presence is often a sign that members will face temptations to behave contrarywise. Their presence is also a clue to the presence of pressures toward social control corruption. Sociologists can draw upon their knowledge of organizations for clues to where dirty data is likely to be found. Certain structural and cultural characteristics can serve as likely barometers of dirty data. The developing literature on organizational deviance contains many clues (Needleman and Needleman, 1979; Sherman, 1980; Finney and Lesieur, 1982). Elements of folk culture such as humor, slang, nick-names, graffiti, and gossip can also offer clues.

Volition

This is a broad category. Whistleblowers, informants, and overt participant and nonparticipant observers share in the willing provision of discrediting information.

Given the prestige of scientific research, it is not surprising that many persons are willing to participate in large-scale anonymous self-report studies regarding their criminal or sexual behavior. Many researchers have followed in the path of Wallerstein and Wyle (1948) and Kinsey et al. (1948) in using this method. More surprising is the extent to which dirty data revelations can come forth without anonymity. Interviews and observation are the major sources for such data. Memoirs, biographies, letters, and other personal documents are important and under-used sources. Social and psychological factors can be conducive to revealing secrets.

Accounts of fieldwork often suggest that, once rapport and trust are established, people are often only too willing to talk (e.g., aside from the legions of investigative reporters, social researchers such as Polsky, 1967; Ianni and Ianni, 1972; Chambliss, 1978; Klockars, 1974; Galliher, 1980; and Millman, 1977). Primary group relations are partly based on sharing information. This can be a means of expressing solidarity. Informants may wish to help. They may have a desire to be understood and to explain their actions. There may be pride in their technical skills for which recognition and aesthetic appreciation is sought. They may feel a need to justify their involvement with dirty data, have a Dostoyevskian compulsion to tell, or enjoy the sense of power noted by Simmel (1950) that comes from sharing secrets. Isolated from opposing definitions and confident in their actions, they may be open because they do not see their behavior as discreditable. Insiders can also be used as researchers to give otherwise unavailable access, e.g., Walker and Lidz's (1977) use of Black street addicts.

The fact that there is frequently a lack of congruence between individual and organizational goals can also be conducive to revelation of secrets. Information is a resource, just like income or authority. It can be used to damage rivals or traded to enhance one's own position. Money and offers of immunity, or other help, can often buy information. There may also be hope of great riches and fame (and perhaps, for the lucky few, a movie or TV series) from writing a book about one's secret activities. In the first six months of 1980 alone, the CIA reviewed 22 manuscripts by former CIA agents.[11]

Whistleblowing is a dramatic form which has increased in the last decade (Westin and Salisbury, 1980; Dudar, 1979; Bok, 1980; Nader et al., 1972; Peter and Taylor, 1972; Government Accountability Project, 1977). New laws and policies have attempted to encourage and protect it. For example, the 1977 Toxic Substances Control Act requires that employees and officials of chemical firms be instructed about their legal obligation to report chemicals posing substantial health or environmental risks. Here, *not* to whistleblow becomes illegal. In many government agencies, employees must report bribe offers.

New anonymous tip and complaint receiving mechanisms make it easier to whistleblow or report improper behavior. These vary from 911 mail boxes in some cities for reports of police abuse (police themselves are often major users), TIP (turn in a pusher) programs, and toll free numbers where violations can be reported to government agencies. The first and best known of the latter is that of the General Accounting Office. It has received about fifty calls a day since it was established in 1979. Following its success, the Office of Management and the Budget has required certain federal agencies to establish such lines. While the initial complaints are not made public, they may result in court cases which are public.

Some whistleblowing comes from highly idealistic persons who are shocked by what they see in the day-to-day operation of their agency. This

---

[11]According to one survey, between 1945 and 1973, over one hundred memoirs were written by persons holding government positions in the area of national security (Halperin, *Bureaucratic Politics and Foreign Policy*, 1974, vol. 11:317–321). A capitalist economic system and a free press, in providing both incentive and means, are very conductive to the dissemination of secretes.

type of whistleblowing is likely to be common in a society such as the United States, with Puritan roots and a highly moralistic political and cultural style. In instances where the occupation attracts idealistic people and where the gap between ideal standards and actual practices is large, whistleblowing is more likely. This seems to be the case for some whistleblowing within law enforcement (e.g., Wall, 1972). Conflicts between the highly educated professional's sense of expertise and bureaucratic and political realities in large organizations is another source of whistleblowing. As both the need for professionals and bureaucratization increase, so too may whistleblowing (Perrucci et al., 1980).

Beyond generating data about which trumpets, let alone whistles, could be blown, organizations also may generate personal motives. Complex organizations do not reward people equally. Some persons are likely to be angered over blocked mobility or rewards they see as insufficient.

Whistleblowing involves a conflict between the person who would tell and the organization (or at least its dominant leaders) who wish to keep things quiet. More subtle and more common is the leak, where the release of discrediting information is a device for serving some other organizational purpose. There is also a category of "give-aways," where persons do not realize they are revealing dirty data. This may be because of its highly technical nature, because its providers don't know that you have other data with which you can match it, or neutral data may become dirty in time, as new developments such as accidents, illness, or environmental spoliation become manifest and lead to reassessment and reinterpretations.[12]

Some dirty data appears at the intersection of several pieces of conventional data which may be easily available. This can be the case with research on the concentration of economic and political power (e.g., Domhoff, 1979; Useem, 1980). Other examples can be seen in the case of people processing institutions (e.g., commitment to mental hospitals) whose formal records describing a person's behavior may conflict with accounts of friends and family and coworkers. When these are juxtaposed and in contradiction, the researcher may wonder about the agency's actions.

The fact that dirty data is often available should not cause us to miss the point that it is less available than clean data. We are dealing with conflict relations and the need for secrecy. The active investigator need not wait for accidents to occur, or whistleblowers to come forward. He or she can also take the initiative. More subject to the control of the researcher are methods involving deception and coercion. These assume an adversarial or conflict model.

---

[12]Such give-away information was probably more common in earlier decades, before public relations specialists and lawyers became such prominent parts of large organizations.

Deception

The use of deception is familiar in social science research, particularly that of a social psychological nature. However, it has been used far less to gather dirty data than for other reasons (e.g., to gain access to worlds normally denied the researcher, to gain data on matters kept private, to not bias responses by telling people what is being studied or that a study is being done, and to manipulate the participant's situation in accordance with notions of causal variables, or, as with candid camera, merely to see what happens). There is a sizeable literature on deception in traditional social psychological experiments, on covert participant observations, and on information collected under false pretenses (Kelman, 1977; Hilbert, 1980; Humphreys, 1975; Warwick, 1975). But there has been little discussion of the role (and power) of deception as an information gathering strategy involving "reality experiments" in dirty data contexts.

Here the logic of the experiment may differ from its more conventional social science usage involving control and experimental groups. There may be no control group, since the goal is empirical description rather than an effort to test causal theory. More refined inquiries, often at a later point in time, or research where the dirty data lies in documenting a pattern of differential treatment by race, sex, offender status, etc., will have the traditional control group.

After a long, relatively dormant period, muckraking journalism has shown increased vigor. Contemporary investigative journalism, whether newspapers such as the *Chicago Sun Times,* or television programs such as "60 Minutes" or "20/20," offer many examples. The *Sun Times* has been a leader in use of the technique. For example in an investigation of insurance fraud, it had its investigators pose as victims of minor accidents with whiplash. They were then led down the road to hospitalization and insurance fraud by unwitting lawyers, doctors, and hospital staff. Chiropractors came to treat "injuries" created by lawyers. In some cases, expenses of $40,000 were generated, treating the essentially healthy investigators. In another case, reporters opened a Chicago bar and documented requests from various government agents for bribes.

Social reform groups have used the tactic to document and publicize problems. For example, the Chicago Better Government Association's inquiry into voter fraud had two investigators assume the life of winos and move into a skid row flop house. They registered under names such as James Joyce and Ernest Hemingway. When the voter lists turned up a short time later, Joyce and Hemingway were on them and actually voted! (*Los Angeles Times,* Oct. 9, 1977.)

There are a great many law enforcement examples. Some of the more elaborate involve police posing as fences, pornographers, or sheiks bearing bribes as in ABSCAM.

The social research literature shows a smattering of deception used in this fashion. Schwartz and Skolnick (1962), in seeking to study the effect of a criminal court record on employment opportunities, had an "employment agent" visit a sample of one hundred employers. The agent presented one of four fictitious employment folders. The folders were exactly the same, with the exception of the criminal record (this varied from no record, to acquitted, to convicted and sentenced). As the seriousness of the record increased, chances for employment decreased: even those who were acquitted had much less chance of being hired. In Los Angeles, Heussenstamm (1971) sought to study claims of police harassment of the Black Panthers. Fifteen "typical" students with "exemplary" driving records agreed to put Black Panther party bumper stickers on their cars. The cars were in good condition and the students drove as they normally did. They received 33 citations in 17 days, and the study had to be stopped. Phil Zimbardo (1969) left what appeared to be abandoned cars on New York City and California thoroughfares and watched to see if they would be dismantled.

The National Wiretap Commission's interest in the availability of illegal wiretaps led its investigators to call 115 randomly chosen private detective agencies in seven large cities. They identified themselves as businessmen interested in tapping a rival's phones. In more than a third of the cases, the agencies contacted offered to install the illegal taps; many that refused offered to "show the callers how to do it themselves"[13] (O'Toole, 1978:75).

Selltiz (1955) reports an early experiment that used matched pairs of Black and White diners to assess discrimination in restaurants. HUD has used an equivalent tactic in studying housing discrimination. Black and White auditors who were otherwise similar responded separately to the same rental-sale opportunities. They found Blacks were systematically treated less favorably and courteously than Whites.[14] The Supreme Court in a

---

[13]Another proposal made to the National Commission on Gambling (which was not followed) was to have investigators take a large number of taxi rides in various cities and ask to be taken to card games.

[14]This is reported in Wienk, et al., (1979). Among the first race relations researchers in this genre was LaPierre. His classic 1934 study did not document discrimination against Chinese travelers. It did, however, call attention to the frequent gap between attitude and behavior. In a time when prejudice was more openly expressed, he found over ninety percent of two hundred fifty hotels and restaurants responded negatively to his questionnaire which asked if Chinese customers were welcomed. Yet in actually visiting these businesses, he and a Chinese couple were refused service only once.

A recent trend in race relations research involves hidden manipulations and unobtrusive measures of racial response in field settings. Unobtrusive studies of race and helping, aggressive, and nonverbal behavior find greater discrimination than would be expected from survey data (Crosby, Bromley and Saxe, 1980). Since the subjects of such research tend to be chosen from diffuse publics (persons walking on the street or shopping in a supermarket), rather than organizations thought to discriminate, the direct relevance of such studies to social problems research or amelioration is limited.

1982 decision ruled that a "tester" who is misled has standing to maintain a claim for damages under the 1968 Fair Housing Act.

Jesilow and O'Brien (1980), in a study of deterrence and automobile repair fraud, had women approach randomly chosen garages with the story that they were moving and their cars would not start. They told the repairmen that the car battery was in the trunk of the borrowed car they were driving, and requested that the battery be tested. The battery, of course, was fine. Depending on the group sampled (experimental, control, pre- or posttest), from five to twenty percent of the time a new battery was recommended.

Pontell et al. (1980) has proposed using patients with prediagnosed common ailments to study fraud in government-funded medical benefit programs. The method involves using patients with equivalent symptoms. Some of the patients are entitled to health care benefits. All are to pay out of their own pockets for services rendered after each visit. The quality of treatment received and suggested would then be rated by a panel of doctors, and records of the insuring agencies checked to see if double-billing occurs. In a related case, investigators (including a U.S. senator) for a Senate Subcommittee on Long-Term Care (1976) visited medical clinics. They complained of colds and other minor symptoms. The inquiry documented numerous examples of fraud, and inferior and unnecessary care.

While not dirty data in the sense of the examples considered here, which have a willful quality, experiments designed to test the quality of professional diagnosis and skills may make similar use of deception. For example, Rosenhan (1973) discovered that healthy "pseudo-patients" who checked themselves into mental hospitals with vague symptoms could be diagnosed as schizophrenic.

Infiltration or covert participant observation is another form of deception. Its main domestic users are police, industrial espionage agents, and occasionally journalists, activists, and researchers. It involves fitting into some ongoing set of activities rather than generating new organizations and activities. To the extent that the infiltrator takes a more active role, trying to consciously influence what happens, the method has some of the quality of an experiment. At one extreme, the observer functions like covert electronic surveillance, merely transmitting what is going on; at the other, is the researcher as agent provocateur.[15]

Coercion

This includes a variety of means that share compulsion as the essential mechanism. People or organizations are required to furnish information

---

[15]The former is rare, regardless of intentions, since the investigator can rarely be certain what impact his or her presence has on the nature of the data elicited; for example, the issues raised by three infiltrators into a small sect predicting the world's end (Festinger et al., 1956).

under threat of various penalities ranging from imprisonment, fines, revocation of license, or withholding of goods, services, or privileges desired by the possessor of the information. Through laws, courts, and policies, government, with its power to coerce, is the major source of institutionalized discovery practices.

Investigations and hearings by congressional, presidential, state and local commissions, and various government agencies such as the General Accounting Office and Office of Management and Budget with subpoena powers are major sources of information. In the case of historical data, most files are open to researchers after 50 years. Annual reports and reports of inspectors general can provide rich data. The Freedom of Information Act is particularly relevant to the needs of researchers, though in most states there is nothing like it at the local level. Reiss and Biderman (1980) have complied a list of federal data sources available for the study of white collar crime.

Court records including indictments, testimony, and evidence can offer valuable information. However, one must know where to look and have resources for generating a transcript from the court record. If the case is not appealed, a transcript will be unavailable. New federal discovery rules require prosecutors to make available to the defense information in their possession relevant to the case. Grand jury data, which in general is kept secret, can be very powerful. Another good source of data lies in the routine reports that many occupational groups are required to file, e.g., for doctors (prescriptions, tissue samples), for police (bribery attempts, use of force, and weapons discharge), and for congressmen (campaign contributions, conflict of interest).

Lawyers and criminal investigators may use coercive confrontation tactics to gain information. These vary from threats to subpoena, arrest, or sue, to blackmail and the use of force. (While less prevalent now in the U.S. than previously, the third degree is one such technique.)

Brief mention can be made of a nonconventional data gathering technique which falls between the above methods: ESP. This method is apparently taken quite seriously by Eastern European and Israeli intelligence agencies, who are engaged in extensive research on it (Deacon, 1977). Police departments also have experimented with the use of psychics. While it raises interesting issues for validity, ethics, and privacy, were it to be used in social research, it is possible that, in the future, ESP may emerge as still another form of gathering dirty data. What type of technique is it? It might be classified as coercion because it is against, or independent of, a person's will; as deception, because it is carried out covertly; or as an uncontrollable contingency, because of the residue or traces given off by thought and behavior which the expert draws on. It is also interesting to speculate on what form counterespionage might take.

PROTECTING DIRTY DATA

The would-be discoverer of dirty data must ask, how do organizations attempt to protect their information? The four methods of discovery we have considered have counterparts in actions taken to protect secrets.

Organizations may attempt to limit the damage from accidental or coincidental discoveries by diffusing and hiding responsibility, by having "need to know" rules (even for those who are highly trusted), by compartmentalizing activities, by using code names and a cell organizational structure, by delegating dirty work in a nontraceable way, by having mechanisms which insulate higher status persons from traceable "contamination," by eliminating witnesses, and by having contingency cover-up plans. Paper shredders and refuse burned under guard are means of thwarting garbage detectives.

Efforts to avoid informing and whistleblowing can be seen in recruitment, socialization, and sanctioning patterns. Background investigations are one means. Recruiting on the basis of ethnicity, or friends and relatives, is also thought to increase reliability. Kinship was a prominent device in underground networks in World War II and is a factor in some criminal enterprises. Loyalty may be cultivated by good working conditions and rewards, as well as appeals to shared values. In a kind of institutionalized blackmail, culpability may be built in by requiring or maneuvering employees into participation in illegal or potentially discrediting actions. To indict the organization would thus be to indict oneself. Long training, testing periods, and, as employees come to prove their reliability, gradual exposure to an organization's secrets are other devices. Contracts binding employees to secrecy and subjecting them to civil and criminal penalties for divulging information are also relevant. The CIA, for example, claims the right to censor what its former employees publish and, under some conditions, can stop them from getting royalties. Violence against informants, stigmatizing the tattletale, psychiatric labeling, dismissal, the loss of a pension, and blackballing are other devices intended to deter the sharing of secrets.

Awareness of deception and institutionalized coercion as information gathering tactics may give rise to a variety of strategic actions designed to mislead and limit what can be discovered. Thus, the deception of the investigator may be matched by the counterespionage of the target who gives out or pemits false data to be discovered. The requirement that reports be filed or testimony given does not insure that they will be accurate. Awareness of legitimate and illegitimate electronic surveillance may mean electronic countersweeping, or restricting key communications to areas where bugs are unlikely. Communications can be faked, guarded, and disguised when a wiretap or bug has been discovered. There is a dialectic between discoverers and keepers of secrets, as they reciprocally adjust their behavior. A discoverer's advantage may be only temporary, or work best on amateurs who have not found a form of neutralization.

CONTRASTING THE METHODS

We have considered four general methods by which researchers can obtain hidden and dirty data.[16] How do these methods compare with respect to criteria such as ethics, representativeness, reactivity, susceptibility to the researcher's initiative, range of topics covered, validity, skill requirements, and costs? Table 3 contrasts the methods with respect to these criteria. Without going over every cell in the table, let us highlight some of the major characteristics of these methods.

The major advantage of the deceptive experiment is, of course, its incredible power to pierce the protective shield of secrecy that is likely to surround those involved with dirty data. It yields primary data, is subject to the researcher's initiative, and permits testing hypotheses. With adequate resources, one can take a sample of appropriate settings or subjects and hence make a case for its representativeness (though of just what can be problematic, as will be noted).

Replication and a degree of control over the variables involved are possible (although with field experiments such control is always limited). Skill requirements are moderate, though imagination is needed to develop the precise tactics, and skill in acting may be required.

The major disadvantage of the method involves questions of ethics and the meaning of the data. There are potentially corrosive and problematic aspects of using such tactics. Deception involves important ethical issues such as lying, invasions of privacy, manipulation, and involving subjects without their consent. In getting at the dirt, one may get dirty oneself. Seeking data on illegal actions may draw the researcher into illegal activities, and he or she may face temptations not usually considered in graduate methodology classes.

For reasons of resources and ethics, a rather narrow range of issues has been covered using the deceptive experiment. For social researchers, it is best used in attempting to document a pattern of victimization of persons that involves specific actions at one point in time. The dirty data appears as

---

[16]There are, of course, other reasons for using such methods beyond the discovery of dirty data. Webb et al. (1966) scarcely mention it in arguing for the use of unobtrusive measures such as physical traces of contrived observation. Instead, they advocate such methods because of belief in "multiple operationalism." Using several methods permits stronger conclusions and some correction for the limitations (e.g., reactivity, faulty memories) present when only one method, such as the interview, is used.

Table 3

Some Criteria for Contrasting Methods for Gathering Dirty Data

| Method | Criteria | | | | |
	Ethics: Researcher's Standpoint	Representativeness	Reactivity	Susceptible to Researcher's Initiative	Range of Issues or Topics Covered
Experiments	Problematic because of deception and tampering without consent	With sufficient resources, not an issue	A problem—"experimenter effects"	Yes	Narrow
Infiltrators	Problematic if researcher is involved in disguised participation observation, less if uses accounts of others	Often problematic, since access rarely random	A problem	Sometimes	Broad
Uncontrollable Contingencies	Not an issue, other than privacy questions	Likely a problem, hard to determine how typical an event is	Not an issue	No, except for reading trace elements	Narrow
Whistleblowers	Ethical issues fall mostly on the whistleblower	Hard to determine, reasons to expect person is atypical	Assuming initial good faith on whistle-blower's part, not a problem	No, though institutional mechanisms may facilitate	Broad
Open Field Work	Can be problematic insofar as involves conflict between loyalty to subjects and demands of outside society	Usually problematic, but with sufficient resources and access need not be	Can be a problem, but more amenable to control than with infiltrators	Yes	Broad

				Intermediate
Matters of Public Record; Freedom of Information Act	Generally not an issue	Hard to determine, with respect to both what is recorded and what survives	An issue, insofar as subjects anticipate their data will become public and may shape it accordingly	Basically, no; researcher must pretty much take whatever was written down and made public
Experiments	Not an issue except for problems of reactivity	Moderate	Moderate to expensive	New data
Infiltrators	Can be problematic—hidden agendas, lack of cross-observer validation	Good acting ability, willingness to take risks, role conflicts	Inexpensive, moderate if researcher is infiltrator	
Uncontrollable Contingencies	Generally not an issue	Moderate	Inexpensive	Lends self best to discovery rather than explanation
Whistleblowers	Researchers must be skeptical and ask what hidden agenda the informant may have	Does not apply	Inexpensive	
Open Field Work	Less of an issue	Highly specialized	Moderate	Unlike other methods, does not assume a conflict relationship
Matters of Public Record	Less an issue of validity than relevance of what gets written down; given knowledge that it may become public can generate methods of institutionalized evasion	Minimal, but you need to know what you are looking for	Generally inexpensive	After-the-fact data, you need an idea of what to look/ask for; can be a useful followup to leads from uncontrollable contingencies or whistleblowers

a result of actions taken by the target relative to a subject, e.g., fake voter registration, discrimination in housing, employment, or law enforcement, or consumer fraud. The dirt can lie in a clear violation of laws or policies, or in a more subtle misuse of discretion. The researcher presents him or herself as a client, patient, stooge, or ally, and sees if the hypothesized behavior is, or appears to be, forthcoming. There are limits here, as the researcher is unlikely to wish to take this to a point where actual damage is done, or the law is violated, as with unnecessary surgery, actually paying a bribe, or purchasing contraband.

It is much easier to become involved in an ongoing setting at one point in time than to create an entirely new setting. Elaborate hoaxes, such as fake criminal enterprises run by police, generally go far beyond the resources and competencies of the researcher. The cost, skill requirements, and risks of discovery increase, the more complex the deception and the longer it goes on.

The data from deceptive experiments can be questioned with respect to both their validity and generalizability. One source of error lies in the strategic actions of those with secrets to protect. They may discover the experiment and take what amounts to counter espionage actions, giving out deceptive information themselves. Thus a finding of no dirty data must always be considered in light of the question, "was the target suspicious and hence behaving in an atypical way?" A second source of error lies in reactivity or entrapment, as subjects respond to subtle or obvious pressure from the researchers. The degree of passivity is an important factor here. Does the researcher merely offer an opportunity, or go beyond this to actively encourage the subject to use it?

Even if the results are valid, the intervention may have an artificial quality, making it unclear what it should be generalized to. As with any experimental undertaking, even those done in natural settings, there is the question of whether it is representative of real-world settings or merely other experimental settings. For example, this seems to be the problem with discovering that persons will respond criminally to deceptively provided opportunities that are appreciably more tempting than those likely to be found in reality, or discovering (using Black and White investigators) that there is housing discrimination against Blacks in elite White areas in which few Blacks may wish, or be in a position, to live in. An important factor here (and one recognized by the courts in criminal cases) is how closely the artificial setting corresponds to those in the real world.

Deception in the case of infiltration shares many of the advantages and disadvantages of the deceptive experiment, yet some differences can be noted. Since it goes on for a longer period of time and is more diffuse, the range of topics or issues covered is likely to be much broader than with experiments.

The risks, ethical issues, and temptations faced are likely to be far more serious than with the onetime experiment, especially those where the researcher is offered as potential victim. Joint illegal actions may be demanded as the price of access, discovery of one's true identity can lead to physical harm, and the researcher with knowledge of others' wrongdoing can be compelled to testify. The researcher does not have the immunity or right to confidentiality that law enforcement, medical, and religious professionals have.

Since there is usually only one covert participant, cross-observer data cannot be a source of validation. Representativeness is also likely to be an issue, since access is often a matter of idiosyncratic local factors related to previous work experience or friendship patterns.

Data obtained through the various means of institutionalized coercion are unlikely to be otherwise available. In general, they do not raise profound ethical issues, are relatively inexpensive (generally involving the cost of photocopying, though where elaborate FOIA searches or the transcription of court records are required, expenses can be large). The data may be available on a scale far beyond what the researcher could normally obtain.

However, the researcher has less initiative, and replication and control of relevant variables are rarely possible. Merely locating the information can be a problem. Court data are not centrally located nor indexed in ways that benefit the researcher. Even with FOIA requests, the researcher needs to know what he or she wants. Because such data is initially gathered for purposes other than research, it tends to have the usual drawbacks of secondary data. This sometimes is avoided by the researcher being able to advise commissions, committees, legislative bodies, and courts as to exactly what data should be gathered. With regularized reporting requirements that apply categorically, representativeness is not an issue. However, with grand jury or court proceedings, issues of representativeness may loom large. Cases for which data is available may represent particularly grievous instances, or idiosyncratic prosecutorial factors.

The validity of data gathered under coercion must be carefully scrutinized, given a conflict setting and the likelihood of strategic responses. In the case of court testimony, those facing criminal charges may have a strong incentive to lie, particularly if they are offered immunity. With respect to records, false or misleading reports may be filed. The former may be a natural response for agencies (e.g., national security or law enforcement) professionally involved in dissimilitude. Awareness that one's documents are subject to the Freedom of Information Act may mean that far less is written down, or that written records are destroyed as soon as possible[17]

---

[17]The FBI was destroying records on a massive scale until a 1980 Federal District Court

(thus, records prior to the 1966 passage of FOIA, or the stronger version of 1974 following Watergate, are likely to have the greatest validity). The concept of "maximum deniability" that surfaced during the Congressional Hearings on U.S. Intelligence activities in the 1970s certainly predates reporting requirements and the FOIA. Even where things are written down, observers should be on guard. As a federal employee with extensive experience in the handling of the kinds of records researchers seek from government observes, "the 'cooking [falsifying] of records' has gone on as long as there has been any government anywhere" (The *New York Times*, July 11, 1982).

As a means of misleading their competition, businesses may patent their failures. Through tricks and subterfuge, reports filed may be technically, but not actually, correct. Thus, assets or conflicts of interest may be hidden. Silent partners may not be listed. Those listed as owners may merely be fronting for others. Bribe offers and payments may be made indirectly through lawyers. The most serious offenders may never file reports (for example, some businesses avoid licensing and reporting requirements by continually changing their name and place of business).

Information which is given voluntarily avoids many of the ethical issues around deception and coercion. To take the case of the whistleblower, the ethical issues fall primarily on the bearer of the data, and much less on the researcher who uses it. Since the whistleblower tends to come forward on his or her own, reactivity is not likely to be an issue. The range of topics covered is likely to be broad, the method is inexpensive, and it does not require a highly skilled researcher to use it.

Yet it clearly has disadvantages. As in the accident, the researcher's role is rather passive. The researcher usually must wait for the whistleblower, though good field workers can sometimes gain equivalent information from their informants. Problems of representativeness are often present. It is difficult to know what the account of the whistleblower represents. The rarity of whistleblowing can be used to argue that the very atypicality of the case was what generated whistleblowing in the first place. Great care must be taken with respect to validity. In coming from the horse's mouth, whistleblowing can have a persuasiveness which anonymous, or outside, data sources lack. The personal motives of the whistleblower can lead to distortions, exaggerations, and outright falsification. Skepticism and a critical attitude are necessary in the face of seeming data gifts, whether from whistleblowers, accidents, or informants. Are they what they appear to be? The researcher must be especially careful when the whistleblower's account supports the researcher's own ideological stance toward the organization or issue in questions.

---

ordered cessation and the development of record retention plans. After the strengthening of the FOIA, some agencies shifted from records in narrative to checklist form (e.g., yes–no).

The uncontrolled contingency does not present serious ethical problems, though dealing with trace elements may involve violations of privacy. Since the data appears independently of the actions of the researcher, reactivity is not a problem, and it is inexpensive. Nor is validity likely to be an issue (though in highly controversial or conflictual areas there is always the possibility that a trace element or accident is not what it appears to be and was created to cover up something else, to damage someone, or to pursue self-interests). The researcher must always ask, was the accident faked, the evidence planted, the dirty artifacts, or data, counterfeited or contrived?

Unlike the other methods, the uncontrolled contingency is not a strategy that the investigator can initiate; replication and control of extraneous variables are rarely possible. Rather, it is an opportunity which the researcher reacts to, although the investigator is aided by knowing where to look.

The occurrence of an accident is, of course, no guarantee that dirty data is present, nor, if it is, that it will become available. Its occurrence may be covered up and access to data about it denied.[18] The discovery of coverups raises the intriguing question of the ratio of discovered to successful coverups. Is success typical and discovery primarily due to incompetence or bad luck? Even if this is not the case, issues of representativeness plague generalizations from accidents. It is difficult to know what they are representative of.

When data are available, there may be major problems with respect to their meaning and interpretation. Seeing smoke does not necessarily tell you what kind of fire is present, nor what caused it, nor how to put it out. Facts do not speak for themselves, though some seem to whisper louder than others. This is part of a more general issue in social problems research. It is much easier to document a problem than to explain it.

Accidents can be a key to *discovering* that dirty data is present. But the collection of data is likely to depend on further actions. The publicity around an accident can mobilize resources and political support to set coercive data collection procedures (courts, grand juries, commissions) in motion.

SOME RESEARCH ISSUES AND NEEDS

My purpose in this paper has been to call attention to a type of data with particular relevance to social problems research and to contrast some meth-

---

[18]For example, the horrifying cover-ups documented in "Paul Jacobs and the Nuclear Gang" presented on public television in 1980. With respect to denial of data, the Union of Concerned Scientists recently had to resort to the FOIA to force the Nuclear Regulatory Commission to release its secret "Nugget File." The file details 230 failures and accidents at nuclear power stations between 1966 and 1976.

ods for obtaining it. Substantively, the topic of dirty data touches many areas, including the sociology of knowledge and science, secrecy, stratification, face-to-face interaction, mass communications, and deviance and social control. It suggests a number of researchable questions:

• From a sociology of knowledge perspective, what are the implications of the differential availability of information? With respect to both popular consciousness and scientific knowledge, what are the areas where we have valid information (whether as a result of systematic social research of personal experience), as against areas where information is invalid or lacking? To what extent is our assessment of the contours of information validity correct?

• How is our image of the world distorted because facts are hidden or deceptively presented? What are the implications of our greater weakness as scientists or interveners in the face of hidden and dirty data?

• How does this type of ignorance (withheld or deceptively presented information) compare in form, process, and consequences to ignorance involving errors of measurement, or theory, things that are knowable but undiscovered (e.g., topics that are dangerous to study), or to things that are unknowable?

For example, contrast (before discovery) what was believed about the Soviet downing of Gary Powers U-2 spy plane, the Tonkin Gulf bombing, the My-Lai massacre, black lung disease, destabilization and the CIA, police and protest groups, and Watergate with what were, or remain, scientific anomalies, e.g., meteorites and sea serpents (Westrum, 1978), or individual or mass delusions. What does it mean that we tend to lack adequate terms for even characterizing types of empirically invalid beliefs?

• Does the greater difficulty in studying dirty data topics (including method limitations) mean we will always have to give greater reliance to the accounts of novelists or journalists, and will these topics always be more contentious because the data are poorer?

• Is there a knowledge product (characteristic of much social problems research) which stands between the novelist, journalist, or detective, and the pure scientist, while drawing from both groups? Such knowledge shares with the former the need to rely on non-rigorous and questionable data sources, the desire to raise issues, sensitize the public, and document problems, and a frequent reliance on individual cases. It shares with the latter respect for the logic of explanation and the need for empirical verification and generalization.

• How do dirty data secrets differ from other types of secrets?

- How is dirty data distributed in the society?
- How do (1) its extensiveness, (2) its form, (3) the ability to protect it, and (4) its consequences relate to social stratification? The presence of dirty data is certainly not restricted to elites, though the social costs of their dirty data and their ability to prevent discovery, are likely much greater than is the case for subordinant groups. What institutional areas or organizations produce the most, e.g., contrast commerce with art, or politics with science (though recent revelations suggest that deception in science is far more widespread than is generally acknowledged). Is an organized adversary present who stands to be harmed by concealment? If so, what are the implications of this?[19]
- How is access and accountability for discrediting information related to stratification? On the one hand, higher status people may give the orders, but on the other, they are likely to be insulated from responsibility. Thus, middle or lower level personnel are more likely to be sanctioned. In addition, certain types of dirty-work are routinely given to lower status members and serve to reenforce their status. Where physical actions are involved, workers close to the scene are likely to know what is going on. Butlers, servants, and maids have historically been the first to know, and are in a good position to be spies and blackmailers.[20]
- How conducive is "insulation from observability" (to use Rose Coser's [1961] long neglected phrase) to rule violations? Put the other way, is sunlight always the best remedy, as Justice Brandeis suggested?
- What is the connection between keeping dirty data secret and legitimacy? A central element in sustaining societal myths (beyond staying in power) may be concealing dirty data. On the other hand, openness (e.g., Jimmy Carter's "I will not lie to you" speech) can be a device for enhancing legitimacy.

---

[19]While perhaps not adversarial in the conventional sense, a fascinating group to study here would be the Aviation Safety Institute. This independent watch dog organization was set up by a test pilot who had little faith in the FAA and its regulatory safety practices. It publishes a newsletter entitled "Monitor." The "cornerstone" of the organization's work is an "anonymous reporting service." Since 1973, 40,000 persons have dialed its toll free phone number to report "unsafe aviation conditions or unsafe acts." Verified accounts are reported in the newsletter. It is interesting that even for something like air safety, when the costs of failure are visible and enormous, there appears to be a need for an independent information gathering organization using an anonymous reporting service.

[20]Hughes (1958:51) observes, ". . . it is by the garbage that the janitor judges, and, as it were, gets power over the tenants who high-hat him. Janitors know about hidden love affairs by bits of torn up letter paper; of impending financial disaster or of financial four-flushing by the presence of many unopened letters in the waste."

• What unintended consequences may accompany the recent efforts to increase openness? For example, the major users of the FOIA are businesses trying to learn about government regulatory practices and those in prison trying to find out who informed. Do open meetings mean less candor and more "premeeting meetings"? Does living in a goldfish bowl mean more and better concealed secrets, as Bennis (1980) argues? Are there conditions where "ignorance is bliss" and "what you don't know, won't hurt you" (Moore and Tumin, 1949)?

• What are the consequences of making it easy to file anonymous complaints? Similar issues are raised with "shield laws" offering immunity to journalists who refuse to reveal their sources. On the one hand, it could be argued that not having the identity of the informant known will produce important and otherwise unavailable information. On the other hand, the very anonymity can stimulate invalid data and trivia, overloading the system, slandering reputations and wreaking havoc, as those who are vindictive, ruthless, irresponsible, cranks, saboteurs or witch hunters take advantage of the protection it offers. Important issues are the ease with which allegations can be kept secret before and (should they prove unfounded) after efforts at verification. Are problems reduced when the identity of the information source is known, but not made public, or is known by trusted intermediaries who are not formally a part of the organization interested in the information? To what extent are problems reduced with a two-step system, where the identity of the complainant is known by certain officials but not made public?

• How do types of society compare? How does a society's degree of openness affect the amount of dirt that there is? When it is relatively easy to get, as in the U.S., do people become indignant and demand change, or cynical and tolerant because "it's everywhere"? Under what conditions might publicizing it serve to stimulate the misbehavior of others through a forbidden fruit effect?

• How does it relate to scandal and social reform?

• How are broad societal changes, whether social, cultural, or technical, affecting the ability to protect and discover dirty data? Are we becoming a more open society? Is the relative amount of dirty data declining or should it best be seen as a moving equilibrium?

Beyond substantive issues, awareness of the topic has practical implications. Social researchers appear to make much less use of dirty data discovery methods than do journalists, detectives, and even historians. This partly reflects differences in goals, resources, and norms. Table 4 contrasts types of secrecy investigator by goals (scientific understanding, news, social reform, planning a counterstrategy, prosecution, and resources for coercion).[21]

Unlike the social researcher, most other secrecy investigators are themselves protected by secrecy, and need publicly document neither their sources nor their methods. These may be protected legally and by professional standards. Indeed, even results may be kept secret or used only as needed. But, given the demands of scientific communication, the researcher is expected to go public. He or she must describe where the data comes from and how it was collected. The standards of evidence for making a scientific claim are higher than for journalism or the law. In the case of journalism, for example, issues of causality, methodological failings, and representativeness generally receive little attention. Social researchers also differ from many government agents in that they cannot offer large sums for information, put together a grand jury, issue a subpoena, compel testimony, offer immunity, nor legally wiretap.[22] The closest we can come is occasionally advising government bodies, as with special commissions or courts that can do these things. Whether considering government agents, or journalists, our resources are more limited and our standards in general are more restrictive with respect to using coercion and decpetion.[23] Academic norms of civility and gentility operate against some of the more roughshod methods of others in the dirty data discovery business.[24]

But beyond these differences, I think social researchers also make less use of these techniques as a result of lack of awareness and familiarity, and perhaps a generally less skeptical and cynical occupational world view than is the case for police, lawyers, and investigative journalists.

There is a small literature on dirty data research issues, particularly in

---

[21]Other professionals excluded from this table, such as religious and psychological counselors and physicians, also deal with secrets. However, this tends to involve personal rather than organizational data, is (at least ideally) in a helping rather than an adversarial or conflict relationship, and publication to other audiences is not a goal. There are exceptions, however, as with the requirement that health workers must report cases of venereal disease.

[22]This is a nice example of how method shapes knowledge. What would the state of social problems knowledge be if we could do these things?

[23]This may seem less clear around *deception*. But the very fact that there is a social science literature debating this indicates its sensitivity. The divergent direction in social science vs. journalism is interesting here. Investigative journalism has become well established, while social scientists seem to be moving in the other direction with concerns over human subjects research.

[24]Social scientists have the advantage of not having to be so concerned about the validity of any specific case, since their interest is in the aggregate, in patterns, and in developing ideal types. However, this is balanced by the need to have a larger number of cases before one can address relevant audiences with authority.

Table 4
Investigators of Secrecy and Goals

Type of Investigator	Organization Serving Goals Sought by Investigators of Secrets*					
	Scientific Understanding	as news	Publicize as a factor in social reform	Plan Counterstrategy	Prosecution	As Resource for Coercion (informants)
Journalists		X				
Lawyers				X	X	X
Public and Private Detectives				X	X	X
Social Reformers			X			
Intelligence Agents				X		X
Social Researchers	X		X			

*Here we exclude private goals such as blackmail, selling secrets, etc.

considerations of field work methods (e.g., *Social Problems,* Feb. 1980), social psychological experiments, and in the substantive areas of political sociology (around the study of power elites) and deviance-criminology. But this literature is restricted and has not dealt adequately with the new issues and opportunities of the last decade. Our methodology textbooks tend to be sadly lacking in guidelines for such research. We can learn a considerable amount from those professionals who routinely seek to discover dirty data. Their results may offer rich materials for secondary analysis. We might also make greater use of their methods for primary analysis, as some historians have done using the FOIA.

The array of methods we use could be broadened. Methodology texts and courses should give more attention to these methods and resources for obtaining dirty data. We should become as familiar with the University of Missouri's CIRE (Center for Investigative Reporters and Editors), as with the University of Chicago's NORC. Students should be taught how to use the Freedom of Information Act (e.g., see Committee on Government Operations, 1977; Center for National Security Studies, 1979), just as they are taught how to draw a sample. We should communicate to our students the joy of discovery and also what a discovery motion in court is. Berman Associates' checklist of Congressional Hearings, and the monthly list of Government Accounting Office reports, should become standard references. We should scan the periodic lists offered by the Nader-sponsored Freedom of Information Clearing House, just as we scan listings of government and foundation grants. The Carrollton Declassified Documents Reference Service should become as well known to us as the Yale Human relations area files. Just as some of us have learned how to contact the Census for demographic data, we should learn how to contact the Clerk of a court for legal documents. Civil and Criminal Court indices should be consulted. The data archives at the Center for National Security Studies should be as well known as those at the Roper Center or the Inter-University Consortium.

While researchers sometimes consult "Who's Who?", they should also be consulting an obscure, formerly classified, publication put together by CIA office of security specialist Harry J. Murphy, entitled, "Where's What— Sources of Information for Federal Investigators." This is a marvelously rich compendium of sources of personal information such as private directories and government files. Methodological stalwarts, such as Lazarsfeld and Hyman, must make room for outsiders such as Mollenhoff's *Investigative Reporting* (1980) and Williams' "Investigative Reporting and Editing" (1977). *First Principles, Mother Jones,* and *7 Days* should take their place alongside the more established academic journals whose contents we skim.

While I do not suggest that we learn to wire tap, if wire tap data presents itself, we should not necessarily ignore it. Furthermore, we should know where to look to find out if it is presenting itself. As Horatio Alger noted, the knock of opportunity does little for those who do not hear it. The ethical problem here is somewhat similar to that raised by whether or not a university or church should accept tainted money (as from a slum lord).

While the ethical issues are not to be taken lightly, and will limit us relative to actions that may be justified in war time, or even those routinely taken by police, I think sociologists can go further and be more imaginative than we have been in the kinds of natural field experiments we attempt. There is a need for standards and discussion in this area to be sure (Kelman, 1977; Klockars and O'Connor, 1979). However, perhaps different standards with respect to deception, privacy, informed consent, and avoiding harm to research subjects ought to apply when the subjects themselves are engaged in deceitful, coercive, and illegal activities, and/or where one is dealing with an institution which is publicly accountable.[25] Even without resorting to ethically questionable methods, an astounding amount can be discovered through intelligence, knowing where to look and what to look for, diligence, and the cultivation of sources. The career of I.F. Stone, with its heavy reliance on congressional hearings, attests to this. Preferring publically available information, and without resorting to deception, he has been a one person discovery machine.

Many of the topics dear to the hearts of social problems researchers could be better illuminated were we to make greater, though restrained, use of methods for discovering dirty data. Yet the researcher in this area must judiciously walk a hazy line between the unacceptable extremes of taking the world at face value and believing that what is unseen is unimportant, as against thinking that nothing is what it appears to be and that whatever is hidden must, therefore, be significant. The presence of secrecy is a guarantee of neither theoretical nor social relevance. Even where dirty data is

---

[25]We lack a clear and agreed upon moral framework which can mesh, balance, or resolve conflict among these elements. Informed consent, for example, can be seen as an equitable measure in that it offers less powerful groups the right not to be studied, a de facto right which higher status groups have tended to have all along. Yet there may be other costs in its categorical application. Duster, Matza, and Wellman (1979:140–141) observe, "in some situations, 'informed consent' may in fact impede the protection of some human subjects, for example, when the question before researchers—and the public—involves possible unethical behavior, like fraud and discrimination . . . to mechanically apply to powerful institutions a bureaucratic rule originally meant to protect the powerless, forgets the reason behind the reform." On the other hand, who is to decide, and by what decision criteria is it appropriate to conclude that a research subject may be deceived? One standard is a kind of reverse golden rule (Marx, 1983). Here persons who violate the public trust are appropriate subjects for investigative tactics that would otherwise be inappropriate. The great Catch-22 comes with the (large?) number of cases for which it is not possible to know beforehand that violations are occurring. To exempt such persons from deceptive tactics until probable cause appears makes it unlikely that the wrongdoing will be discovered.

scientifically and socially relevant, respect for the law and individuals' rights must be carefully balanced against the scholar's concern with discovering the truth and contributing to reform. There are many instances where the former will preclude the latter. In spite of such concerns, increased attention to dirty data methods, topics, and issues is one factor required for better understanding of social problems.

REFERENCES

Anderson, D. and P. Benjaminson
    1976   Investigative Reporting. Bloomington, IN: Indiana University Press.
Bennis, W.
    1980   "The cult of candor." Atlantic (September): 89–91.
Blakey, G. R. and R. N. Billings
    1981   The Plot to Kill the President. New York: Times Books.
Bok, S.
    1978   Lying. New York: Random House.
    1980   "Whistleblowing and professional responsibility." New York University Education
            Quarterly 11 (summer):2–8.
Center for National Security Studies
    1979   Using the Freedom of Information Act: A Step by Step Guide. Washington, DC
Chambliss, W.
    1978   On the Take. Bloomington, IN: Indiana University Press.
Committee on Government Operations
    1977   A Citizen's Guide on How to Use the Freedom of Information Act in Requesting
            Government Documents. United States Congress, Washington, DC: United States
            Government Printing Office.
Coser, R.
    1961   "Insulation from observability and type of social conformity." American So-
            ciological Review 26 (February): 28–39.
Crosby, R. S. Bromley, and L. Saxe
    1980   "Recent unobtrusive studies of black and white discrimination and prejudice: A
            literature review." Psychological Bulletin 87, 3: 546–63.
Deacon, R.
    1977   The Israeli Secret Service. New York: Taplinger.
Domhoff, W. G.
    1979   The Powers that Be: Processes of Ruling Class Domination in America. New York:
            Random House.
Douglas, J.
    1976   Investigative Social Research. Beverly Hills, CA: Sage.
Downes, A.
    1967   Inside Bureaucracy. Boston, MA: Little Brown.
Dudar, H.
    1979   "The price of blowing the whistle." New York Times Magazine (October): 41–54.
Duster, T., D. Matza, and D. Wellman
    1979   "Field work and the protection of human subjects." The American Sociologist
            (August): 136–142.

Emerson, R. and M. Pollner
     1976   "Dirty work designations: Their features and consequences in a psychiatric set-
              ting." Social Problems 24 (February): 243–254.
Festinger, Leon, H. W. Riecken, and S. Schachter
     1956   When Prophecy Fails. Minneapolis, MN: University of Minnesota Press.
Finney, H. and H. Lesieur
     1982   "A contingency theory of organizational crime." Pp. 255–299 in S. Bachrach (ed.)
              Current Perspectives in Organizational Sociology. Greenwich, CT: JAI Press.
Galliher, J. F.
     1980   "Social scientists' ethical responsibilities to superordinates: Looking upward
              meekly." Social Problems 27,3: 298–308.
Goffman, E.
     1963   Stigma: Notes on the Management of Spoiled Identity. Englewood Cliffs, NJ: Pren-
              tice-Hall.
Government Accountability Project
     1977   A Whistleblower's Guide to the Federal Bureaucracy. Washington, DC: Institute for
              Policy Studies.
Halperin, M. H.
     1974   Bureaucratic Politics and Foreign Policy. Washington, DC: Brookings Institute.
Heussenstamm, F. K.
     1971   "Bumper stickers and the cops." Trans-Action 8 (February): 32–33.
Hilbert, R.
     1980   "Covert participant observation." Urban Life 9 (April): 51–78.
Hughes, E. C.
     1958   Men and Their Work. Glencoe, IL: Free Press.
     1971   The Sociological Eye: Selected Papers. Chicago, IL: Aldine.
Humphreys, L.
     1975   Tearoom Trade: Impersonal Sex in Public Places. Chicago, IL: Aldine.
Ianni, F. and E. R. Ianni
     1972   A Family Business. New York: Russell Sage Foundation.
Jesilow, P. and M. J. O'Brien
     1980   "Deterring automobile repair fraud: A field experiment." Paper presented at Ameri-
              can Sociological Association meetings, New York.
Kelman, H. C.
     1977   "Privacy and research with human beings." Journal of Social Issues 33,3: 169–
              195.
Kinsey, A. C., W. B. Pomeroy, and C. E. Martin
     1948   Sexual Behavior in the Human Male. Philadelphia: Saunders.
Kitsuse, J.
     1980   "Coming out all over: Deviants and the politics of social problems." Social Prob-
              lems 28,4: 1–13.
Klockars, C. and F. O'Connor
     1979   Deviance and Decency. Beverly Hills, CA: Sage.
LaPierre, R. T.
     1934   "Attitudes vs. actions." Social Forces 13:230–237.
Lenzner, Terry
     1980   Newsweek. April 21: 104.
Lowry, R.
     1972   "Toward a sociology of secrecy and security systems." Social Problems 19: 437–
              450.
Marx, G. T.
     1971   Muckraking Sociology: Research As Social Criticism. New York: Dutton.

1974 "Thoughts on a neglected category of social movement participant: Agent provocateurs and informants." American Journal of Sociology 80,2: 402–442.

1980 "The new police undercover work." Urban Life and Culture 8,4: 400–446.

1983 "Undercover police work: Ethical deception or deceptive ethics?" In W. Hefferman and T. Stroup (eds.) Police Ethics: Hard Choices in Law Enforcement. New York: John Jay Press.

Millman, M.
1977 The Unkindest Cut. New York: Morrow.

Mollenhoff, C.
1980 Investigative Reporting. New York: Macmillan.

Molotch, H. and M. Lester
1974 "News as purposive behavior: On the strategic use of routine events, accidents, and scandals." American Sociological Review 39 (February): 101–112.

Moore, W. E. and M. Tumin
1949 "Some social functions of ignorance." American Sociological Review 14 (December): 787–795.

Murphy, H. J.
1977 Where's What—Sources of Information for Federal Investigators. New York: Warner.

Nader, R., P. J. Petkas, and K. Blackwell
1972 Whistle Blowing. New York: Grossman.

Needleman, N. and C. Needleman
1979 "Organizational crime: Two models of criminogenesis." Sociological Quarterly 20: 517–528.

O'Toole, G.
1978 The Private Sector: Rent-a-Cop, Private Spies, and the Industrial Complex. New York: Norton.

Perrucci, R., R. Anderson, D. Schendel and L. Trachtman
1980 "Whistle blowing: Professionals' resistance to organizational authority." Social Problems 27,2: 149–164.

Peter, C. and B. Taylor
1972 Blowing the Whistle. New York: Praeger.

Polsky, N.
1967 Hustlers, Beats and Others. New York: Free Press.

Pontell, H., G. Geis, P. Jesilow, and M. J. O'Brien
1980 "Practitioner fraud and abuse in government-funded medical benefit programs." Unpublished paper. University of California, Irvine.

Privacy Protection Study Commission
1979 Personal Privacy in an Information Society. Washington, DC: U.S. Government Printing Office.

Reiss, A. and A. Biderman
1980 Data Sources on White Collar Law Breaking. Washington, DC: National Institute of Justice.

Rosenhan, D. C.
1973 "On being sane in insane places." Science 79: 250–258.

Schwartz, R. and J. Skolnick
1962 "Two studies of legal stigma." Social Problems 10 (fall): 133–138.

Selltiz, C.
1955 "The use of survey methods in a citizen's campaign against discrimination." Human Organization 14,3: 19–25.

Sherick, L. C.
1978 How To Use the Freedom of Information Act. New York: Arco.

Sherman, L.
  1978   Scandal and Reform. Berkeley, CA: University of California Press.
  1980   "Three models of organizational corruption in agencies of social control." Social
          Problems 27,4: 478–491.
Shils, E.
  1966   "Privacy: Its constitution and vicissitudes." Law and Contemporary Problems 31:
          281–306.
Simmel, G.
  1950   The Sociology of George Simmel. K. H. Wolff (ed.) New York: Free Press.
Snepp, F.
  1977   Decent Interval. New York: Random House.
Subcommittee on Long-Term Care, Special Committee on Aging Fraud and Abuse Among
      Practitioners Participating in the Medicaid Program.
  1976   Report. 94th Congress. Washington, DC: U.S. Government Printing Office.
Tefft, S.
  1980   Secrecy, New York: Human Sciences Press.
Useem, M.
  1980   "Corporations and the corporate elite." Annual Review of Sociology. 6: 41–78.
Van Maanen, J.
  1979   "The fact of fiction in organizational ethnography." Administrative Quarterly 24
          (December): 539–550.
Walker, A. L. and C. W. Lidz
  1977   "Methodological notes on the employment of indigenous observers." Pp. 103–123
          in R. S. Weppner (ed.) Street Ethnography. Beverly Hills, CA: Sage.
Wall, R.
  1972   "Special agent for the FBI." New York Review of Books (January 27): 12–18.
Wallerstein, J. S. and L. Wyle
  1947   "Our law-abiding law breakers." Federal Probation 25 (March–April): 107–112.
Warren, C. and B. Laslett
  1980   "Privacy and secrecy: A conceptual comparison." In S. Tefft (ed.) Secrecy. New
          York: Human Sciences Press.
Warwick, D.
  1975   "Tearoom trade: Means and ends in social research." In L. Humphreys, Tearoom
          Trade: Impersonal Sex in Public Places. Chicago, IL: Aldine.
Webb, E., D. Campbell, R. Schwartz, and L. Sechrest
  1966   Unobtrusive Measures: Nonreactive Research in the Social Sciences. Chicago, IL:
          Rand McNally.
Westin, A. and S. Salisbury
  1980   Individual Rights in the Corporation. New York: Pantheon.
Westrum, R.
  1978   "Science and social intelligence about anomalies: The case of meteorites." Social
          Studies of Science 8: 461–493.
Wienk, R., C. Reid, J. Simonson, and F. Eggers
  1979   Measuring Racial Discrimination in American Housing Markets: The Housing Mar-
          ket Practices Survey. Washington, DC: Department of Housing and Urban
          Development.
Williams, P.
  1977   Investigative Reporting and Editing. Englewood Cliffs, NJ: Prentice-Hall.

Zimbardo, P.
1969   "The human choice: Individuation, reason, and order versus deindividuation, impulse, and chaos." Pp. 237–307 in W. Arnold and D. Levine (eds.) Nebraska Symposium on Motivation. Lincoln, NE: University of Nebraska Press.
Zweigenhaft, R.
1978   "Deception research in social psychology: A call for a ten-year moratorium." Peace and Change 5 (fall): 34–45.

5 When is a "problem" not a problem?: Deflection activities in a clandestine motel

Richard A. Ball
West Virginia University

J. Robert Lilly
Northern Kentucky University

Although a great deal of attention has been given to the process by which social problems come into existence, relatively little has been paid to the converse—how is it that *potential problems* may never arise as such? For present purposes, we define potential problems as *activities which might reasonably be expected to provoke claims-making responses* (Spector and Kitsuse, 1977). An examination of negative cases, situations in which the potential is not realized, might shed light on the typical developmental processes involved in the emergence and growth of social problems. Our intention is to examine one such negative case, a clandestine motel which has operated unmolested for more than twenty-five years while providing a sanctuary for heterosexual relationships on the sly. Since we wish to deal with social problems (as contrasted with societal problems) by concentrating upon activities rather than upon conditions (Spector and Kitsuse, 1977) while seeking some means of generalization with respect to these activities, our approach will bring to the tradition of Symbolic Interactionism certain propositions derived from General Systems Theory.

Symbolic Interactionism has displayed a deep appreciation for the subtleties of social process, subtleties sometimes obscured by the "normative paradigm" positing an overly socialized actor reflecting reified norms internalized during earlier socialization (Wilson, 1970). Although it is true that such a perspective on social life risks being accused of having an "astructural bias" (Gouldner, 1970; Reynolds and Reynolds, 1973), any such tendency seems to be more a result of intense interest in ongoing, everyday life than of some inherent reductionism. Perhaps this can be made clearer through recourse to General Systems Theory, which also stresses a sensitivity to context, an essentially acausal orientation, a nonlinear perspective, a processual focus, and a concern for emergent ordering phenomena (Ball, 1978; Stover, 1979). Like Symbolic Interactionism, General Systems Theory is concerned with the patterning of activities, especially with the search for possible generalizations which might assist us in comparing across different sets of patterned activity.

Klapp (1973:294) has stressed that the applicability of General Systems Theory and its allied perspectives (e.g., cybernetics, information theory) to Symbolic Interactionism depends upon the extent to which the former remain flexible enough to "handle the subtler aspects of transactions, of constructing and interpreting definitions of situations" instead of falling into a mechanistic, "push–pull" approach to social order. Such a tendency is exemplified by much "functionalism" as well as by the reductionistic practice of "systems analysis" (Boguslaw, 1965), an extremely "positivistic" approach which is too often confused with the processual perspective advocated by such theorists as Buckley (1967), Laszlo (1972) and von Bertalanffy (1968). The latter approach does not represent some artificial imposition of a social structural perspective upon Symbolic Interactionism but merely seeks to elucidate the constraints under which mutual activities develop (Maines, 1977). Thus, for example, social structure itself is seen as controlled by social actors engaged in ongoing negative processes constrained by the nature of available information and the patterning of perceived alternatives (Burns and Buckley, 1976). The act of social organization therefore appears in adjustive processes rather than in formal structure (Maines, 1977), so that social order becomes a "structural process" as described by Glaser and Strauss (1968). This is as different from the older, mechanistic modeling running through Pareto to Parsons (1951) and Homans (1961) as it is from the organic modeling associated with Spencer and his various disciples.

THE MOTEL AS A POTENTIAL PROBLEM

The establishment with which we are concerned is located in a major urban center in the Southwest. It consists of forty-one rooms, most of which have private garages, entrance to which is controlled from an electronic switchboard located in the office. The building is surrounded on three sides by an eight-foot high stone wall. Patrons typically enter their rooms by first driving into the garage opened by the office staff, entering their rooms only after the garage door has been closed. Garage doors face the outer wall, with the rooms themselves facing a central courtyard. Although each room has a door opening onto the courtyard, these are rarely used. Rental fees may be paid at the office, but it is more common for a member of the staff to come to the room itself and to pick up the fee through a special slot in the door. Two sets of rooms have joining doors for those who want to arrange especially complicated activity. Ten have television sets which show closed-circuit, "X-rated" films. The entire facility is organized to facilitate secrecy and deflect trouble, and it has been remarkably successful. Although similar operations within the immediate area have been defined as major social problems, exposed to public assault, and forced to close, this particular setting has thrived during anti-vice campaigns of all sorts, and for much longer than any of the others. Its success is far from accidental, being rather the consequence of particularly effective adaptations. Since we have described the establishment in some detail elsewhere (Lilly and Ball, 1980; Lilly and Ball, 1981), we shall concentrate our attention here on what may be called *deflection processes.*

In his classic description of the process by which unproblematic social interaction was made possible, Mead (1934) outlined it from the point of view of the actor learning to take the role of the other, as in a game. When one understood not only the rules of the game but the role of each different player within the total context, one stood in possession of a complete set of expectations around which to organize activity. General Systems Theory operates in a similar vein. As Churchman (1968:231) puts it, "The systems approach begins when first you see the world through the eyes of another," adding that it goes on "to discovering that every world view is terribly limited." In terms of General Systems Theory, the community in which the motel is located may be understood as a complex "ecology of games" (Long, 1961) in which different clusters of actors play circumscribed games of their own, but always within the overall web by which the interaction games are related. As long as the overall ecology of games is going smoothly, there are no problems.

Given the analytical issue, the principal drawback of the negative case approach is obvious. How are we to speak of a set of circumstances as a "potential" problem? If it has not become a problem, who is to say that it contains the potential to become one? By what criteria is a "potential" problem determined, and how are we to get agreement that our example represents such a case? The theoretical issue here is cloudy, partly because the orthodox, functionalist orientation has succeeded in grasping the idea that any system is sustained by a balance of internal relationships (i.e., latent functions), while failing to notice that empirical systems typically incorporate antithetical forces or *latent potentials* which may alter the system (Ball, 1979). From both the General Systems Theory and the Symbolic Interactionist points of view, change is not the result of analytic variables taken one by one, but of conjunctions of forces which form new and powerful configurations whose strength rests largely on interaction effects. These potentials produce change either by interfering with traditional negative feedback of the sort that maintains a relatively steady state, or by generating sufficient positive feedback to alter the trajectory of the game, or by some combination of both. In the case of the facility in question, we feel on reasonably safe ground in treating it as a potential social problem simply because similar operations within the same community have emerged as clearly defined problems subjected to considerable claims-making activity—to the extent that some have been forced to close because of public pressure and police intervention.

It may be worthwhile to examine the typical process by which these other facilities have been successfully "exposed," labeled, pressured, and eliminated. In every instance during the past decade, the exposure and denunciations sequence has been triggered by a specific *catalyst* (Wright and Weiss, 1980). One such situation, for example, resulted from an accident. Not understanding the special nature of the scene, someone reserved a block of rooms in a local "no-tell motel" to provide overnight accommodations for the annual "senior trip" that would bring a group of out-of-town high school students for an excursion to the city. The class chaperones learned what they had stumbled onto only after their charges had settled in to enjoy the pornographic films on closed-circuit television. Either out of genuine horror or because of the need to protect themselves by deflecting attention from their oversight, the chaperones made vigorous complaints not only to the local police but to the ministerial association. Sensing a good "story," one television station produced a "special" claiming to identify and "expose" all "adult motels" in the city. Editorials appeared in city newspapers, and pickets became a common sight at each facility identified. The most seriously stigmatized actually closed and eventually was sold, while others were either closed for several months or forced by police pressure and threats of lawsuits, arrests, and continued picketing to remove all "X-rated" films.

As part of an intensive research effort which included interviews with all employees, participant observation, and close association with the proprietor over more than six years, the authors were also able to analyze rental records for a seven year period. Never during this time was the motel in any serious difficulty. Rental fluctuations were only minimally affected by the turmoil surrounding the curtailing of competitive operations, and even in the heat of claims and counterclaims accompanying media exposure, this facility was never included in the various complaints. No pickets appeared to disrupt activities or harrass patrons. Indeed, it was never even mentioned in all the newspaper and television exposes. Yet it is the oldest such operation in the city, was managed for many years by one of the most colorful characters in town, and has served some of the most prominent people in the area.

Claims making may be expected to involve those segments of a community with concerns related to some aspects of the activities at issue. Since the classic definition of a "public" describes such an aggregation as a group formed out of mutual concern with a particular issue, we maintain that claims are most likely to be made by what we will term "relevant publics." Our investigation has led us to the conclusion that the motel is not likely to become a social problem until at least one of its three distinct "publics" is sufficiently aroused to make claims against it. Beyond the normal management functions characteristic of any hotel or motel, it is the responsibility of the proprietor and his staff to control the situations so as to deflect *trouble with any of these relevant publics,* which include (a) the "morally concerned citizenry," (b) the police, and (c) the patrons.

We suggest that the emergence of social problems will be less the result of the inherent conditions or properties of related systems than of the relationships among them. To counter tendencies toward problematic status, those who comprise a given system (i.e., interaction cluster) must learn to manage *boundary relationships* (Emery, 1969:9). Such management processes are more judgemental than technical (Kitsuse and Spector, 1973). In the case of the motel, General Systems Theory (Vickers, 1967) suggests that we concentrate upon three judgemental foci: (a) *reality judgements* (which have to do with accurate mapping of social reality), (b) *value judgements* (which have to do with decisions as to what is desirable), and (c) *action judgements* (which have to do with selection among behavioral options).

According to General Systems Theory (Vickers, 1967), the three standard modes of control by which these various judgements can be implemented can be designated as (a) control by error, (b) control by rule, and (c) control by goal. The first and the third depend for their success upon effective feedback processes by which relevant publics can be "scanned" for necessary information. Social problems theory has for some time stressed the impact of such *contingencies,* and Weiner (1956) has noted that systems capable of dealing with contingencies must have considerable organizational freedom. Adaptive capacity depends to a considerable extent upon "requisite variety" (Ashby, 1956) or internal flexibility sufficient to assimilate and process shifting environmental input without overload. In the case of the motel, requisite variety exists through a pattern of more than sixty years of collective staff experience under all sorts of pressures and environmental changes. No matter what happens, those managing the operation seem to recall a previously successful strategy, i.e., they may identify an appropriate contact, or develop a successful response based on personal initiative, understanding, confidence, experience, and access to information. Since the design of adequate feedback loops to allow for *control by error* demands an understanding of the parameters of possible disturbance (Miller, 1965), it is crucial that the proprietor and staff make accurate estimates of these situations and undertake realigning actions (Goffman, 1959). Otherwise, disturbances might easily "get out of hand" and become unmanageable, as has happened from time to time with similar establishments in the area.

Control by rule depends much less upon external feedback than upon standardized operating procedures. With its reliance upon rules or norms, it is the mode most congenial to traditional functionalist theorists and those managing classic, bureaucratic organizations. The principal advantage of such a mode of control lies in its capacity for error reduction through maximization of predictability. The principal disadvantage lies in its tendency to produce systemic rigidity, with a consequent reduction in capacity to adapt to "error" or develop its own "goal-seeking" potentials. Since systems representing potential social problems are quite vulnerable to shifts in their environments, those guiding them cannot rely too much on control by rigid rule. This means that, in the event some rule fails to serve the purpose, those operating the motel must immediately fall back on control by error or shift to a control by goal mode.

In the more traditional "systems" theory of many exchange or functionalist models, *control by goal* is usually conceived of in terms of a narrow, linear logic far removed from either the logic of Symbolic Interactionism or that of General Systems Theory. Linear logic tends to assume both *linearity* and *continuity*, as illustrated by Merton's (1957) well-known treatment of social problems within a framework of *anomie*, which he redefined as *ends-means discontinuity*. Here, social problems result from a breakdown of some theoretically continuous, linear relationship between previously established goals and the stable, institutionalized means for their achievement. According to General Systems Theory, an empirically more common process of control by goal in open systems is the process of *equifinality*, by which the goal is pursued through means which shift to fit circumstances. This is a model of shifting strategy rather than of institutionalized techniques, of plans modifiable within certain limits so as to accomplish essentially the same end in spite of alterations in surrounding environmental activities. In the case of the motel control by goal proceeds in term of such *equifinality*, with the proprietor and staff assuming a generally unflappable perspective, realizing that there are "many ways to skin a cat" and developing a familiarity with most of them.

THE "MORALLY CONCERNED CITIZENRY"

The most serious danger facing the motel, the one carrying the greatest likelihood that the facility will be exposed and denounced as a social problem, lies in the existence of a segment of the community we have called the "morally concerned citizenry." These people constitute the first of the relevant publics with which the motel must deal. They have staked a claim for themselves as watchdogs of community morality, and stand ready to do battle if aroused. Most of them seem willing, however, to overlook the motel and concentrate attention on what they perceive as more pressing moral concerns as long as the establishment seems to offer no immediate, visible threat. Since it is not the nature of the act so much as the context that determines social reaction, acts committed in private are not perceived the same as when committed in a situation, such as a public restroom, where the "innocent" might stumble into stigmatized copresence, to be "contaminated" by the behavior (Humphreys, 1970). Thus, the "social visibility" (Reiss, 1960:319) of the activity is important. Social invisibility amounts to much more than mere invisibility, for it depends in some ways upon the degree to which the activity can be admitted and discussed without stigmatizing those who are coarse enough to "drag it into the open." As long as motel activities are conducted with discretion, even the "morally concerned citizenry" might be accused of "stirring up trouble" if they insisted upon exposing them. To do such a thing is to risk the loss of credibility and the suspicion that one is simply a "busybody" rather than a moral bulwark.

Reality Judgements

To the extent that the proprietor and staff of the motel can develop an accurate image of reality as perceived by the relevant public of "morally concerned citizenry," those operating the facility are in an excellent position to judge which tactics are likely to provoke moral crusades and to avoid them. When the proprietor was asked why his own establishment, the oldest in the city, was not even identified in the series of media exposures described above, he replied that the "reality of the situation" was that only those motels which advertised themselves in an obvious way were ever so stigmatized. What we must remember is that there are dangers of libel suits in such cases. Bedrooms have an almost sacred character according to the law, and a motel is essentially a set of managed bedrooms, so that issues of invasion of privacy are legally significant here (Bostwick, 1976). Furthermore, any tendency toward excessive condemnation can always be interpreted as defamation (Hill, 1976). Moralistic outbursts are more legally dangerous than they once were, a change that itself reflects movement toward greater recognition of acceptable variations within a pluralistic society. This motel can actually "get away with" more questionable activities than can many others, simply because such realities are recognized and taken into account.

Just as those managing the motel must be able to "read" the realities of its relevant publics, so must they develop a capacity for deflecting those definitions along desirable lines, a capacity for impression management.

Such a capacity rests upon considerable information control. There are two separate processes of information control which combine to project the image desired. The first may be referred to as the *evasion process,* the second as the *persuasion process.* The evasion process consists of a variety of mechanisms by which a system avoids the exposure of information which would reflect upon it negatively. The persuasion process consists of a variety of mechanisms by which a system disseminates information which reflects upon it positively. In either case, the content of the information may be true or false. Thus, for example, false rumors sometimes grow up about alleged occurrences at the motel, rumors which could do much damage to its reputation and which might even trigger action on the part of the "morally concerned citizenry" or the police. It is important that these rumors be squelched. Both proprietor and staff maintain open communication lines so as to pick up early warning signals and keep up necessary "contacts" so that matters can be "set straight." At the same time, some of the information disseminated by the motel may be less than totally accurate, including for example, gossip about celebrity patrons, huge tips, or other signals of "first-class" status.

These two processes contribute to both *normalization* (Schwartz, 1957) and *normification* (Goffman, 1963) imagery. Through the first, the "morally concerned citizenry" are led to treat the motel *as if* it were morally respectable by ignoring it. Through the second, they are led toward an extended tolerance threshold. This is facilitated by the capacity of the motel to control its *obtrusiveness* (Goffman, 1963), defined as the extent to which its visibility interferes with the institutionalized flow of interaction considered proper by the "morally concerned citizenry." As long as the proprietor and staff can avoid any interpretation defining it as "interfering with" the socialization of the young, the sanctity of marriage, and other interests dear to them, the facility offers no direct challenge to their moral order. Thus, for example, the staff is careful to watch for youngsters who occasionally ride their bicycles near the office in obvious attempts to catch sight of some of the pornographic scenery displayed on television and to react immediately by shooing them away and turning off the set for a few minutes. Unlike most of its competitors, the motel does not advertise, so that it can hardly be accused of tempting the weak and destroying their marriages. Indeed, there is some sense that its extreme attention to bourgeois discretion may actually preserve some marriages by keeping spouses ignorant of occasional moral lapses among their mates, something that may earn a certain grudging respect from its relevant publics. The capacity of proprietor and staff to detect and react to danger signals and to sustain a "quaint" rather than a "pushy" image gives the motel an especially effective *circumspection gloss* (Goffman, 1971) which signals its respect for community standards even as it facilitates their violation.

In his discussion of the arts of impression management, Goffman (1959) points out that dramaturgical loyalty and dramaturgical discipline are as important as dramaturgical circumspection. The motel is as effective in the first two realms as it is in the latter. There are, for example, many secrets which, if revealed, would almost certainly propel the motel into the arena of social problems. These include "dark secrets," "strategic secrets," "inside secrets," and "entrusted secrets" (Goffman, 1959). Dark secrets, those which are incompatible with the image the motel attempts to project, are safe because of the loyalty of the staff and the discipline flowing from this loyalty and their long experience. Strategic secrets regarding the intentions and capacities of the facility, as illustrated by the manner in which the existence of a "special room" has been hidden from many of the patrons and from the "morally concerned citizenry," are equally safe. The many inside secrets which separate those who "know what's going on" from those who do not are carefully managed so that penetration of the inside secrets of the facility become linked to an elaborate "information game" (Scott, 1968). Because the three sisters making up the key staff are themselves so closely linked to one another, and because they share vulnerability, the motel is particularly successful in protecting its entrusted secrets, those which members of the staff are obligated to keep by virtue of relationships among the members of the team managing the dangerous information.

The sensitivity of the motel system is perhaps most clearly manifested in its handling of "free secrets" (Goffman, 1959), those which might be of importance outside the motel but which could be disclosed without discrediting the operation itself. The motel staff actually shares with such professions as law and medicine the possibility of benefiting from the disclosure of the secrets of individuals who render themselves vulnerable by placing these secrets at the disposal of those who have offered them assistance in some highly personal matter (Bates, 1964). Despite the widespread pattern of blackmail (Hepworth, 1975) and pervasive temptation toward the double-cross (Masterman, 1972) which are so characteristic of institutional relationships in contemporary society, never to our knowledge has any patron of the motel been compromised as a result of actions of the proprietor or staff. There are patrons whose wives are known to members of the staff, and there are some who hold respectable positions in the neighborhood. There are laws broken, and secrets having nothing to do with the motel that may be exposed. Several clients have serious "alcohol problems" or manifest behaviors which might suggest psychiatric symptoms to some, but they are ignored. Much of the success of the facility in its efforts to understand the definitions of reality held by its relevant publics and to project an image of subtle deviance disavowal (Davis, 1961), can be traced to the genuine conviction of the staff, to their "sincerity of belief" in their own performance (Goffman, 1959).

Value Judgements

To explain activities by asserting that they spring from a more abstract level of "values" takes us no further than the old ethological theories which insisted that human behavior resulted from the fact that certain more basic "instincts" (e.g., gregariousness or self-preservation) manifested themselves at some times, with other instincts dominant on other occasions, never *specifying the processes* by which these alleged "manifestations" occurred. Thus, the use of the concept of higher level "values" to explain why people engage in activities generating social problems is usually an explanation by fiat (Spector and Kitsuse, 1977). According to General Systems Theory, the term "values" must be operationalized in terms of specific determinations of priority (Vickers, 1967). As Kitsuse and Spector (1973) have pointed out, any sound theoretical approach to understanding of social problems as activities must rest in part upon an adequate theory of interests. Conceived of as priorities (ranked interests), "values" are determined by the perceived interests of concerned social actors as filtered through their images of the environment. It is, however, incumbent on us to attempt some specification of the actual *processes* by which such judgements are made, the processes by which specific priorities are determined.

As we employ the concept, value judgements are not simply sub-propositions derived from more general value propositions held by social actors. They are determinations of priorities based upon concomitant reality judgements, especially those with respect to the perceived priorities of those with whom one wishes to interact. Those who operate the motel cannot make their value judgements in isolation; they must relate their own interests to those of the "morally concerned citizenry." Since these shift periodically, considerable flexibility becomes a necessity. Resulting value judgements depend upon the nature of the *relationship* between the two activity clusters rather than upon the inherent properties of either.

What is even more interesting is the way in which successful impression management based on evasion and persuasion processes of information control have operated to produce a special image for the motel, an image which has important implications for the value judgements of the "morally concerned citizenry." The point is that exposure within the context of one image is not as dangerous as exposure within the context of another. We observed one example when a late-night fire brought fire trucks, police, and considerable news coverage, undermining the usual social invisibility. Although no one was injured, the fire drew heavy coverage on local news programs because, as one newscaster put it, the motel really is "one of our city's best-known establishments." Local disk jockeys teased each other and some well-known city residents for several days, joking about how fortunate they were to have escaped with their clothes and pretending to threaten disclosures to their wives. While one cited the motel in almost sentimental terms as the "ole place," another referred to it laughingly as "the riding academy." Another establishment might have provoked a very different reaction.

For a few weeks after the fire, curious spectators could be seen driving around the grounds to inspect the damage and share in the risqué atmosphere created by the media. During this period, the motel staff simply "covered up" by turning off the television, being even more careful than usual about their admissions policy and their telephone conversations, and presenting an especially businesslike face. As the proprietor had predicted, the temporary publicity actually had the effect of increasing occupancy rates over the next several months. The image of the facility, along with its symbiotic ties, appears to have protected it from the negative evaluations which could have surfaced in such a situation.

Action Judgements

If the motel is to avoid denunciation based upon claims lodged by the "morally concerned citizenry," those operating the establishment must know how to act upon their reality judgement and priority determinations. One example of such action may be seen in the reversal of the usual arrangement of "back regions" (Goffman, 1959) where performances are constructed and potentially embarrassing preparations contained. Thus, for example, the motel laundry, which would usually be located at the rear of the facility, has been placed in the front, so that laundry workers will not interfere with the "real secret" of the establishment. Deliveries are also made in front, at a kitchen adjacent to the office. These arrangements are geared toward protecting the patron, the assumption being that there is a higher priority on secrecy than upon decorum. Should a delivery be made by someone from among the "morally concerned citizenry," possibilities of exposure are minimized, and the motel certainly cannot be accused of forcing such a person to enter into the heart of some despised activity at the cost of losing a job.

Those who operate the motel must take a variety of actions to make secrecy effective. This is done through a secondary elaboration of security subsystems (Lowry, 1972) different from those of the typical motel operations. But these measures must not be too obvious, or the facility runs the risk of increasing the apparent value of the information which is being denied the "morally concerned citizenry." This might arouse their interest and provoke attempts at espionage (Hamilton, 1967), a common response of those maintaining a social system who feel its vital interests to be affected by the unknown policies of those maintaining another system. For the same reason, those operating the motel deliberately avoid any appearance of being too successful. Evidence that "immorality" is well rewarded would constitute an excessive challenge to a relevant public organized around the

defense of morality. Operations which become too ostentatious or too obviously concerned with security embellishments are more likely to be defined and processed as community problems.

The major threat to any system which depends upon information control for its survival lies in the possibility of effective *evaluation of information* by those controlling potentially threatening systems (Ind, 1963). Close
scrutiny must be deflected so that the projected image will be taken for
granted with no real effort of potentially dangerous opponents to evaluate
these projections. Evaluation will arise with either fear or mistrust. It is
therefore important for the proprietor and staff even when aiding and abet-
ting "immorality" to act in such a way that the facility apparently has nothing
more than the obvious to hide. For years the establishment has operated
without harassment partly by virtue of its low-key image, with such a sub-
dued appearance that it has been accepted by the community at face value.

Modes of Control

As in many successful systems, those operating the motel combine control
by error, control by rule, and control by goal. Each of these modes of control
is crucial to relationships between the establishment and the "morally concerned citizenry." Although errors are held to a minimum, they cannot be
eliminated entirely. A successful system must not deny its errors but must
learn from them, must make use of them as signals guiding adaptation. One
illustrative example may be taken from the recent history of the motel operation, its adaptation to problems signaled by the impetus of racial integration.
During its early years, the facility had catered to Whites only and had included a restraurant on the premises. Much of the turbulence surrounding
racial integration in this area had centered around eating establishments.
Incidents at the motel had begun to arouse the "morally concerned citizenry," who may have been troubled more by the possibility of eventual sexual
integration than anything else. In any event, the restaurant was sacrificed,
and within a few years the facility had shifted toward a catering pattern
which now draws mostly Black patrons. Troublesome feedback was simply
absorbed and employed to redirect the course of operations.

The way in which the proprietor and staff also control interaction with
the "morally concerned citizenry" by using highly evolved operating rules
will become more obvious when we examine interaction with patrons. Nevertheless, one central point needs to be made here. Although a well-de-
signed system existing in a fluctuating environment might be expected to do
better through reliance upon a combination of control by goal (which will
keep it moving in an appropriate direction regardless of environmental fluctuations) and control by error (which will allow it to adjust its trajectory so as
to correct for such fluctuations), there is an additional consideration: This is
the demand of those in related systems for some measure of predictability, a

demand which necessitates a larger measure of control by rule than might seem desirable to the systems theorist who is concerned only with that single system and neglects the requirements of those with which it must interact. The proprietor and staff seem to understand this, for they go out of their way to remain predictable.

In its relationships with relevant publics, however, those managing the motel risk either denunciation or decline unless they also rely upon control by goal. They seek survival and profit, and they must not be so overly cautious that they find neither. The motel seems to have much in common with other successful, "open systems" (Katz and Kahn, 1969). Much of the total capacity to avoid either decline or denunciation appears to depend, for example, upon one special characteristic of most successful systems, the "span of foresight" (Schutzenberger, 1969). This is critical to activities aimed at a goal. Given the fact that the guidance given by those who operate the facility is based on long-term considerations the motel as a system has been able to take shortterm pressures more or less in stride.

THE POLICE

Relationships to each public are both *symbiotic* and *symbolic.* The former amount to exchanges of mutual benefit, the latter to manipulations of imagery. The symbiotic relationship between this particular motel and the police establishment is long-standing and well understood by all concerned. There is much that the police can do to ensure the survival of the facility, and there is much that those managing the facility can do to make police work easier. The police are perfectly willing to ignore the operation as long as mutual obligations are honored. "Trouble" must be held below a certain threshold or it will be necessary for the police system, which survives on continuing funding from the community, to react by doing its "duty." And a reasonable level of "favors" is to be expected. The most effective of these is a "special" room—the walls, floor and ceiling of which are covered with gold carpeting, except for a large mirror mounted on the ceiling above the bed. The room itself is circular, as is the bed, and the room is equipped with television built into the ceiling, an elaborate stereo system, a luxury bath with sauna, and a fully stocked bar. The room is available free-of-charge to certain local officials, including influential law enforcement officers, and is in frequent use. The proprietor and staff remain on friendly relations with the police of the neighborhood, who can count upon other favors such as free bottles of whiskey at Christmas.

Reality Judgements

If the motel is to avoid becoming a social problem, those who manage it must make reasonably accurate reality judgements with respect to the second of its relevant publics—the police. This is necessary to permit easy interfacing and smooth communication. Similar facilities in the city have been unable to maintain this conjunction over a long period. The success of the establishment in question is apparently the outcome of two special capabilities—those of the proprietor and those of the staff.

The original builder and proprietor was a successful gambler and devotee of local "nightlife" with acquaintances in nearly every segment of the population. Long years of experience had produced a finely tuned appreciation for "how different people see things." He constructed the motel with emphasis upon secrecy, and the first patrons were friends and acquaintances who had frequented the city's "red-light district" prior to the "cleanup," which eliminated it. His operation seems to have conformed closely to one particular assumption about the relationship of the citizenry to the "problem" of vice: the assumption that the community is actually ambivalent about the question and will be satisfied with a "containment policy." The management problem has to do with periodic fluctuations in the containment threshold. There are times when "the lid is on," with the various vice functions tightly constrained, and there are times when patterns are relatively "open" and expansion is possible. It is not enough to maintain an organizational flexibility which will allow for adaptability to such shifts without undo strain on system boundaries; one must also be able to *predict* within satisfactory limits the occurrence of shifts. This demands special sensitivity to signals from the police system, as well as from the "morally concerned citizenry." The current proprietor has also "been around" and has developed crucial contacts and communication networks. He is particularly skilled at separating critical signals from random "noise," and at decoding them.

The capacities of the staff are in many ways more important than those of the proprietor. While his systemic responsibilities are strategic, theirs are tactical. They must monitor reality minute-by-minute. Thus, the original proprietor gave a great deal of attention to staff selection. The "key staff" includes three middle-aged, Black sisters who have been with the establishment for many years. They rotate shifts in such a way that one is always on duty. The "cleared staff" consists of a variety of clerks, maids, laundry workers and maintenance personnel, all of whom have been "checked out," and many of whom are relatives of key staff. The relationships among staff members amounts to more than a paid employee system, the symbiotic connections being quite close. Nepotism tends to guarantee more loyalty to the establishment and to provide for greater system stability under environmental pressures. These people know the community very well, and they are sophisticated at the business of interpreting police behavior and signaling understanding and compliance with the game.

Value Judgements

One reason for the success of the facility under examination is the skill of the proprietor and staff in assessing their own priorities vis-à-vis those of the police. The chief priority of the proprietor and staff is survival; the chief priority of the police is order. To survive is to put a high priority on orderliness, the prevention of disruptions. Those operating the motel must see to procedures which admit as many acceptable customers as possible (for survival also depends upon a certain profit margin) while screening out potentially troublesome patrons, and must control patrons who have gained entrance. Thus, an elaborate screening process has evolved. Anyone entering the office might immediately suspect that this is a "different" motel. The potential patron comes face-to-face with a bullet-proof glass shield with one small opening suitable for exchanging money. Instead of the usual arrangement of pigeonholes for room keys and messages, there is behind the desk a 12-gauge-pump shotgun hung next to a television monitor featuring ongoing pornographic films. Outside a sign reads: "Adult Movies Available Upon Request. Inquire at Office." There are no chairs, maps, telephones, coffee shops or other typical conveniences. Rather than a hearty greeting, the unfamiliar are welcomed by a distant, questioning glance.

Inexperienced customers who persist are subjected to what amounts to an interrogation. If the individual, having been asked how long he (such persons are almost always male) plans to stay, answers either several days or even just a night, he will almost always be turned away with the explanation that no rooms are available. This is because all rooms are rented in four and one half hour blocks, something that a "safe" patron would be expected to know. In doubtful cases, elaborate measures are taken to insure that the facility is "covered" in case of "trouble." The clerk is careful to ascertain that the individual(s) is at least twenty-one years old, and at least three sources of identification are required even though payment is demanded in advance. Every precaution is taken to assure that no one will be admitted who might later experience (or claim to experience) moral shock. The motel can never be accused of "tempting the unwary." Activities taking place there may be disapproved by some, but they are nevertheless under tight control. On the other hand, similar facilities which have made faulty value judgement (e.g., arranging their priorities so that the "fast buck" takes precedence over a careful interfacing with police priorities) have seen themselves designated as social problems. Several have ignored warning signals only to find themselves closed because their activities have brought too much "pressure" on the police. The rules of the political game require the police to reaffirm "law and order" when such an establishment comes to be defined as *disorderly* (a term which remains more common to the legal definition of social problems than the more recent term "deviant").

Action Judgements

Adequate reality judgements and adaptive value judgements are of little advantage unless followed by reasonable action judgements. There are those whose picture of reality meshes with the images of others with whom they must deal and whose priorities can be worked out to fit the priorities of these others, but this does not insure that they can both understand the action which is required under the circumstances and can bring off that action. Here the General Systems Theory concept of *feedback* related quite nicely to the interactionist concept of *reciprocity*. From a cybernetic perspective, successful action depends upon self-stabilizing controls operating by error-reducing *negative* feedback, the most common example of which is the thermostat which "steers" a system in dynamic equilibrium between designated tolerance limits, a drop in temperature providing negative feedback triggering a heating unit with a rise in temperature providing negative feedback triggering a cooling unit. From the larger General Systems Theory perspective (which embraces and expands the cybernetic approach), stability is also gained by processes which interfere with *positive* feedback, defined as feedback which amplifies deviating tendencies, one example of which would be Lemert's (1951) notion of the way in which primary deviation is amplified into secondary deviation through overreactive feedback. If we conceptualize the question of motel "stability" as the successful avoidance of claims-making activity which might convert it into a social problem, we can see that the proprietor and staff succeed both by facilitating error-reducing negative feedback and by short-circuiting any buildup of dangerous positive feedback.

If a system shows a consistent tendency to return to some particular state or condition after being disturbed, General Systems Theory suggests that we seek to discover sets of two items whose relationship is *direct one way and inverse the other*. There are many such examples governing the stability of the motel, but perhaps one may suffice as an illustration. When any relevant public begins to complain (X), the proprietor and staff react by implementing well practiced processes of mollification (Y). This is to say that an increase in X brings an increase in Y. But the reverse does not hold; an increase in Y (mollification) does not bring a further increase in X (complaining). Such a relationship might be found in situations usually derogated as appeasement, where signs of mollification may be interpreted as signals of "weakness," but it does not happen in the case of the motel, and the proprietor and staff are experienced enough to realize it. Otherwise, the sort of stage progression described by Spector and Kitsuse (1977) might be expected, since the continuing claims (X) of any relevant public will tend to be contingent upon the response (Y) of the motel, with the result that a "social problem" comes into existence through escalation of claim and counterclaim. By quickly surrendering at any sign of battle, those managing the motel win the war of survival.

Modes of Control

This description of relationships between the motel and the police should make it clear that control by error is especially important here. Those operating the facility are well aware that occasional mistakes of judgement will be made. They succeed in deflecting trouble by concentrating upon quick detection and correction of errors and by a process that has been described as "error-embracing" (Michael, 1973:131–143). Rather than to ignore or overreact to disruptions, both the proprietors and the staff seem to accept them as messages carrying "lessons." In this way they become an opportunity for learning and a source of information allowing for adaptation before "real problems" arise.

Control by rule is illustrated by the policy which instructs the staff to call the proprietor in the event of any police "harassment." He himself has developed a set of rules which can "take care of it" according to a Standard Operating Procedure of his own. From time to time, for example, a patrol car may pull into the motel parking lot. If it remains for long, the consequence is a sharp decline in patronage. This will provoke a call to the proprietor, who is usually at some other place of business, and he will in turn call a "contact," someone who can see to it that the car is removed. This process proceeds with impressive efficiency, and the patrol car moves away within a few minutes of the proprietor's call. The testing procedure serves to remind the staff of the symbiotic importance of police cooperation and to reassure the police that the proprietor has kept his "connections" intact.

Those who manage the establishment are in general much more concerned with survival and profit than with attachment to any particular means for their realization. Thus, control by goal becomes the chief mode of system management. This requires a good deal of flexibility and a familiarity with a number of alternative strategies. Since those operating the motel are in no position to wax self-righteous with the police, they must here depend upon means other than an image of respectability. If some potential problem cannot be deflected by one telephone call, perhaps another one will serve. If telephoning itself will not provide a solution, perhaps a favor to someone at the right time will do the job. Part of the trick in operating through control by goal is to know *when* the time is "right," *who* needs a favor, and *what* sort of favor might be most appreciated.

THE PATRONS

If the proprietor and staff are to relate successfully with motel patrons, they must first admit only those who cannot be expected to make claims labeling the establishment problematic. As we have seen, this will require strict attention to boundary maintenance. In addition, the facility must "deliver the goods" in the form of experiences matching patrons' expectations and must prevent or at least contain disruptions. Patrons are in a position to make claims precisely because the motel is part of a network of "patterned evasions" based on "contravening norms" which operate sub rosa, but which are no less binding for their apparently aberrant character (Williams, 1958). We generally recognize rights to "privacy" with respect to sexual activities. Moore and Tumin (1949) have gone so far as to assert that all social systems depend upon a certain level of ignorance as a sort of tacit agreement to remain officially unaware of goings-on that might introduce too much dissonance into everyday interaction. Although the motel patrons may be engaging in what would be considered "deviant behavior" by a substantial segment of citizens, these activities are not so stigmatized as to put them beyond the pale, without the right, for example, to police protection in the event of a robbery on the motel premises. In this sense the motel is treated as are many prostitutes—the situation is ignored as long as the "rules of the game" are honored. Those operating this particular establishment have assumed what amounts to an obligation to protect its patrons, many of whom have been coming there for years.

Reality Judgements

To succeed with motel patrons, to avoid any claims-making, the proprietor and staff must become familiar enough with them to understand their wishes and special problems without "invading privacy." This is something competitors seem to give shorter shrift. On one occasion, for example, a taxi driver entered the motel grounds and began knocking on doors, asking for someone by name. Several patrons complained, and a policy was immediately developed so as to force drivers to stop at the office. Although most experienced patrons call ahead to reserve a room, there are those who for one reason or another wish to enter the grounds on foot and to obtain a room without going into the office. Pay phones are discreetly placed about the grounds for just such purposes. On another occasion, a woman arrived by taxi, telling the driver that she did not know what room her "boyfriend" had rented and asking if he could drive around the grounds so that she might locate his car. The staff directed him to leave immediately, suspecting that this woman might be searching for her husband's car. Such courtesies are much appreciated and tend to foster loyalty among patrons, to the extent that some who might have complained about "bad experiences" have refused to force the issue. "Good will" is a major source of protection for vulnerable systems which run constant risk of exposure and denunciation. And such good will depends upon capacity to map the environment and to understand the realities faced by patrons.

Upon close examination, it becomes apparent that those who manage the motel have evolved a highly functional management information system with an appropriate *"quality filter"* and a well-developed *retrieval mechanism* (Churchman, 1968). The proprietor and staff have been able to draw upon information from a wide variety of sources and to evaluate these sources over many years as data were synthesized, sources were compared, and criteria were discovered for assessment of reliability and adequacy of incoming information. During our observations, we were reminded again and again that some input is "crap" but that the staff is "all ears" in other instances. As to retrieval mechanism, the most effective appears to operate at the level of conversation and "comparing notes" that goes on among the staff and between the staff and proprietor. If none of them can recall the specific information which might shed light on some set of events, certain of the "old customers" may be enlisted, for they too are interested in protecting the establishment.

Value Judgements

In their relations with motel patrons, the proprietor and staff must sacrifice some "values" for others. They must develop and implement priorities of interest, always keeping in mind potential vulnerability. Perhaps these issues can be best illustrated by attention to the dilemma faced by the members of the key staff. Tactical adaptability requires that the staff be granted as much flexibility as possible. One of the principal reasons for the success of this operation and its ability to avoid exposure and public denunciation is the foresight of the original proprietor in his selection of staff. Our impression is that staffing patterns of competitive establishments show younger people and that staff turnover is pronounced. Such staffs have been characterized as "undependable." The sort of operation we are describing puts considerable power in the hands of the staff. Because of the unique records problem, it would be relatively easy for them to skim profits. Blackmail is a real temptation. Lack of dedication to the job, to the "little things" that make the difference, is a daily danger. Such dangers are held to a minimum in this facility, partly because of staff loyalty and partly because of the symbiotic advantages offered by nepotism.

Research into socially disapproved establishments, such as this motel, has tended to assume more "deviance" on the part of the people who staff them than may be the rule, particularly for those that survive. For the latter, the very "respectability" of the staff may be a source of *role strain* (Goode, 1960) as much as a source of stability and adaptability. Aside from their work, for example, the three members of the key staff who virtually "run the place" on a day-to-day basis are preoccupied with matters of family and religion. All of them express some concern about the "goings-on" at the motel, and they have a special distaste for what they term the "freaky" activities that are a part of the scene. While attending to the desk, much of their time is spent in Bible reading. They have never reconciled themselves to the pornographic films shown on the office television set and the proprietor has to "remind" them to attend to it. They react by displaying what Humphreys (1970:134) has called "refulgent respectability," that compensatory righteousness that serves as a moral shield. Male patrons are referred to euphemistically as "customers," their sexual partners are called "dates," or "lady friends," or simply "friends." Although prostitutes are discouraged from working the motel as another matter of priority (the risk being greater than the gain), those who do are referred to as "working girls."

Action Judgements

Even if the reality judgements made by a given system are reasonably accurate, and even if priorities are adequately determined, there is still the question of satisfactory *execution*. Since the major concerns with respect to patron relationships revolve around admission procedures and processes by which disruptions can be prevented or contained, it may be useful to examine these in somewhat more detail. Those operating the motel must execute a satisfactory role release (Goffman, 1963:38–39) which will free the patron(s) from customary obligations for a specified period of time and do it smoothly, with a minimum of intersystemic friction. With the "tearoom trade" described by Humphreys (1970), the process is relatively uncomplicated; one makes a quick stop at a public restroom where partners are encountered more or less at random. The motel is faced with a much more complex management problem.

"Old customers" are never asked for identification. It is clear that they are entering a special zone of situated morality (Weinberg, 1970) where dramaturgical anonymity (Young and Massey, 1978) is at issue. The survival of the motel depends upon ability to control boundaries while guaranteeing this anonymity. Every social setting, of course, has its rules for entering and exiting (Schwartz, 1968). In cases such as this, we can expect the successful system to solve the problems by means of some especially effective *information coding* matrix. The staff must cooperate with the patron so as to allow for maintenance of an *involvement shield* (Goffman, 1963) which restricts the nature of the copresence and allows the patron to present a "paper self" (Manning, 1972) which might not survive demands for documentation. Unless the motel is to become problematic, the proprietor and staff must manage all this successfully.

Most "old customers" call ahead for reservations, often requesting a particular room and usually specifying whether or not "movies" are necessary. This coded message is sufficient to identify the caller as an "insider." If such a code is not presented, a few questions such as, "Have you been here before?" or "How long will you be staying?" will clear matters up. When the patron arrives, the car is directed around the motel in a clockwise direction so as to avoid outgoing traffic until the open garage door is reached and the car has entered. This routine seems to serve both security and symbolic functions, assuring the patron that the facility is "well-organized" and dependable. In such ways, the establishment has earned respect. The function it performs may be "shady," but it does it well. That counts for a great deal in a world where one finds so many moral inadequacies in the most respected institutions.

Modes of Control

The various judgements made by the proprietor of the motel and its staff must be implemented through rules, goalseeking processes and error-reaction processes. Beginning with the latter, which are not as overloaded as they appear to be in some similar operations, we find that the motel thrives partly because those who operate it correct errors before they escalate into full-blown claims-making activities. The staff devotes considerable attention to the identification of the "problem people," patrons who are the major source of disruptions or other "trouble." Such patrons require attention far out of proportion to their numbers, but they are not easy to turn away, especially if they are "old customers" who have become problematic but might turn on the establishment if barred. Some patrons drink too much and become boisterous, something that cannot be tolerated for long. Some actually have learned to use the motel as a place for a binge. They are a special source of concern, for they are a common source of hotel and motel fires. In a few cases, staff members will break even the most hallowed rule and enter the room to "check on" the patron. In the case of at least one robbery by a prostitute, the patron was reimbursed with a warning to "watch out for bad hookers." While many organizations make a practice of systematically denying upsetting feedback from clientele, the motel survives by seeking it out so as to adapt as quickly as possible.

Control by rule can be observed more clearly in staff–patron relationships than in perhaps any other sphere of interaction. We have already examined some of the rules for entry, but the entire architectural layout of the motel is actually an excellent example of control by rule, for the structure was designed from the beginning to constrain patrons' movements and to control visibility. Thus, the very architecture *rules out* the possibility of looking into windows, at least on the outer walls, where there are none. And when there *are* rules for interaction, such as the prohibition against staring at other patrons, they are *reinforced* by the "rules" built into the physical structure, such as placement of windows, use of heavy shrubbery, deliberate construction of overhanging porticos around the central courtyard so as to keep the areas near the rooms in shadows, and a variety of other architectural devices.

Another tangible example of control by rule can be found in the measures taken to defend against theft, which is a serious threat. Many patrons do not register at all, and many of those who do use phony names and addresses. The very nature of the system makes the motel much more vulnerable than is the more conventional establishment, and to complain to the police might lead them to label the motel as a "source of trouble." The proprietor, however, has solved the dilemma reasonably well by bolting both air conditioners and television sets in place and attaching electronic monitors which signal the office in the event of tampering, thus building even more control onto the scene.

Since the goal of the entire establishment is to "serve the customer" in such a way as to make a profit while maintaining continuing relationships with various segments of the community who are useful in a variety of ways, rules are occasionally bent, with the staff going out of its way to serve particular needs of patrons even if this requires circumvention of standard operating procedures. There is, for example, a general rule against permitting prostitution on the premises, a rule which exists because of a distinction in the larger community between simple adultery (which is officially disapproved but considered to be more of a moral than legal issue) and prostitution (which is considered to be very close to serious criminal activity). It is one thing for the police to condone a rendevous involving a couple one or both of whom are married to others, and something quite different for them to be charged with "condoning prostitution." The police seem to appreciate staff efforts to keep prostitution out of the establishment, for it makes their job easier. On the other hand, the fact that they regard perfect control as impossible allows the staff to occasionally overlook a situation in which a "good customer" who is temporarily without a "lady friend" has had to turn to a "working girl."

The considerable authority delegated to the staff allows them to adapt quickly to the needs of patrons, so that the rules can hold errors to a minimum without interfering too much with the goal of "customer service." This seems to give the patrons some sense that the facility "respects" them. Since to show respect is to be respectable, the establishment gains a certain legitimation from its capacity to control by goal. It is able to demonstrate organization while maintaining a human face, an achievement which is appreciated rather than condemned.

CONCLUSION

It is important to stress that social actors engaged in the construction and negotiation of social reality are also engaged in the development of elaborate systems of interaction and in the interfacing of these systems with other systems to which they must relate. Social problems may be expected to arise from friction associated with these activities. Different systems tend to express different principles of organization; those composing one system can only synchronize their activities with another if these principles are honored. Otherwise, there will be mutual withdrawal or patterned conflict. If the latter, then the emergence of a "social problem" will depend upon which system is more successful in asserting its claims against the definitions of the other.

Seen in terms of General Systems Theory, it would appear that social problems are likely to emerge in the event of inadequate reality judgements, inappropriate value judgements which produce an unworkable set of priorities, or faulty execution of action judgements. Those involved in a system of interaction which takes advantage of more modes of control, employing control by error along with control by rule and control by goal, stand a good chance of avoiding exposure and denunciation even if their activities appear to hold considerable potential for such labeling. The clandestine motel described above represents one such system. By remaining open to environmental feedback, the proprietor and staff have been able to develop an image of reality which gives them an advantage, an image which includes a clear and reasonably accurate assessment of the pictures of the world held by the relevant publics to which they must relate. Through judicious adjustment to its priorities, and a willingness to modify them somewhat so as to mesh with the priorities of related systems, those operating the facility have succeeded in building up a powerful set of symbiotic interchanges. Since the loyalty and experience of the staff guarantee effective execution of policy, the system is rather well protected despite a threatening environment.

The success of the motel is sustained by its capacity for deflecting deviation-amplification processes (Wilkins, 1964). The paradox here is that, while the facility must operate on one level as an extremely closed system, it has still been able to maintain the essential characteristics of an *open system* connected to its environment by mutual interactionism (Buckley, 1967). Furthermore, there is a nice mesh between the overall goals of the system and the individual goals of its members, something that cannot be assumed for most systems (Katz and Kahn, 1969). The urge for respectability on the part of the staff tends to reduce any tendency toward alienation which might result in further drift into activities stigmatized by the "morally concerned citizenry," and their integration into the conventional community by virtue of family ties and religious concerns provides another buffer. Given the situation, there is little likelihood that the staff will generate a moral system counter to that prevailing in the community, little likelihood of their provoking community reaction by moves resulting from concomitant frustration in their dealings with it, and a sharp reduction in any tendency for the motel to become grounds for social problems activities.

REFERENCES

Ashby, W. Ross
    1956   Introduction to Cybernetics. New York: Wiley.
Ball, Richard A.
    1978   "Sociology and general systems theory." The American Sociologist 13:65–72.
    1979   "The dialetical method: Its application to social theory." Social Forces 57:785–798.
Bates, Alan P.
    1964   "Privacy—a useful concept?" Social Forces 42:429–434.
Bostwick, L.
    1976   "A taxonomy of privacy: Repose, sanctuary, and intimate decision." California Law
            Review 64:1447–1483.
Boguslaw, Robert
    1965   The New Utopians. Englewood Cliffs, NJ: Prentice-Hall.
Boulding, Kenneth
    1964   The Image. Ann Arbor, MI: University of Michigan Press.
Buckley, Walter
    1967   Sociology and Modern Systems Theory. Englewood Cliffs, NJ: Prentice-Hall.
Burns, T. and Walter C. Buckley (eds.)
    1976   Power and Control. Beverly Hills, CA: Sage.
Churchman, C. West
    1968   The Systems Approach. New York: Dell.
Davis, Fred
    1961   "Deviance disavowal: The management of strained interaction by the visibly handi-
            capped." Social Problems 9:120–132.
Emery, F. E.
    1969   "Introduction." Pp. 7–13 in F. E. Emery (ed.), Systems Thinking. Baltimore, MD:
            Penguin.
Glaser, Barney and Anselm Strauss
    1968   Time for Dying. Chicago, IL: Aldine.
Goffman, Erving
    1959   The Presentation for Self in Everyday Life. New York: Doubleday Anchor.
    1963   Stigma. Englewood Cliffs, NJ: Prentice-Hall.
    1971   Relations in Public. New York: Basic Books.
Goode, William J.
    1960   "A theory of role strain." American Sociological Review 25:483–496.
Gouldner, Alvin
    1970   The Coming Crisis in Western Sociology. New York: Basic Books.
Hamilton, P.
    1967   Espionage and Subversion in an Industrial Society. London: Hutchison.
Hepworth, M.
    1975   Blackmail: Publicity and Secrecy in Everyday Life. London: Routledge and Kegan
            Paul.
Hill, A.
    1976   "Defamation and privacy under the first amendment." Columbia Law Review
            76:1205–1313.
Homans, George C.
    1961   Social Behavior: Its Elementary Forms. New York: Harcourt, Brace, and World.
Humphreys, Laud
    1970   Tearoom Trade. Chicago, IL: Aldine.

Ind, A.
    1963   A short History of Espionage. New York: McKay.
Katz, Daniel and R. L. Kahn
    1969   "Common characteristics of open systems." Pp. 86–104 in R. E. Emery (eds.),
            Systems Thinking. Baltimore, MD: Penguin.
Kitsuse, John I. and Malcolm Spector
    1973   "Toward a sociology of social problems: Social conditions, value judgements, and
            social problems." Social Problems 20:407–419.
Klapp, Orrin
    1973   Models of Social Order. Palo Alto, CA: National Press.
Laszlo, Ervin
    1972   Introduction to Systems Philosophy. New York: Harper and Row.
Lemert, Edwin
    1951   Social Pathology. New York: McGraw-Hill.
Lilly, J. Robert and Richard A. Ball
    1980   "Challenges to situated morality." Qualitative Sociology 3:205–222.
    1981   "No-tell motel: The management of social invisibility." Urban Life. 2:179–
            98.
Long, Norton
    1961   "The local community as an ecology of games." Pp. 400–413 in Edward Banfield
            (ed.), Urban Government. A reader in Administration and Politics. Glencoe, IL: Free
            Press.
Lowry, Richie P.
    1972   "Toward a sociology of secrecy and security systems." Social Problems 19:437–
            450.
Maines, David R.
    1977   "Social organization and social structure in symbolic interactionist thought." Pp.
            235–59 in Alex Inkeles, James Coleman and Neil Smelser (eds.), Annual Review of
            Sociology, Vol. 3. Palo Alto, CA: Annual Reviews, Sociology.
Manning, Peter
    1972   "Locks and keys: An essay on privacy." Pp. 83–94 in James M. Henslin (ed.), Down
            to Earth Sociology. New York: Free Press.
Masterman, J. C.
    1972   The Doublecross System. New Haven, CT: Yale University Press.
Mead, George H.
    1934   Mind, Self, and Society. Chicago, IL: University of Chicago Press.
Merton, Robert K.
    1957   "Social structure and anomie." Pp. 131–160 in Robert K. Merton, Social Theory and
            Social Structure. Glencoe, IL: Free Press.
Michael, Donald
    1973   On Learning to Plan—and Planning to Learn. San Francisco, CA: Jossey-Bass.
Miller, J. G.
    1965   "Living systems: Cross-level hypothesis." Behavioral Science 10:380–411.
Moore, Wilbert and Melvin Tumin
    1949   "Some social functions of ignorance." American Sociological Review 14: 780–792.
Parsons, Talcott
    1951   The Social System. New York: Free Press of Glencoe.
Reiss, A. J., Jr
    1960   "Sex offenses: The marginal status of the adolescent." Law and Contemporary
            Problems 25:312–319.

Reynolds, Janice and Larry T. Reynolds
    1973   "Interactionism, complicity and the astructural bias." Catalyst 7:76–85.
Schwartz, C. G.
    1957   "Perspectives on deviance—wives' definition of their husbands' mental illness."
            Psychiatry 20:275–291.
Schutzenberger, M. P.
    1969   "A tentative classification of goal-seeking behaviors." Pp. 205–213 in F. E. Emery
            (ed.), Systems Thinking. Baltimore, MD: Penguin.
Scott, Marvin B.
    1968   The Racing Game. Chicago, IL: Aldine.
Simon, Herbert A.
    1956   "Rational choice and the structure of the environment." Psychological Review
            63:129–138.
Spector, Malcolm and John I. Kitsuse
    1977   Constructing Social Problems. Menlo Park, CA: Cummings.
Stover, Stewart S.
    1979   "Convergences between symbolic interactionism and systems theory." Symbolic
            Interaction 5:89–103.
Vickers, Geoffrey
    1967   Towards a Sociology of Management. New York: Basic Books.
von Bertalanffy, Ludwig
    1968   General System Theory. New York: Braziller.
Weiner, Norbert
    1956   I am a Mathematician. New York: Doubleday.
Weinberg, Martin S.
    1970   "The nudist management of respectability: Strategies for and consequences of the
            construction of situated morality." Pp. 375–403 in Jack D. Douglas (ed.), Deviance
            and Respectability. New York: Basic Books.
Wilkins, Leslie
    1964   Social Deviance. London: Tavistock.
Williams, Robin
    1958   American Society. New York: Knopf.
Wilson, Thomas P.
    1970   "Normative and interpretive paradigms in sociology." Pp. 57–79 in Jack D. Douglas
            (ed.), Understanding Everyday Life. Chicago, IL: Aldine.
Wright, Burton and John P. Weiss
    1980   Social Problems. Boston, MA: Little-Brown.
Young, T. R. and G. Massey
    1968   "The dramaturgical society: A macroanalytic approach to dramaturgical analysis."
            Qualitative Sociology 1:78–98.

6 From accommodation to rebellion: Tertiary deviance and the radical redefinition of lesbianism*

Rose Weitz
Arizona State University

Sociological analysis begins from the premise that individual identity develops through social interaction. How this occurs has long been a central concern among sociologists, particularly among those working from an interactionist perspective. These researchers theorize that identity develops through a looking-glass self process (Cooley, 1967), as individuals respond to and typically internalize the reactions of significant others towards themselves, eventually taking the perspective of the generalized other (Mead, 1934).

Beginning most importantly with Lemert (1951), sociologists have used this same theory to explain the adoption of deviant identity. Persons whose activities meet with disapproval and who lack supportive subcultural interpretations for their behavior may incorporate the negative reactions of others into their self-concept. Subsequently, they may defensively stabilize their behavior into a deviant role, becoming what Lemert (1951), has called "secondary deviants." Alternatively, individuals who engage in discreditable behaviors may accommodate themselves to society, trying to deflect social sanctions either through stigma management techniques (Goffman, 1963) or

---

*This manuscript has benefited greatly from the suggestions of Miriam Axelrod, Leonard Gordon, Barbara Grier, Mary Laner, Joanne Nigg, and the editors of this volume. My thanks also to Terri Atkins for her assistance in the data analysis.

through vocabularies of motive which excuse or justify their actions (Scott and Lyman, 1968).

Although this perspective has increased our understanding of deviance, the emphasis on reactive aspects of deviance has obscured the active role of individuals in negotiating their own social position, as various scholars have noted (Kitsuse, 1981; Levitin, 1975; Turner, 1972). Far from passively accepting others' valuations, deviants may actively engage in the production of definitions of their own behavior—definitions which may differ greatly from the dominant perspective in the society.

In his seminal article, "Coming Out All Over: Deviants and the Politics of Social Problems," Kitsuse (1980) analyzes this definitional process. He uses the term "tertiary deviance" to refer to "the deviant's confrontation, assessment, and rejection of the negative identity embedded in secondary deviation, and the transformation of that identity into a positive and viable self-conception" (1980:9). Tertiary deviants reject accommodative strategies and argue that their difference from the norm should in no way limit their civil rights or social worth. As I will show in this paper, the most rebellious of these deviants may go on to develop a radical critique of society, condemning their condemners and substituting a new ethic which affirms their behavior as sensible, moral, and preferable.

Kitsuse's article leaves unclear the attitudes of tertiary deviants towards their deviance per se. While he suggests in some places that tertiary deviants regard their deviance "as a valued identity and . . . profess and advocate the lives they live" (1980:8), some of the people he discusses at other points (such as rape victims and paraplegics) do not seem likely to do so. I believe it necessary, therefore, to separate out the attitude of deviants towards their deviance from the attitude towards their essential selves. Thus, disabled persons might not feel proud to be disabled and might certainly wish to be otherwise, yet they would still be tertiary deviants if they reject society's negative valuation of them as "cripples," refuse to accommodate (by, for example, wearing an uncomfortable false leg to avoid offending anyone), and develop a sense of self as worthy individuals deserving of all civil and social rights.

As Kitsuse notes, the development of tertiary deviance among various deviant groups during the 1960s and 1970s could not have been predicted by classic interactionist theory, and has remained largely unstudied by sociologists of deviance. A crucial problem for sociologists, then, is to understand the nature and sources of this phenomenon. This chapter describes the historical development of tertiary deviance among lesbians, focusing on the development of ingroup definitions of deviant behavior rather than on the sources of the behavior itself, and on the political consequences of those definitions, regardless of their validity.

METHODOLOGY

This chapter is based on a content analysis of *The Ladder,* the first significant lesbian periodical in America.[1] *The Ladder* appeared almost every
month from October 1956 through September 1967, and every two months
thereafter until it ended in 1972. Published by the Daughters of Bilitis (DOB),
the first lesbian organization in the United States, *The Ladder* contained a
variety of features ranging from political essays and news announcements to
poetry, short stories, and book reviews. Among its contributors were DOB
founder Del Martin, playwright Lorraine Hansberry, and well-known authors
Rita Mae Brown, Jane Rule, and Mary Renault.[2] Joan Nestle, of the Lesbian
Herstory Archives, has recently described *The Ladder* (which eventually
reached 3800 subscribers) as "the most sustaining Lesbian cultural creation
of this period" (1981:24). The only previous research using these data is
Lillian Faderman's (1981) brief historical overview of the periodical's
radicalization.

   For most of their history, *The Ladder* and DOB were the only outlets for
lesbian writing and the only forum for the development of lesbian philosophy in this country. Although one periodical cannot represent the entire
lesbian community, an analysis of *The Ladder* is crucial for understanding
the shifting in-group meanings of lesbianism during this time period.

   This research focuses on changing definitions of lesbianism, the relationship of these definitions to tbe homophile and feminist movements, and
the consequences of changing definitions for lesbian political activism. As a
first step, I took a random sample of 16 issues (one from each volume of *The
Ladder*) and tabulated the nomenclature used by lesbian writers to describe
female homosexuals (e.g., homosexual, lesbian, variant, gay). I searched all
volumes for statements regarding the cause of lesbianism; the statements
were then categorized as describing homosexuality as conscious or uncon-
scious choice, biologically determined, or unchangeably set in early childhood. Fictional accounts of lesbian life and relationships were classified as
pessimistic or nonpessimistic; pessimistic stories emphasized isolation,
suicide, blackmail, loss of lovers, or rejection by family or friends.

   I looked for data regarding the writers' attitudes towards, and level of

---

[1]The only previous lesbian periodical, *Vice Versa,* was privately published by Lisa Ben
and distributed in the Los Angeles area from June 1947 to February 1948 (Martin and Lyon,
1972).

   [2]In January 1957, *The Ladder*'s first editor, Phyllis Lyon, formally published a statement
announcing her true identity and dropping the pseudonym "Ann Ferguson" which she had used
in the preceding issues. However, many subsequent writers and editors continued to publish
under pseudonyms or only initials for reasons including realistic fear of repercussions, enjoy-
ment of the romance of belonging to a "secret society," and inflating the perceived size of *The
Ladder*'s staff.

interest in, male homosexuals and the homophile movement. Similarly, the number of feminist articles and editorials per volume was counted; items were defined as feminist if they demonstrated an awareness of women as a social group subject to unequal and unjust treatment, or discussed the feminist movement sympathetically. These articles were further divided into those which did and did not discuss lesbian concerns. A straightforward review of *The Feminine Mystique,* for example, would have been coded feminist with no lesbian content. If that review had applied the concept of the feminine mystique to lesbians, it would have been coded feminist with lesbian content. Items in the news section of *The Ladder* ("Crosscurrents") were divided by the same definitions into those which were feminist with no lesbian content, feminist with lesbian content, and lesbian with no feminist content.

Articles and editorials which discussed how best to improve lesbians' position in society were divided according to their suggested policies. Two broad groups of policies resulted: those which focused on changing lesbians, and those focused on changing society. The former included advocating outward conformity, adjustment to society, reduction in hostility towards heterosexuals, education of lesbians, and the development of greater selfacceptance among lesbians. The latter included advocating decriminalization, research, education of the public, improvement in the status of women, and encouragement of social diversity.

PROLOGUE: THE EARLY HOMOPHILE MOVEMENT

While homosexual social clubs have existed for hundreds of years, the organized homophile movement only developed in the United States during the 1950s. According to Humphreys (1972), this movement became conceivable only after the publication of the Kinsey Report on male sexuality demonstrated the prevalence of homosexual behavior (Kinsey, Pomeroy and Martin, 1948). This in turn reduced individuals' sense of isolation, assisted in the redefinition of homosexuality from a personal problem to a social issue, and created the belief that organization for change was possible. The first lasting homophile organization, the Mattachine Foundation (later reorganized as the Mattachine Society) began in 1950. Two years later, ONE, Inc. started as an offshoot of Mattachine (Humphreys, 1972). Both organizations were in principle open to women but had almost no women members.

The Daughters of Bilitis began in October 1955, when four lesbian couples met to organize a social club as an alternative to the lesbian bars. At that time, the women of DOB had no knowledge of ONE or Mattachine. The group soon decided to stress educational as well as social functions, and in October 1956 began publishing *The Ladder* (Martin and Lyon, 1972).

Apolitical Definitions and Accommodative Strategies

From its start in 1956 through the early 1960s, the writings in *The Ladder* demonstrate strong ties with the male homosexual community and suggest that homosexuality rather than womanhood forms the most salient aspect of lesbian identity. While *The Ladder*'s audience is overwhelmingly female and its emphasis is on concerns of the female homosexual, the periodical's broader loyalties under editors Del Martin and Phyllis Lyon (and later Barbara Gittings) connect it to the male-dominated homophile movement. Various statements suggest that the founders of DOB and *The Ladder* were motivated neither by feminist sympathies nor by an interest in a separatist lesbian movement, but by the belief that a women's organization and journal were the most effective ways to "draw the lesbian into the homophile movement" (October 1958: 5). Periodic notices announce events organized by ONE and Mattachine, as well as joint meetings between those groups and DOB. Most of these events feature as speakers male experts in areas such as psychiatry and the law; summaries of the events appear regularly in the pages of *The Ladder*.

Since *The Ladder* works towards developing a stronger, more unified homophile movement, rather than towards a separatist lesbian movement, it encourages male participation in DOB and interest in *The Ladder*:

> We feel that the time has come for still another step in our growth . . . that of working our programs to include the male homosexual. This does not mean membership, but it does mean offering them some of the same situations for group enjoyment and acceptance. We are re-opening our public discussion groups, planning Gab 'n' Javas periodically to include the male homosexual, and are now increasing the social functions which they may attend. . . . Although our magazine has always worked to be of interest to both men and women, we are now running a special "Masculine Viewpoint" section in which we more than ever welcome opinions from our male readers. (October 1961:9)

The Ladder's writers seem typically to view lesbians and male homosexuals as belonging to the same membership group and subject to the same socially created fates. Their language accentuates ties to male homosexuals and downplays any specifically female elements involved. The authors typically use male pronouns as generics to describe the homosexual community without questioning the appropriateness of those pronouns, and use "homosexual" or the more sanitized "homophile" more often than "lesbian" as self-descriptors.

Only vague glimmerings of a feminist consciousness—an awareness of women as a social group subject to unequal and unjust treatment—appear during these years. Rare exceptions do occur, however, in such divergent places as a review of *The Feminine Mystique* and a biographical piece on the troubles of a nineteenth century lesbian artist.

Since these pages contain almost no analysis of women's status, *The Ladder* cannot develop any theory connecting that status to lesbianism. Instead, reflecting the then dominant medical model, articles repeatedly describe lesbianism as a "process of development, and *not a matter of choice*" (e.g., September 1958:6, Emphasis in original.). Early childhood experiences in some unspecified way establish an unchangeable sexual pattern; lesbianism is not biologically caused, yet is beyond the individual's control and hence not the individual's responsibility. From *The Ladder*'s perspective, one cannot—and certainly should not—choose to become a lesbian; lesbians are not evil persons, but victims of forces beyond their control. This posture reflects significant ambivalence: If the writers truly regarded lesbianism as morally nonproblematic, they would not need to stress lack of responsibility for it.

This ambivalence is seen also through the fiction writing in *The Ladder*. More than half of the stories from 1956–1964 which describe lesbian life and relationships do so pessimistically, focusing on isolation, suicide, blackmail, rejection by family and friends, or the loss of lovers—particularly to a more "natural" love with a man. In a story published in February 1959, for example, rumors start about two young women. In the wake of these rumors, the protagonist leaves her woman friend, is abandoned by her family, moves away to avoid gossip and ridicule, and slowly dies of a broken heart.

In the absence of a political critique of society, *The Ladder* aims to integrate the lesbian into existing society and holds lesbians rather than heterosexual society responsible for reducing homophobic prejudice and discrimination:

> The tendency for the other organizations in the homophile movement is to lay the onus of the problem at the door of a hostile heterosexual society. "They" are the ones who must change, who must learn to understand, because it is "They" who malign, because it is "They" who persecute and prosecute. And above all, it is "They" who fail to view homosexuals as persons—human beings. . . . For his own salvation, the homosexual must learn that his life is not directed by the great god, "They," who [sic] he worships and condemns at one and the same time. The homosexual's life is self-directed. . . . He is the product of his own thought, and what others see in him is the image which he projects. If he is hostile, "They" will be hostile. If he hides from himself, "They" will hide from him. If he is fearful, "They" will fear him. If he is hateful, "They" will hate him. (January 1963:22)

Similarly:

> While ONE and Mattachine have concerned themselves chiefly with public attitudes, this particular approach has been of secondary importance in DOB's concept. Members of DOB have always felt that we can't wait for society to

change. Our needs are *now*, and it is possible for homosexuals to accept themselves and the society in which they live and so become productive citizens of the community . . . We need not wait for society to accept us; we can accept the challenge of society and help to bridge the gap of seeming separation by our own awareness of ourselves as human beings in a society of human beings. *If the public has an image of the homosexual, it is because the homosexual has created this image and continued to project this image.* As our own attitudes change, so will society's attitudes change. (May 1962: 9. Emphasis mine)

Presenting a good image thus becomes all-important. When, for example, in 1960 ONE, Inc. calls for a homosexual bill of rights, numerous editorials and articles in *The Ladder* strongly oppose it on the grounds that it would call attention to the homosexual community and incite the wrath of heterosexual society:

> Such a "Bill of Rights" is unnecessary, irrelevant, and likely to set the homo- phile movement back into oblivion. In the first place, drawing up a "homosex- ual bill of rights" implies that this document would be a statement represen- tative of this entire minority group. Nothing could be further from the truth. It further implies a demanding attitude toward society. This does not correspond to the feelings of many of us. It carries the flavor of an ultimatum, which of course we would be powerless to enforce. It implies, that we want exclusive rights–yet we want no rights for ourselves which we would not extent to others. For all of these reasons such a "Bill of Rights," if drawn up, would leave us wide open as a target of ridicule from those who already dislike us and would make it much harder for our friends to continue helping us. . . . It might also only serve to reinforce the paranoid tendencies some homosexuals already have! (January 1961:4)

Instead of a "Bill of Rights," *The Ladder* suggests that the various organiza- tions write "a statement of the purposes and goals of the homophile move- ment [which would] . . . devote as much space to spelling out the obliga- tions of homosexuals to society as it does to describing society's obligations to the homosexual" (January 1961: 4–5). Thus, *The Ladder* rejects any con- frontational tactics and instead advocates a policy similar to that adopted by those German Jews who believed persecution would eventually cease if they quietly demonstrated their good citizenship.

To achieve its goal of integration into society, *The Ladder* stresses the lack of important differences between lesbians and heterosexuals, and en- courages a reduction in surface differences, so as to reduce the saliency of their deviance. Numerous editorials and nonfiction articles from these years declare that lesbians differ from heterosexuals only in their sexual preference:

> The Lesbian is a woman endowed with all the attributes of any other woman.

. . . Her only difference lies in her choice of a love partner. . . . To the informed this difference merely means another form of individual adjustment to
self and society. (November 1956:8)

Remember you are a human being first. Your difference in only in choice of
love object, and actually your feelings, emotions, and problems are the same
as any heterosexual's. (August 1957:6)

To facilitate acceptance, lesbians are encouraged to minimize the differences and appear as much like traditional heterosexual females as possible. For example, a 1956 letter from a reader declares, "the kids in fly-front
pants and with the butch haircuts and mannish manner are the worst publicity that we can get." DOB President D. Griffin replies:

Very true. Our organization has already touched on that matter and has con-
verted a few to remembering that they are women first and a butch or fem
secondly, so their attire should be that which society will accept. Contrary to
belief, we have shown them that there is a place for them in society, but only if
they wish to make it so. (November 1956:3)

From this perspective, the homosexual should not deny her "nature," but
should realize that visible nonconformity will only create further difficulties,
while outward conformity and adjustment will eventually produce tolerance.

In sum, during these early years *The Ladder* does not encourage pride
in a unique and positively chosen lifestyle, nor does it present a political
critique of society. Instead, it advocates restraint and self-acceptance among
lesbians as a means of reducing the saliency of the label "lesbian" and thus
developing tolerance among heterosexuals. At the same time, *The Ladder*
urges heterosexuals to refrain from condemning lesbians, since lesbians
differ from heterosexuals only in minor ways and do not choose their unfortunate–but not immoral—fate.

Not just DOB and *The Ladder*, but the homophile movement as a
whole, emphasize outward conformity as the route to social tolerance during these years (Humphreys, 1972). This conservative stance must be evaluated in the context of the political climate of those times. Both the popular
culture and the government connected the heresies of communism and
homosexuality (Humphreys, 1972), making employment difficult if not impossible for any known or suspected homosexual:

DOB, like the Mattachine Society, and ONE, was born in the shadow of the Joe
McCarthy witch-hunts and the sweeping purges of homosexuals from the U.S.
State Department. Constantly harassed by the police, many gays were beaten
up and ordered to leave town or face imprisonment. Gay bars, our only social
meeting place, were subject to periodic raids. We never knew when the paddy
wagon would pull up in front and all of the patrons would be loaded in and
taken to the station. They were usually charged with "visiting a house of ill

repute" or "disturbing the peace." Police notified employers when they made
such arrests. Most homosexuals pleaded guilty to get off with a suspended
sentence and a small fine. But they had a police record, which counted against
them when seeking employment. Additionally, both female and male undercover agents frequented gay bars to entice patrons into making a pass so that
they could make arrests for "lewd and lascivious" behavior or solicitation.
(Martin and Lyon, 1978:124)

In this context, anything but the most respectably conformist tactics seemed
self-destructive.

THE DEVELOPMENT OF TERTIARY DEVIANCE

The years 1965 and 1966 see an increased emphasis in the pages of *The
Ladder* on the broader homophile movement. This emphasis reflects the
loyalties of then editor Barbara Gittings, who eventually left DOB to work for
the Mattachine Society and who has continued to work with mixed-sex gay
groups rather than with lesbian or feminist groups (Tobin and Wicker, 1975).
During these years, few statements appear from either the editor or DOB.
Instead, *The Ladder* seems to become a forum for announcements and
position papers from the East Coast Homophile Organizations (ECHO) and
the Mattachine Society. Coverage of the 1965 ECHO conference, for example,
fills almost half the pages of three consecutive issues of *The Ladder*. The
"Masculine Viewpoint" column continues, and Frank Kameny, president of
the Mattachine Society of Washington, becomes a regular *Ladder* contributor.
"Homosexual" remains the most common self-descriptor, although the term
"lesbian" appears more frequently than in earlier volumes.

The homophile movement of the mid-1960s appears strongly influenced by the growing Black civil rights movement, as witnessed by the
frequent comparisons between homosexuals and Blacks. For example:

> The drive to eliminate discrimination against homosexuals (sex fascism) is a
> direct parallel to the drive to eliminate discrimination against Negroes (race
> fascism). These minority movements are not attempts to overthrow the white
> race, or to destroy the institution of the family, but to allow a fuller growth of
> human potential, breaking down the barriers against a strange race or sexu-
> ality. (December 1965: 8)

Taking their cue from the Black civil rights movement, *The Ladder*'s writers
now focus on actively fighting discrimination against homosexuals in the
legal code and in employment (particularly in civil service) so as to obtain
their rights as citizens. While in 1960, DOB had strongly opposed the idea of
a bill of homosexual rights, now DOB joins fourteen other homophile organizations in issuing the following statement:

Laws against homosexual conduct between consenting adults in private should be removed from the criminal code. Homosexual American citizens should have precise equality with all other citizens before the law and are entitled to social and economic equality of opportunity. Each homosexual should be judged as an individual on his qualifications for Federal and all other employment. The disqualification of homosexuals as a group or class from receipt of security clearances is unjustified and contrary to fundamental American principles. Homosexual American citizens have the same duties and the same right to serve in the armed forces as do all other citizens. . . . For too long, homosexuals have been deprived of these rights on the basis of cultural prejudices, myth, folklore and superstition. Professional opinion is in complete disagreement as to the cause and nature of homosexuality. Those objective research projects undertaken thus far have indicated that findings of homosexual undesirability are based on opinion, value judgments, or emotional reaction, rather than on scientific evidence or fact. A substantial number of American people are subjected to a second class citizenship, to the Gestapo-like "purges" of governmental agencies, and to local police harassment. It is time that the American public reexamines its attitudes and its laws concerning the homosexual. (April 1966:4–5)

By this point, then, *The Ladder* no longer emphasizes the need to change the behaviors and attitudes of homosexuals as a precondition for social acceptance. However, accommodative strategies are not overtly rejected, as can be seen in the positive comments made regarding the (mandated) conventional dress of protesters at homosexual rights demonstrations.

Articles from the mid-1960s rarely discuss causation of homosexuality beyond stressing that it is not an illness; writers seem to feel less need than in earlier years to justify their sexual orientation. Ambivalence towards homosexuality continues to crop up in the fiction writing, however; sixty-one percent of the stories from 1965 through 1969 present a pessimistic view of lesbian life and relationships.

In October 1966, "Helen Sanders" (pseudonym) replaces Barbara Gittings as editor of *The Ladder*. At this point, it is announced that:

Certain changes in editorial policy are anticipated. To date emphasis has been on the Lesbian's role in the homophile movement. Her identity as a woman in our society has not yet been explored in depth. It is often stated in explaining "Who is a Lesbian?" that she is a human being first, a woman second, and a Lesbian only thirdly. The third aspect has been expounded at length. Now it is time to step up *The Ladder* to the second rung. (October 1966: 24)

Subsequent issues typically contain one or two articles regarding discrimination against women in law and employment. These articles stress that "the Lesbian is discriminated against not only because she is a Lesbian, but because she is a woman" (November 1966:17). At the same time, *The Ladder* begins printing in its news section items regarding the women's movement and women's place in society without explicitly relating those items to lesbians. Thus, *The Ladder* implicitly suggests that lesbians share a common fate with all women, and should work for both women's and homosexuals' rights. This in turn provides the necessary pre-condition for the subsequent feminist redefinition of lesbianism.

After this first spate of feminist articles, *The Ladder* becomes generally apolitical, printing few policy statements of any sort and devoting an increased number of pages to fiction, humor, and poetry. *The Ladder* only gradually shifts back towards a more political stance in 1969, under new editor Barbara Grier ("Gene Damon").

During this same year (1969), an event takes place which radically affects the consciousness of male homosexuals. The coverage of this event in *The Ladder* suggests the changing relationship between *The Ladder* and the homophile movement.

The homosexual community has always accepted police raids on gay bars as a fact of life. In June 1969, however, police raiding the Stonewall, a gay male bar in Greenwhich Village, meet with fierce physical resistance from the patrons, which results in four days of sporadic rioting. This marks the birth of the gay liberation movement (Humphreys, 1972).

Prior to this time, the male homophile movement, like DOB, has had as its goal tolerance from the wider society and eventual assimilation into that society. It has generally used tactics designed not to upset or challenge heterosexuals. The new gay liberation movement, by contrast, uses tactics of confrontation adopted from the New Left in order to demand acceptance rather than tolerance, and liberation rather than assimilation into an "unliberated" society.

The Ladder has a lengthy summary of events at the Stonewall in the news section at the back of its October/November 1969 issue. The topic is not, however, picked up in the front pages of that or any subsequent issue, nor is it mentioned in subsequent news sections. By contrast, gay male activists identify the Stonewall Rebellion as marking a crucial turning point in their ideological world. It seems, then, that events in the gay male world have greatly decreased in significance for the writers of *The Ladder*.

The 1969 discussions regarding DOB's potential membership in the North American Conference of Homophile Organizations (NACHO) provide further evidence for the decreasing importance of the homophile movement to *The Ladder*. Writers uniformly agree that, while DOB and the male homophile groups should work together when it is to their mutual benefit, DOB must first work for the improvement of the status of lesbians and should not dissipate its resources by joining an alliance which focuses on issues of concern only to male homosexuals. This argument will resurface in much stronger form in 1970, when the break with the homophile movement is completed.

THE RADICAL REDEFINITION OF LESBIANISM

The growing feminist movement of the early 1970s affected not just hetero-sexual society, but the lesbian world as well. In August 1970, with Barbara Grier as *Ladder* editor, *The Ladder* breaks its ties to DOB in order to officially change from a lesbian periodical to a feminist magazine openly supportive of lesbians. According to the new frontispiece: "Initially, *The Ladder*'s goal was limited to achieving the rights accorded heterosexual women, that is, full second-class citizenship. . . . *The Ladder*'s purpose today is to raise all women to full human status." Thus the focus for change moves officially from the individual lesbian to society as a whole and from homophobia to sexism.

As *The Ladder*'s broader orientation shifts from the homophile to the feminist movement, "lesbian" gradually replaces "homosexual" as the most common self-descriptor, while connections to gay men are deemphasized and ridiculed. From 1970 on, various editorials exhort lesbians to stop act-ing as "the Ladies' Auxiliary to the homophile movement" (Au-gust/September 1970:4). Concurrently, a series of vituperative statements appear (with approving comments) from women who denounce and re-nounce the homophile movement as male-dominated and sexist and who reject the possibility of cooperation between lesbians and gay males. For example, a letter to the editor printed in the August/September 1971 issue declares:

> All right guys, gentlemen, "brothers" . . . I am leaving at last . . .
>
> Leaving because this organization and this movement offer me nothing. Why should I be interested in homosexual rights —they're based on (male) homosexual problems: entrapment, police harassment, blackmail, tea room assignations, veneral disease. Christ, I can't relate to that kind of shit; it has no meaning whatsoever for me . . .
>
> I'm tired of being called a "girl." I ceased being a "girl" several years ago. I am on my own now, I support myself, and I conduct myself in an adult manner—I deserve to be called a woman, and I have many more claims on that title than many of you do to the appellation "man" . . . .
>
> You faggots, and I use that word with every ounce of malice I possess, could care less about women. And you will suffer for it . . . .
>
> Isn't the worst thing that can be said about a man is that "He's acting just like a woman?" Don't you all strive to rid yourselves of effeminacy, for it's wrong to seem like a woman. Woman is *not* nigger, gentlemen, but as long as you continue to believe it is so, you rip open your own bellies.

> Gay Liberation will never succeed until Women's Liberation succeeds.
> Your fate hinges on that of women, like it or not. Male homosexuals will not be
> equal until women are equal . . .

> Liberation? Gay Liberation? Liberate yourselves, my friends. For myself, I
> don't need you or it.

An editorial note accompanying the letter states that:

> Nancy Tucker has been . . . active in the gay movement for many years.
> Like most women she is deserting the homophile movement because of its
> uselessness to Lesbians. Nancy has long been a "friend" to THE LADDER, and
> we are happy to run this "farewell."

By this point, then, the focus of *The Ladder* has shifted from homophile to
women's liberation, as womanhood becomes a more salient aspect of lesbian identity than homosexuality. Numerous features appear during this
period which describe the oppressed position of women in society and do
not discuss lesbians at all—implicitly stressing solidarity among women
regardless of sexual preference; issues published during *The Ladder*'s last
year contain more such feminist, nonlesbian news items than lesbian, non-
feminist items.

New, politicized definitions emerge in these issues, both of women as
an oppressed minority and of lesbians as the original (if sometimes non-
conscious) feminists:

> In the 1950's women as a whole were as yet unaware of their oppression. The
> Lesbian knew. And she wondered silently when her sisters would realize that
> they, too, shared many of the Lesbian's handicaps, those that pertained to
> being a woman. (Frontispiece, *The Ladder,* all issues from August 1970 to
> September 1972)

No longer seen as an unfortunate and unchosen fate, lesbianism is now
defined as a choice women make in response to a sexist society:

> The male party line concerning lesbians is that women become lesbians out of
> reaction to men. This is a pathetic illustration of the male ego's inflated
> proportions. I became a lesbian because the culture that I live in is violently
> antiwoman. How could I, a woman, participate in a culture that denies my
> humanity? (April/May 1972:17).

This new definition of lesbianism is formalized in an article entitled "Woman-Identified Woman":

> What is a Lesbian? A Lesbian is the rage of all women condensed to the point
> of explosion. She is the woman who, often beginning at an extremely early
> age, acts in accordance with her inner compulsion to be a more complete and
> more free human being than her society–perhaps then, but certainly later—

> cares to allow her. . . . She may not be fully conscious of the political implica-
> tions of what for her began as personal necessity, but on some level she has
> not been able to accept the limitations and oppression laid on her by the most
> basic role of her society—the female role. (August/September 1970:6)

This statement was simultaneously published in a number of feminist journals and widely circulated in feminist circles. From that point on, "woman-
identified woman" became used as a term for women whose self-concept is
independent of their relationships with men, and whose primary energies
and loyalties flow towards other women. Although some believe it to be
theoretically applicable to heterosexual women, the term seems generally
used within the feminist community as synonymous with lesbian-feminist.

Once lesbianism becomes defined as a sensible choice, it becomes
reasonable to encourage women to choose lesbianism. "Woman-Identified
Woman" ends with a call for women to become lesbians as a step towards
liberation:

> As the source of self-hate and the lack of real self are rooted in our male-given
> identity, we must create a new sense of self . . . . For this we must be available
> and supportive to one another, give our commitment and our love, give the
> emotional support necessary to sustain this movement. Our energies must
> flow toward our sisters, not backwards toward our oppressors. As long as
> women's liberation tries to free women without facing the basic heterosexual
> structure that binds us in one-to-one relationship with our own oppressors,
> tremendous energies will continue to flow into trying to straighten up each
> particular relationship with a man, how to get better sex, how to turn his head
> around—into trying to make the "new man" out of him, in the delusion that
> this will allow us to be the "new woman." This obviously splits our energies
> and commitments, leaving us unable to be committed to the construction of
> the new patterns which will liberate us.
>
> It is the primacy of women relating to women, of women creating a new
> consciousness of and with each other which is at the heart of women's libera-
> tion, and the basis for the cultural revolution. Together we must find, reinforce
> and validate our authentic selves. (August/September 1970:8)

Political lesbianism—the conscious, politically motivated choice to live as a
lesbian—is thus encouraged as a way to "dump all roles as much as possible . . . forget the male power system, and . . . give women primacy in your
life" (April/May 1972:21).

In sum, the development of a feminist analysis leads to a radical
redefinition of lesbianism. Lesbian relationships are extolled because of
their potential for equality and personal growth, while heterosexual relationships, mainstream society, and male homosexual society are condemned as sexist and oppressive. The new pride in lesbianism is reflected
in the fiction writing; only thirty-nine percent of the fiction stories describe
lesbian life and relationships pessimistically in the issues published after

The Ladder became a feminist periodical, compared to more than half of the stories published before then.

From these new definitions of the situation, a new political strategy in turn emerges. Editorials and articles describe lesbian and women's liberation as interdependent; a new utopian vision calls for not only the abolition of the taboo on same-sex relationships, but the abolition of traditional sex roles. Solidarity between lesbians and straight women is therefore essential. Lesbians must understand the costs paid by heterosexual women in living with men on a daily basis, while "straight" feminist groups such as the National Organization for Women must support lesbian rights, particularly since lesbians—the one group "throughout history . . . [which] has had no interest in furthering male power"—form the backbone of the feminist workforce (August/September 1970:4).

Various statements in these last three volumes explicitly disavow previous tactics of conformity. No longer emphasizing similarities between all persons regardless of sex or sexual preference, *The Ladder* now stresses pride in difference—pride in choosing women in a society which values only men. For example, in an autobiographical account of a rape trial, a woman recalls responding affirmatively and proudly when asked by the defense attorney if she was a lesbian:

> I have never, never before been so proud of that fact and never will again be so proud of anything I have publicly done or said. I had said, look at me, gentlemen. I am unique. I am no man's wife, daughter, or mother. I belong to myself. (December/January 1971:26)

Whereas earlier issues chastize women for hostility towards society, once society is defined as misogynist, lesbians' hostility becomes defined as true class consciousness.

The increasing politicization of *The Ladder* during these years reflects—and perhaps helps create—changes in the broader lesbian world. The changing definition of lesbianism occurs concurrently with the development of lesbian/feminist organizations such as Radicalesbians, which begin appearing in 1970, and sets the stage for one further change in strategy. In the April/May 1972 issue, Rita Mae Brown calls for a separatist lesbian/feminist movement. Her statement follows logically from the new definition of lesbianism. If lesbianism is a choice, then those who continue to relate to men may be defined as those who refuse to choose (for an elaboration of this position, see Bunch, 1978). The greatest distrust and hostility on the part of lesbians will be reserved for bisexuals, since these women know they can relate sexually and emotionally with women yet willfully "consort with the enemy" every time they become involved with men (Blumstein and Schwartz, 1974).

Editorial policy of *The Ladder* opposes separatism as self-defeating;

the article following Brown's describes in glowing terms the possibilities for cooperation between lesbian and heterosexual feminists. Nonetheless, the reality of a separatist movement beginning around this time and based in these definitions is documented not just by occasional writings in *The Ladder*, but by such divergent happenings as concerts open only to lesbians, the marketing of books and records for sale only to lesbians, and the establishment of lesbian-only housing at the annual National Women's Studies Association conference.

DISCUSSION

In Kitsuse's conception, the typical tertiary deviant comes out of the proverbial closet "not . . . to assume the role of social critic [but] . . . to claim the right to go in and stay in *just like everybody else*" (1981:10, Emphasis in original). Thus the tertiary deviant desires simply integration into the existing society rather than any radical changes in the social structure.

As this research has shown, however, tertiary deviants are not limited to an egalitarian ethic and libertarian political movements. Instead, deviants may define their situation in such a way that radical ideology and activism result. While Kitsuse notes that individuals may use their deviance as a springboard for a radical critique of society, he describes these "radical deviants" as atypical, isolated extremists such as Jean Genet, who revel in their deviance rather than attempt to change their social situation. He thus underestimates the potential of tertiary deviance as a base for radical social movements.

Radical Deviance
Why do some tertiary deviants go on to become radical critics of society, while others remain content to work for equal rights within the existing social structure?[3] Like other tertiary deviants, radical deviants reject prior negative valuations of themselves and substitute new and positive self-conceptions. Radical deviants differ from other tertiary deviants, however, in defining society as corrupt and regarding their actions as hidden resistance to that corruption. The following paragraphs delineate some of the factors which may encourage or hinder the development of radical deviance.

First, the option of radical deviance will only be available to those who can logically state that they choose their deviant actions, whether consciously or unconsciously. Those such as the disabled or rape victims,

---

[3]I am not here discussing those countercultural groups whose deviance is initially and overtly defined as political, but rather those groups in which political definitions of deviance only emerge over time to supplant prior negative and apolitical definitions.

whose deviance does not result from their own choosing, cannot define their deviance as politically motivated action.

In the case described in this paper, radical deviance becomes possible when the feminist movement provides the intellectual tools for politically analyzing womanhood, lesbianism, and society. The feminist movement was and is based on the concept that "the personal is political." Working from this principle, heterosexual feminists analyzed all aspects of life as political phenomena, including areas as seemingly private as sexuality (e.g., Koedt, 1970). Contact with the emerging faminist movement enabled lesbians to develop politicized counterdefinitions of their own sexuality—definitions which encouraged pride in that sexuality. At the same time, the feminist movement provided a vocabulary which neutralized the dominant society as sexist and corrupt. Thus, lesbians were able to redefine their actions as political resistance and their problems with society as injustice rather than merely personal misfortune—definitions crucial to the development of a political movement (Turner and Killian, 1972; Cloward and Piven, 1979).

Comparisons between gay male and lesbian activists during the early 1970s demonstrate the importance of a new world view—in this case, feminism—in developing radical definitions of deviance. As the gay liberation movement developed from the homophile movement, gay males adopted in varying degrees from the hippie counterculture a belief in the value of personal diversity. Yet, unlike lesbians, gay males had no larger ideology in terms of which to understand their homosexuality. Thus, the male gay liberation movement never truly developed a political theory of homosexuality and homophobia, but simply a more activist civil libertarian position. A reading of Laud Humphreys' (1972) history of the gay liberation movement and of the various statements generated by that movement (Teal, 1971) amply demonstrates the lack of any political theory comparable to that developed among lesbian/feminists.

While a political analysis of lesbianism led *The Ladder*'s writers to eventually promote and glorify lesbianism as resistance, political analyses of other forms of deviance may result in their abandonment. *The Autobiography of Malcolm X,* for example, suggests that a growing understanding of racism led Malcolm X to redefine his past criminal actions as resistance to an oppressive system, while awakening him to the self-destructive and ineffective nature of this resistance. The Black Muslims' addiction treatment program, as he describes it, was designed to have the same effect:

> The addict first was brought to admit to himself that he was an addict. Secondly, he was taught *why* he used narcotics. Every addict takes junk to escape something, the Muslim explains. He explains that most black junkies really are trying to narcotize themselves against being a black man in the white man's America. But actually, the Muslim says, the black man taking dope is only

helping the white man to "prove" that the black man is nothing. The Muslim talks confidentially, and straight. " . . . Man, what's a black man buying Whitey's dope for but to make Whitey richer—killing yourself?" The Muslim can tell when his quarry is ready to be shown that the way for him to quit dope is through joining the Nation of Islam. (1964:260–261)

Similarly, while most fat liberationists define fatness as mere biological diversity and hence work for equal rights and social acceptance (Millman, 1980), feminist fat liberationists define their fatness as an act of hidden resistance to sexist society:

> Fat is a response to the many oppressive manifestations of a sexist culture. Fat is a way of saying "no" to powerlessness and self-denial, to a limiting sexual expression which demands that females look and act a certain way, and to an image of womanhood that defines a specific social role. Fat offends Western ideals of female beauty and as such, every "overweight" woman creates a crack in the popular culture's ability to make us mere products. (Orbach, 1978:21)

Yet being overweight also has obvious costs in terms of health, social interactions, and sexual attractiveness when desired:

> While fat serves the symbolic function of rejecting the way by which society distorts women and their relationships with others . . . , getting fat remains an unhappy and unsatisfactory attempt to resolve those conflicts. It is a painful price to pay, whether a woman is trying to conform to society's expectations or attempting to forge a new identity. . . . Fat is an adaptation to the oppression of women, and, as such, it may be an unsatisfying personal solution and an ineffectual political attack. (Orbach, 1978:22)

In situations such as these, then, the political reinterpretation of deviance may lead to the rejection of the deviant actions, and the development of more direct social change strategies.

Finally, as with any political movement, radical deviance only becomes possible when a community of like individuals exists. Within a community, individuals can share experiences, discover common themes, and hence redefine personal troubles as social problems. The community can subsequently provide a network of significant others to help maintain the newly developed politicized definitions of the situation.

Given the importance of community, those whose deviance is hidden and individualistic (e.g., compulsive binge-purge eaters or "bulimarexics") will have more difficulty developing a radical stance than will those whose deviance brings them together (as in the unofficial gathering places of the gay community). Within a single deviant group, other factors can encourage or inhibit the development of community; the disabled in Berkeley, who form fourteen percent of the population and have an accessible transportation system (*Newsweek*, 2/8/82:84), have much more potential for developing a shared ideology than do disabled individuals scattered in other locations and kept apart by inaccessible transportation and architectural barriers. Similarly, among minority groups heterosexual woman have had much more difficulty establishing an in-group definition of their problems as political than have Blacks; women are isolated from each other by nuclear families and maintain their strongest ties to men, rather than to other women. Hence women, but not Blacks, have needed consciousness raising groups to develop an understanding of their oppressed social position.

In sum, the development of radical deviance requires a supportive community sharing a definition of society as corrupt and in need of radical change, and a definition of deviance as politically motivated, not self-destructive, and an effective means of resisting society. These conditions are not unique to lesbian-feminists. These same conditions would be met, for example, by some of those involved in the American deserters' movement in Canada and Sweden. Unlike draft resisters, most deserters were lower-class and uneducated and did not (at the time of either induction or desertion) have moral or political objections to the Vietnam conflict (Baskir, 1978). Instead, they viewed their desertion as stemming from the need for personal survival—and perhaps also from personal weakness or cowardice. Once in Canada or Sweden, some of these deserters developed a new community in exile, in which desertion was radically redefined as a moral response to an immoral situation. These radicalized deserters rejected amnesty on the grounds that the government and not they had committed criminal acts. Rather than desiring reintegration into American society, they viewed themselves as expatriates from a corrupt regime, and urged others to join them in their actions.

Deviants, Tertiary Deviants, and Minority Groups

In developing the concepts of tertiary and radical deviance, the boundaries between deviant and minority groups become increasingly thin. Traditionally, sociologists have defined deviants as persons stigmatized because of their individual behavior, and minorities as groups judged negatively on a collective basis. Thus the prostitute is ostracized because of her own actions, while the Jew is stigmatized because of group background, and the myth that all members of that group share certain negative characteristics. Sociologists have also traditionally restricted the term "minority group" to those groups which share a sense of themselves "as objects of collective discrimination" (Wirth, 1945:347), while assuming that deviants typically deal with stigma as isolated individuals.

From these definitions, tertiary deviants appear to lie analytically midway between minority groups and other deviants. Like other deviants, tertiary deviants are stigmatized first and foremost because of their individual actions or attributes. Tertiary deviants differ, however, in sharing a sense of belonging to an oppressed group. Rather than attempting to change or hide their group membership (or simply being unaware of like-situated others), tertiary deviants declare that their group membership should in no way limit their social worth or civil rights. Hence, they aim to convince society at large that they are a minority rather than a deviant group, and to define their oppression as a social problem. A successful campaign by tertiary deviants might, for example, result in the social acceptance of homosexuality and the definition of homophobia as a social problem. Evidence for such a trend can be seen in the American Psychiatric Association's removal of homosexuality per se from its list of illnesses, and the development of psychological research into the nature, causes, and "cures" of homophobia (reviewed in Morin and Garfinkle, 1978).

SUMMARY AND CONCLUSIONS

This article has used material from *The Ladder* to illustrate the development of tertiary deviance among lesbians. These data demonstrate the way lesbian writers actively structured their world, developing accounts for their behavior and political strategies based on those accounts. During its early years, *The Ladder* advocated an accommodative stance towards society, urging lesbians to censor outward differences between themselves and heterosexuals and to stress the unimportance of differences that did exist so as to become more acceptable to the dominant society. (Similar strategies are used by the disabled, who may also claim lack of responsibility for their deviance [Levitin, 1975; Davis, 1961].) With the development of tertiary deviance, lesbians viewed themselves as entitled to civil rights without having to resort to any accommodative strategies. Finally, as a radical deviant stance emerged, deviance was celebrated as honorable resistance, and the locus for desired change shifted unequivocally from the individual deviant to the society.

This paper has focused on the changing in-group definitions of deviant behavior and the political consequences of these shifts. The data suggest the need for research into the psychological effects of tertiary deviance on the individual. Isolated individuals who join a supportive community may well benefit from reduced feelings of guilt and increased feelings of self-worth regardless of the politics of that community. When deviants stress accommodation and work towards acceptance by the dominant society, however, their self-worth may depend upon others' grudging toleration. With tertiary deviance, on the other hand, self-worth is based on self-evaluation. Hence, accommodative deviants may have less control over their own self-concept, and a less stable sense of self-worth, than tertiary deviants.

In focusing on secondary deviants, sociologists have tended to view deviants as passive acceptors of their stigmatized fates. This and other research suggest the need to move beyond an "over-socialized" conception of deviants, and to study the processes through which deviants actively create definitions of their own behavior and political strategies based on those definitions.

REFERENCES

Baskir, Lawrence M.
    1978   Chance and Circumstance. New York: Knopf.
Blumstein, Philip and Pepper Schwartz
    1974   "Lesbianism and bisexuality." In E. Goode and R. Troiden (eds.), Sexual Deviance and Sexual Deviants. New York: Morrow.
Bunch, Charlotte
    1978   "Lesbians in revolt." In Alison Jaggar and Paula Struhl (eds.), Feminist Frameworks. New York: McGraw-Hill.
Cooley, Charles H.
    1967   "Looking glass self," In Jerome G. Manis and Bernard N. Meltzer (eds.), Symbolic Interaction: A Reader in Social Psychology. Boston, MA: Allyn and Bacon.
Cloward, Richard A. and Frances Fox Piven
    1979   "Hidden protest: The channeling of female innovation and resistance" Signs: Journal of Women in Culture and Society 4(4):651–669.
Daughters of Bilitis
    1975   The Ladder. Reprinted as part of the general series, Homosexuality: Lesbians and Gay Men in Society, History and Literature. Jonathan Katz, general editor, New York: Arno Press.
Davis, Fred
    1961   "Deviance disavowal: The management of strained interaction by the visibly handicapped." Social Problems 9:120–32.
Faderman, Lillian
    1981   Surpassing the Love of Men. New York: William Morrow and Co.
Goffman, Erving
    1963   Stigma: Notes on the Management of Spoiled Identity. Englewood Cliffs, NJ: Prentice Hall.
Humphreys, Laud
    1972   Out of the Closets: The sociology of homosexual liberation. Englewood Cliffs, NJ: Prentice Hall.
Kinsey, Alfred, Wardell Pomeroy and Clyde Martin
    1948   Sexual Behavior in the Human Male. Philadelphia, PA: Saunders.
Kitsuse, John
    1980   "Coming out all over: Deviants and the politics of social problems." Social Problems 28(October):1–13.
Koedt, Anne
    1970   "The myth of the vaginal orgasm." In Leslie B. Tanner (ed.), Voices from Women's Liberation. New York: New American Library.
Lemert, Edwin
    1951   Social Pathology: A Systematic Approach to the Theory of Sociopathic Behavior. New York: McGraw Hill.

Levitin, Teresa E.
   1975   "Deviants as active participants in the labeling process." Social Problems
           22(April):548–557.
Martin, Del and Phyllis Lyon
   1972   Lesbian/Woman. San Francisco, CA: Glide Publications.
   1978   "Reminiscences of two female homophiles." In Ginny Vida (ed.), Our Right to
           Love. Englewood Cliffs, NJ: Prentice-Hall.
Mead, George H.
   1934   On Social Psychology. Chicago, IL: University of Chicago Press.
Millman, Marcia
   1980   Such a Pretty Face. New York: Norton.
Morin, Stephen and E. M. Garfinkle
   1978   "Male homophobia." Journal of Social Issues 34(1):29–47.
Nestle, Joan
   1981   "Butch-fem relationships: Sexual courage in the 1950's." Heresies 3 (4) Issue 12.
Orbach, Susie
   1978   Fat is a Feminist Issue. New York: Berkley Publishing Corp.
Scott, Marvin B. and Stanford M. Lyman
   1968   "Accounts." American Sociological Review 33 (February): 46–62.
Teal, Donn
   1971   The Gay Militants. New York: Stein and Day.
Tobin, Kay and Randy Wicker
   1975   The Gay Crusaders. New York: Arno Press.
Turner, Ralph H.
   1972   "Deviance avowal as neutralization of commitment." Social Problems 19 (Winter):
           308–321.
Turner, Ralph H. and Lewis M. Killian
   1972   Collective Behavior (2nd ed.). Englewood Cliffs, NJ: Prentice-Hall.
X, Malcolm
   1964   The Autobiography of Malcolm X. New York: Grove Press.
Wirth, Louis
   1945   "The problem of minority groups," In Ralph Linton (ed.), The Science of Man in the
           World Crisis. New York: Columbia University Press.

7 *Kikokushijo:* The emergence and institutionalization of an educational problem in Japan*

John I. Kitsuse
University of Calfiornia, Santa Cruz

Anne E. Murase
Sophia University

Yoshiaki Yamamura
University of Tsukuba

INTRODUCTION

The "constructionist" approach to the study of social problems has identified and proposed a number of issues that should be addressed for the development of a theory of social problems. Central among these is the question of the relationship between the social conditions that are asserted to exist and definitions of those conditions as problematic and in need of some sort of collective action. Stating this issue in an extreme form, Spector and Kitsuse (1977) have attempted to delineate the logical implications of the analytic as well as empirical independence of the conditions and definitions of them as social problems. In this chapter, we propose to explore this relationship with reference to the emergence and development of a social

*We gratefully acknowledge the support of Faculty Research Grants from the University of California, Santa Cruz, and University of Tsukuba.

problem in Japan known as *kikokushijo mondai* ("the returning student problem").

In our initial exchange of ideas for this binational research effort, our collaboration (part of an ongoing association of some twenty years)[1] on this project was based on a common interest in the sociology of education. The stimulus for the study began with an item appearing in an American newspaper in 1978 citing a study by Anne Murase of a small but growing number of school children called *kikokushijo* in Japan. Ranging in age from beginning elementary to high school seniors, these children were said to face a variety of difficulties on their return to Japan from residence and education abroad, some for periods as brief as several months, and others for many years. These difficulties were reported by school officials and others to pose "problems of adjustment" not only for the reentry of the *kikokushijo* into the Japanese educational system, but more broadly their present and future status in the larger society.

From an American perspective, the social and educational differentiation of the *kikokushijo* as a special category of student was puzzling. Further, our constructionist orientation to the study of social problems directed us to examine the terms in which the so-called problem has been cast, discussed, analyzed, and interpreted within the society. How is it that these children have come to be characterized as "too aggressive," individualistic, displaying odd manners in public without regard for the language, culture, and history of their native land? And how is it that these same children are also positively characterized as offering the possibility of "internationalizing" the educational system and the society at large by introducing new perspectives and orientations acquired during their sojourn abroad? In what situations are such attributions made of these children, and by whom? What are considered to be the "causes" of these problems and possibilities, and what groups, organizations, and institutions are conceived to be the appropriate agencies for responding to them? These questions reflected an "outside" American perspective that became the occasion for examining the taken-for-granted conceptions of the various parties involved in the social problem.

Investigation of these taken-for-granted conceptions required a methodology that would specify the various persons and agencies engaged in identifying and describing the educational situation, and more generally the social status, of this population as problematic, and organizing groups to articulate and sponsor proposals to ameliorate the conditions described. In short, our research moved in the direction of investigating how the charac-

---

[1]Kitsuse and Yemamura have collaborated on research projects in Japan since 1961, while our joint effort with Anne Murase is of more recent date.

terizations, analyses, policy proposals, and institutional responses were interrelated in the production of "the *kikokushijo* problem."

Our initial inquiries were directed to the Ministry of Education, through which the educational system from preschool programs through graduate and professional training is centrally controlled. Extensive interviews with personnel in charge of various sections of the Ministry led us to a wide network of public and private organizations that were and continue to be active in defining, sponsoring, and pressing for institutional responses to various representations of "the *kikokushijo* problem". Our primary source of data was interviews (supplemented by government documents, school records, conference reports, mass media accounts) conducted with officials and spokespersons of more than fifty organizations.

The schools, of course, have been the direct setting in which "the *kikokushijo* problem" has been identified and characterized, but our initial inquiries in 1979 about the "cast of characters" (Spector and Kitsuse, 1977) who have been concerned with the problem yielded a formidable list of government bureaus, business corporations, university administrators, women's organizations, corporate-funded foundations, counseling services, newspapers, and social research groups, in addition to schools at all levels of the educational system. Our informants described and commented not only on the policies and practices of schools with regard to *kikokushijo,* but also referred to the interests and concerns expressed in the actions of organizations representing various aspects of "the problem."

THE EDUCATIONAL CONTEXT OF "THE PROBLEM"

The bases of these interests and concerns can perhaps best be seen in the context of the organization of the Japanese educational system. It is highly standardized and universally perceived as *the* instrument for gaining access to prestigious occupational positions in government and business organizations. This close articulation of the educational and occupational systems in Japan is at the core of the perceptions and concerns that animate the various actors involved in the definitions of the *kikokushijo* as a social problem.

Although school attendance in Japan is compulsory only through middle school, ninety-four percent of the high school age population go on to complete a secondary education (Vogel, 1979). This compares with seventy-five to eighty percent of American children who are generally required to attend school until the age of sixteen. The national mania for education in Japan is apparent in numerous ways, including the highly developed parallel system of private schools through all grade levels. These schools offer ambitious parents the promise of quality as well as status-differentiated education at approximately five times the cost of public education.

The availability of even some prestigious private schools does not mean, however, that "alternative" education is available. While there are several so-called "international schools" in Japan, parents who enroll their children in these schools are technically in violation of the law, which requires all compulsory school-age children to attend schools approved by the Ministry of Education. Such approval is contingent on the maintenance of the standard curriculum and the use of Japanese as the language of instruction, which in "international schools" is usually English. The importance of attending schools accredited by the Ministry of Education is further underlined by the fact that entrance examinations for national universities are restricted to candidates who are products of approved Japanese secondary schools.

Another feature of the Japanese educational system that bears on the discussion and activities surrounding the situation of the *kikokushijo* is that high schools and universities, like almost everything else in Japan, from bean paste to automobiles, are evaluated and assigned positions in a highly consensual ranking system. "Graduates of the elite schools tend to form academic cliques (*gakubatsu*) in which the interpersonal relationships can become crucial in various aspects of life, especially in business connections and in securing desirable employment"[2] (Murase, 1983). One consequence of this stratified system of educational institutions is, of course, an intense competition for admission into the "very best" schools, which are public and thus accessible to successful applicants at minimal cost relative to the costly tuition required by private schools.

Admission to all of these schools, private as well as public, is conditional on performance on standardized, largely "objective" examinations, although even prestigious private schools have been known to accommodate low-scoring applicants from affluent backgrounds. Examinations that mark the movement and redistribution of students into and among the hierarchy of middle schools, high schools, and colleges and universities are administered every spring. These examinations are so fiercely competitive that they are known as "examination hell" (*shiken jigoku*). Middle school students devote their last year to preparation for entrance examinations to the most desirable high schools, just as students in those high schools devote their senior year to cramming for examinations that will admit them to the prestigious universities. As one of our informants, an experienced university administrator, observed:

---

[2]"Access to what is conceived to be quality (college/university-prep) schooling is possible only (except in cases of bribes or extraordinary concessions) if the child successfully negotiates a series of progressively more difficult entrance examinations" (Murase, 1978:10).

The college entrance examinations are becoming a burden to everyone. It is a torture for the faculty who have to devise new exams every year on more or less the same materials that are presented in the texts used by the schools throughout the land. The exams are annually printed and distributed to the schools, which then become the basis for the teachers' preparation of their students. The examination questions are tricky and have to be changed every year.

Although the examination system is almost universally the object of complaint and grumbling, it nevertheless is tacitly approved as the mechanism by which educational opportunity is distributed on the basis of talent and achievement. As will be seen, this system presents the most formidable barrier to the reentry of the *kikokushijo* at all levels of public educational institutions, and is most resistant to demands that the *kikokushijo* be made exempt from the competitive entrance examinations.

In an effort to reduce the uncertainties and traumas of their children's progress through the educational system, Japanese parents expend substantial sums of money to provide tutoring as well as indulgences to motivate and sustain interest in academic performance. This has given rise to the stereotyped caricature of the "education mother" (*kyoiku mama*), characterized as hovering, anxious, and tirelessly solicitous of her (usually male) child, and who constantly monitors his classroom and examination performance. The extremity of the efforts of these *kyoiku mama* to gain advantageous placement in the educational (and hopefully the occupational) system has stimulated the development of an auxiliary educational institution called the *juku* which offers tutoring oriented primarily toward performance on entrance examinations to schools at all levels.

The proliferation of *juku* (as well as an organizational form called *yobiko* specialized to serve a clientele preparing for university entrance examinations) has been extensive and has become "industrialized." They provide extraschool tutoring, for preschool students to those studying for university entrance examinations.[3] The preschool *juku* serve an eager clientele of mothers seeking tutors to prepare their children for elementary school examinations. Most desirable among these elementary schools are those that have affiliated junior and high schools, and sometimes universities, which reduces the problematic character of admission and movement through each level of the educational system.

Inevitably, the system of *juku* has been the object of the aforementioned Japanese predilection for ranking their institutions, position in this hierarchy being determined by the "track record" of their clientele in gaining

---

[3]A woman who has been active in efforts to ameliorate the situation of *kikokushijo* remarked that she thought it was a joke when she first heard about mothers sending their preschool children to *juku* in order to insure admission to the kindergarten of the "best" schools. "It was no joke," she said sadly.

admission to the most desirable schools. To maintain their rank, the "very best" *juku* have instituted a practice of administering examinations to applicants, thus opening the possibility of an infinite regress of entrance examinations in the system of *juku*. The single-minded efforts of parents to promote educational opportunities for their children is astonishing. The mass media frequently chronicles the lastest fads and fashions of the educational mania. They have reported the case of two children from Osaka who were transported every weekend via air to Tokyo (at a cost of approximately $120) to attend a *juku* preparatory to sitting for a high school entrance examination. The financial costs entailed in the maintenance of the *juku* industry must be substantial. The social and psychic costs for those who have made the investment and failed to gain admission to the school of choice are less calculable. The "failures" may find some consolation, however, in a practice, mentioned by one of our informants, of recording the name of prestigious *juku* on the Japanese equivalent of the individual's curriculum vitae.

THE EDUCATIONAL REENTRY OF KIKOKUSHIJO

This brief description of the intense concern, anxiety, and activity surrounding the movement of children through the Japanese school system will suggest the context of the issues that have emerged within the past fifteen years with reference to the *kikokushijo*. On their return from residence abroad, these students and their parents are confronted with the frenzy of entrance examinations described above. In this competitive atmosphere, they are made painfully aware of lacking the preparation provided their peers by the standard, rigorous, national Japanese school curriculum and the supplementary benefits of the *juku* system. From a curricular point of view, their disadvantage is real and serious. For students returning from schools in California, for example, the curriculum in Japan is substantially more demanding. One student of the Japanese educational system states:

> College-bound Japanese students study math every year in high school and attain a level of sophistication beyond trigonometry. Only 5% of high school students in California reach trigonometry. Moreover, the University of California requires only one year of science and two years of math for admission, a standard not even close to entrance requirements at comparable Japanese universities. . . . Japan requires all of its high school students to take an extensive language and social studies curriculum including ethics, civics, history, political science and economics. (Kirst, 1981:707)

Indeed, the standardized curriculum is so elaborate and demanding that even the long Japanese school year which runs for approximately ten months appears to be insufficient to provide instruction time; hence the extensive use of *juku*. Since examinations at each level presuppose exposure if not mastery of this curriculum, most *kikokushijo* are characterized as severely disadvantaged in competing with their Japanese peers. They are thought most importantly to be disadvantaged by the bilingual environment from which they have returned, rendering them deficient in the formal use of Japanese as well as the foreign language used in the schools attended abroad.

Specifically, the *kikokushijo* are considered generally to lack knowledge and facility with regard to *kokugo* (the language of instruction and, of critical importance, of the entrance examinations) as well as *nihongo*, the spoken everyday form of the language. Review of their transcripts from abroad and their present performance capabilities serves to document the interpretation of deficiencies in math and science, not to mention the arts and social studies which are elements of the Japanese curriculum from primary through the secondary schools. Acquisition of a second language, which might be considered the most likely academic benefit of the *kikokushijo's* foreign experience, is evaluated in the case of most to be less than fluent in any form of use.

Ezra Vogel, a noted Japanologist, commenting on the treatment of *kikokushijo*, observes:

> Japanese children who study abroad and learn foreign languages are given virtually no recognition for their achievements. Even Japanese children who have studied abroad and become fluent in English may be required by their teachers in Japan to go through various archaic exercises to prepare for English entrance examinations rather than encouraged to continue to develop their natural fluency. (Vogel, 1979:243)

The status of *kikokushijo* in Japanese schools is an ambiguous one. In family background and physical appearance they are clearly Japanese, but, among those that deal with them in the school setting, they are considered inadequately prepared socially as well as academically. Questioned about this judgment of inadequacy, the teachers and administrators we have interviewed commonly characterize the *kikokushijo* as too individualistic, too aggressively vocal in their expression of opinion, untrained in the requirements of cooperative activity, vulgar in their public behavior, and so forth. Such characterizations of *kikokushijo* have laid the basis for the conception of them among school personnel as an "educational problem" requiring special counseling programs, teaching techniques, and instruction in "human relations" (*ningen kankei*) which *kikokushijo* are frequently said to be lacking.

Peculiarities of speech and diction are attributed to the *kikokushijo*, making them objects of derisive imputations by peers and others expressed in epithets such as *hen japa* ("strange Japanese"), *han japa* ("half Japanese") and the more extreme *katawa na kodomo* ("crippled children," with the implication, as one of the mothers complained bitterly, that they are damaged, inferior merchandise). These characterizations have also become reflected in the research formulations of psychologists, psychiatrists, and social scientists who posit various psychological manifestations of stress as concomitants of the situation of the *kikokushijo*. Although these characterizations are made most particularly of *kikokushijo* returning from the United States, it is generally applied to them without regard to the countries from which they have returned, or the length of their sojourn abroad. Since they are considered to be burdened with these academic as well as cultural and social deficiencies, it is not surprising to find that *kikokushijo* are assumed to be faced with difficult problems of "adaptation."

The reluctance of schools to accommodate *kikokushijo* with regard to their putative educational problems have reinforced the concerns of their parents about the consequences of taking school children abroad. There is virtually unanimous agreement among the various organizations and agencies which have been drawn into this problem that to take leave of the Japanese educational system is to suffer immediate as well as long-term disadvantage. This assessment view is fostered, first of all, by the many parents of children overseas (called *kaigaishijo*), whose concerned and persistent efforts to reproduce an educational environment as close to Japanese school as feasible are dedicated to ameliorate those putative problems. Some parents are so intent on minimizing the "disadvantages" of their children's education abroad that they have enrolled them in the local full-time Japanese schools *and* the weekend supplementary schools, mirroring the intensity of the *kyoiku mama* in Japan. Indeed, the availability of such educational facilities for Japanese children abroad is in no small part a product of the appeals of such parents to the Government through their husbands' corporate affiliations.

The aforementioned study by Anne Murase (1979) is notable as the only investigation that has sought to examine systematically the putative "problems of adaptation" experienced by *kikokushijo*. Using a rigorous design permitting comparisons between "returnee" students and comparable Japanese students who have never been abroad, her data show that the *kikokushijo* are not the troubled and anxious students as they have commonly been described to be. On the contrary, responses to a modified version of the General Anxiety Test showed no significant differences between the two populations.

THE SOCIAL PRODUCTION OF "THE KIKOKUSHIJO PROBLEM"

Our informants date the beginning of the *"kikokushijo mondai"* in the early 1960s. Mr. S., an educationist on the staff of the International Educational

Exchange Center (an organization that offers consultation services to personnel of international business corporations), is widely recognized as knowledgeable in detail concerning the background and history of the *kikokushijo* problem. He traces the beginnings of the problem as follows:

> It depends on whether we're talking about the government or private groups and organizations. The private interests began to talk about it as a problem about 1960. At first, the Foreign Ministry personnel returning from abroad found that they could not get their kids into school, and that's when they began to talk about it as a problem. UN personnel and academics coming back after five or six years also found no schools for these kids.

As indicated in these comments, those who were first involved in identifying a social condition and defining it as a problem were relatively high-ranking government and academic professionals.

> These people made it a problem, or saw it as a problem from the point of view of parents. Officially the Culture section of the Ministry of Education and the Foreign Ministry got together and formed the *Kikokushijo* Research Center. This was 1964, so there was a lag between private and government interest in this problem.

> (Was it because the kids couldn't get into schools that the *kikokushijo* were viewed as a problem?)

> Yes, although there is a distinction made today [1979] between *kaigai* [i.e., overseas] and *kikoku* [returnee], in the beginning it was the *kikoku* that was viewed as a problem.

> (What kinds of problems emerged in 1960 to make the *kikokushijo* a social problem?)

> The kids came back with language problems and academic achievement levels such that they were one or two grades behind their age grade. If these kids had been accepted by the school that would have been one thing, but there was an attitude of rejecting these students for admission to the schools. About that time a high official of the Foreign Ministry was quoted as saying that even though he serves his country abroad and pays taxes in Japan, when returning home with his children, they are not taken in. What kind of treatment is that, he wanted to know. In these circumstances, the parents felt that if they put their children in public schools [which were legally required to accept them, subject to placement at below grade level] they would not receive individualized attention. On the other hand, the private schools that they preferred for their children were not too receptive of the *kikokushijo* since they presented educational problems.

Other interviewees confirm the view that the educational situation of returning students was the concern of a small elite group, "internationalist" in outlook, yet parochial in their concern for admission of their children to prestigious Japanese schools as the sine qua non of prospective status in Japanese society. As members of the achieving upper middle class, they epitomize the intensely education-oriented parents described in the preceding section. They were articulate and organizationally sophisticated. These concerned parents, connected through their professions within the influential Foreign Ministry and educational establishment, were able significantly to shape the definitions and issues of the *kikokushijo* problem, the terms in which it has been promoted, and the groups, organizations, and institutions that have been mobilized to create a "solution" for the problem.

As early as 1962, when the movement of Japanese personnel overseas had just begun and the number of students returning from abroad were fewer than a hundred, the definition of the educational situation of the *kikokushijo* as a social problem was sponsored by a formally organized "committee" called the *Zaigai Kimmusha Shijo Taisaku Kondan Kai* (Overseas Employee's Children's Adaptation Organization). With a membership of about twenty people composed of personnel in the Foreign Ministry, international trading companies, and news media, this committee was chaired by Mr. W., a high ranking diplomat who had recently returned with two young children from a post in Washington, D.C. In classic Millsian (Mills, 1959) fashion, he transformed his personal experience of frustrating encounters with schools officials into a public issue.

Utilizing his prestigious connections in the government bureaucracies, as well as the business, cultural, and social worlds, Mr. W. mobilized their collective resources to disseminate the committee's conception of the *kikokushijo* problem. The committee proposed that (a) Japanese schools should be established abroad where sizable numbers of government and corporate business personnel are posted, and provide their children with instruction in the standard Japanese curriculum. As dependents of parents assigned to overseas posts for diplomatic activities, the committee argued that the children should not be handicapped by their absence from schools in Japan. (b) That special classes and procedures be established in Japan to accommodate the integration of *kikokushijo* into the educational system without prejudice or disadvantage. They should have the opportunity to rectify whatever curricular deficiencies they might have incurred as a consequence of their absence from Japan, and be provided with classroom tutorials toward that end. (c) That boarding schools be established in Japan where parents might enroll their children during the period of foreign assignment, with the British institutions as a model.

The committee's proposals, issued as a set of public policy recommendations to the Ministry of Education and the Foreign Ministry, has spawned and guided the claims-making activities of countless organizations. Parents of overseas school children (officially designated as *kaigaishijo*), and particularly the mothers returning with their children from abroad, were active in calling for recognition of the situation of the *kikokushijo* as a social problem. Interviews with representatives of diverse groups involved in the *kikokushijo* problem are uniform in characterizing the mothers as "movers of the system" through their demands for institutional recognition and accommodation of their children's educational situation. The claims advanced by these mothers with regard to the educational situation of their children varied. Some were single-minded in focusing on the need for sympathetic acceptance of their children by school and society. Others demanded modification of the curriculum to rectify the negative and parochial views reflected in school policies with regard to their children's "international experience." The mothers were generally united, however, in their criticism of the educational system's failure to accommodate the return of their children without prejudice or penalty.

Within Japan, an organization of women, wives of Foreign Ministry personnel, has been particularly active and effective in defining the educational problem of overseas and returning children. As veterans of moving to and from foreign post assignments, they have frequently experienced the educational dislocations of their children's reentry into the Japanese school system. Organized as the Association for the Study of the Education of Children (*Shijo Kyoiku wo Kangaeru Kai*), this volunteer group of women has obtained quasi-official recognition by the Foreign Ministry and office space provided for their activities, no mean achievement in a ministry that is punctilious about extending perquisites of organizational status.

The association established a network of communication with wives of personnel at foreign posts through the publication of a newsletter that reports developments in educational policies, facilities, and services for returning school children and those who are abroad. One measure of the effectiveness of this energetic and well organized group of women is that it has succeeded in obtaining funds through the Foreign Ministry to erect dormitory facilities for female school children comparable to those which have been available for many years to their male siblings when they were left in Japan during their fathers' overseas assignments. They also have been instrumental in persuading the Ministry to provide travel funds for children to be reunited periodically with the families from whom they have been separated.

Mothers of *kikokushijo* operating from within the business corporations have been less visible and formally organized, but no less effective in pressing their definition of the *kikokushijo* problem. As wives of middle-level corporate business personnel known as *sarari man* (white collar workers employed on annual salary basis), they are particularly cognizant of Japan as a society in which the primary determinant of occupational and social status is the relative prestige of the university from which one has graduated (*gakureki shakai*). Their anxieties about the educational consequences of removing their children from the Japanese school system has, in turn, created difficulties for corporations in assigning personnel to foreign posts.

These difficulties have increased with the phenomenal development of the Japanese economy, which has made the corporate home offices the major arena for career advancement. The Japan Overseas Enterprises Association (JOEA), formed in 1971 as a nonprofit organization funded by three hundred, seventy major corporations doing business abroad, has established the International Cooperation Department to research, interpret, and voice the concerns of their membership to government agencies about the educational problems of overseas and returning children. In our interview with Mr. T., director of this department, he immediately launched into a statement of the *kikokushijo* problem. Asserting that Japan is an education-oriented society, he emphasized that for the *kikokushijo*, getting into Japanese universities is a crucial problem because life chances are tied not only to higher education, but to admission to the *particular* university attended. The reluctance of corporate personnel to accept assignment to offices abroad reflects a recognition of the consequences of such foreign service for their children's educational opportunities. When asked in what way corporations confront the *kikokushijo* as a problem, Mr. T. observed that when personnel go abroad concerned about the consequences of their leave for their children's future prospects, this seriously affects the employees' ability to do their work. The children come to be viewed as having been sacrificed by the parents, leading them to press for shorter tours of duty abroad than the three years that corporations generally consider to be a minimum as a matter of efficiency, especially for foreign assignments requiring acquisition of a difficult language.

INSTITUTIONAL RESPONSES TO "THE KIKOKUSHIJO PROBLEM"

As an organization representing powerful business interests, the JOEA serves as the "interface" between its members and the government, most particularly the Ministry of Education and the Foreign Ministry, in defining the *kikokushijo* problem. JOEA has taken the view that, since these children must go abroad as dependents of their parents, and since they are required by law in Japan to attend school through middle school, the government should assume the obligation to provide educational facilities so that they do not suffer disadvantage in the *gekugeki shakai* to which they must return (Kobayashi, 1978).

Over a period of years, the JOEA has been an active and effective champion of the *kikokushijo*, negotiating with the government to establish Japanese educational facilities and services through the middle schools overseas, where sizable populations of Japanese nationals reside. Where numbers cannot support a full time Japanese school, the JOEA has proposed that supplementary schools be established to instruct overseas students in Japanese, calling also for the recruitment for those schools of quality teachers through salary and other inducements. On the domestic front, JOEA has recommended special facilities in private universities with government subsidies for *kikokushijo*, emphasizing the development of curricula to remedy deficiencies. Encouraged by the government's positive responses to these proposals, the JOEA has more recently suggested the need for improving the educational quality of the overseas Japanese schools, and the establishment of centrally located boarding schools in foreign countries.

That the JOEA was able to gain and continues to maintain ready access to the Foreign Ministry and the Ministry of Education, and to mobilize them in the interests of overseas and returning students, is a commentary on the persistence of the *kyoiku mama*. The reasonable character of their definition of their collective experience of concern as a public problem has been tacitly acknowledged in the progressive extension by the Ministry of Education of a policy of grants in aid for the education of Japanese children abroad. The expenditure of public monies for this purpose has been politically sensitive, since it raises the question of whether the national obligation to provide "obligatory" education (*gimu kyoiku*) extends to children of citizens living abroad in pursuit of private interests. Nevertheless, by 1967 public assistance to overseas children included:

- Subsidies for rental of school buildings.
- Return trip expenses for teachers sent from Japan.
- Overseas allowance for teachers sent from Japan.
- Subsidies for salaries of instructors who were appointed locally (i.e., by overseas residents) in Japanese supplementary schools.
- Partial funding for equipment and teaching materials.
- Production and distribution of guidebooks for teachers and parents.
- Free distribution of textbooks to all overseas children.
- Establishment and maintenance of a special class for returning children at a public middle school in Japan.
- Subsidies for selected public and private elementary, middle, and high schools which receive returning children upon reentry to Japan (Kobayashi, 1978).

Although these facilities have been gratefully received and utilized by a large majority of the parents of overseas children, they are generally considered by those parents as well as school officials in Japan to be second rate as preparatory schools for the "examination hell" the students face on their return. It is not uncommon for this assessment of these schools to persuade mothers that they should return to Japan with their children, leaving their husbands at their foreign posts. In her study of Japanese residents in Los Angeles, Minoura (1979:171) quotes from an interview with the mother of two teenage children:

> I want my son to graduate from a good Japanese university. Everybody says that one should go to a Japanese university if one wants to live in Japan. . . . If we are to live in Japan as Japanese, children will be better off in Japan with a B.A. from a good Japanese university, since there is said to be *gakubatsu* [the "old boy network"]. . . . In order to acquire academic excellence to pass an entrance examination to a good university, my son has to pass an exam to a high school with high academic standard. That's why we decided to leave now, so that he has one year and a half before the high school exam season.

However, return to Japan in such circumstances has not been without its difficulties. Parental decision to return to Japan is often imposed on resistant children, reluctant to leave their lives abroad and resentful of the restrictions of life in Japan.

By 1982, parents returning with such children found substantial institutional recognition and accommodation of the educational situation of the *kikokushijo*. Through an impressive mobilization and expenditure of economic, social, and political resources, the diverse interests involved in this problem had moved government agencies to establish seventy "reception schools" (*ukeireko*) throughout Japan to facilitate the reentry of *kikokushijo* into the school system at a maintenance cost of approximately sixty million yen. Several boarding schools have been constructed for *kikokushijo* and children left in Japan (*zanryushijo*) by their overseas parents. In addition, fifteen business corporations have built such facilities for children of their personnel. In response to demands for the amelioration of the *kikokushijo*'s competitive disadvantage in gaining admission to the universities, special admissions procedures have been instituted by which they are exempted from the usual examinations.

As in the case of the reception schools that accommodate the admission of junior and high school *kikokushijo*, universities that have established special admissions procedures are private institutions, with the exception of the recently established national University of Tsukuba, and, in a more limited way, Kyoto University. Tsukuba, which is part of a vast government research and development complex located in a "new town" approximately sixty kilometers from Tokyo, has been exceptionally responsive to the educational situation of the *kikokushijo*. In commenting on Tsukuba's accommodation of the *kikokushijo*, the president of the University explained in an interview that the charter of Tsukuba is distinctive, in that, unlike the rest of the Japanese national universities, authority over educational as well as organizational policies is vested in the administration. As a consequence, Tsukuba is able to be more responsive to public policy porposals from the Ministry of Education to deal with emergent educational problems. For example, although the academic year in Japan begins in April, Tsukuba has instituted a program that provides for admission of *kikokushijo* in September to accommodate returnees from foreign institutions.[4] In 1982, the first class of *kikokushijo* admitted under this program was graduated in a June commencement exercise.

The decision in 1982 of the faculty of law at Kyoto University (which ranks with Tokyo University as the most prestigious educational institution in Japan) to provide alternate admission procedures has been viewed by *kikokushijo* advocates as a hopeful sign of a breach in the formidable barrier of the examination system. However, the various faculties that control and govern the national universities have strongly resisted the relaxation of admissions procedures and standards. This resistance reflects an ideological commitment to the examination system as the universalistic mechanism for the realization of equal educational opportunity. The maintenance of the examination system is also reinforced by the limited facilities of public institutions of higher education. In an intensely education-oriented society, the public universities are able to admit only twenty percent of the population of college and university students. Thus, any policy that exempts a category of applicants from an economically and socially privileged background has been rejected on political as well as ideological grounds as elitist and particularistic by faculties of public institutions.

Our informants, assessing the developments from various perspectives, express the judgment that, with the accommodation of the *kikokushijo* at all levels of the system, the immediate concerns about their *educational* situation have been alleviated. The expansion and development of overseas Japanese school facilities (representing an expenditure of more than 112.5 billion yen), availability of publicly and privately supported counseling services and "reception schools" to facilitate the re-entry of *kikokushijo* on their return, and most importantly, the beginning of special admissions procedures at the university level have routinized the institutional processing of "the *kikokushijo* problems." The accommodations have provided their parents with an institutional system for the expression of concerns, the recognition of those concerns as legitimate claims, and a variety of organizations and services to seek amelioration of their perceived problems.

---

[4]This is not a minor accommodation, since it entails considerable reorganization of the curricula and coordination of course schedules. Perhaps even more significant is the institutional effort directed toward articulating the modified academic calendar with the national practice by which public and private organizations annually recruit and induct new cohorts of employees each spring.

THE INSTITUTIONAL INTEGRATION OF "THE KIKOKUSHIJO PROBLEM"

From the perspective of the "natural history" of social problems (Spector and Kitsuse, 1977) we suggest that the development of "the *kikokushijo* problem" may be interpreted as having moved into stage two. The stage one activities of concerned parents and others identifying the educational situation of the *kikokushijo* as a public issue, defining the disadvantages it imposed as prejudicial and unjust, and mobilizing their resources to seek official recognition of their claims has elicited legitimation of their claims in the form of substantial institutional accommodations. These accommodations have been particularly responsive to those groups that defined the situation of the *kikokushijo* as disadvantaged with reference to the *existing organization of the educational system in Japan.* Those who pressed this definition of "the problem" have been coopted by institutional responses that emphasize the conception of the *kikokushijo* as one requiring corrective, rehabilitative programs.

The alternative definition of the *kikokushijo* and their educational experience as a positive social and cultural asset rather than an individual deficiency and competitive disadvantage has received only rhetorical acknowledgement. Although, in establishing programs for the *kikokushijo*, official statements affirming the importance of their "international experience" have routinely been made, the programs do not contain provisions for integrating, developing, or maintaining the multicultural experience they may have acquired. Thus, there has been little programmatic recognition given to the potentially positive individual or group benefits to be derived from the *kikokushijo*'s exposure abroad, or to the possibility of infusing the existing curriculum with the "international experience" that they are said to have brought back to Japan.

Against the prevailing conception of the *kikokushijo* as an "educational problem," those who hold this alternative definition have proposed that the presence of the *kikokushijo* in the schools presents an opportunity for "internationalizing" the system, and that they provide the basis for creating the first generation of "international persons" (*kokusaijin*) essential for the future political, social, and economic development of Japan. In expressing this view, they are critical of the monolithic character of the Japanese system, and the pervasive examinations that organize teaching and learning in the schools.

The rhetoric in which the discussion about *kokusaijin* is cast has struck a sympathetic chord even among those who seek only to gain admission and acceptance for *kikokushijo* within the existing system. In a period when Japan's economic dependence on international trade is a constant theme in media reports and commentaries on national and international affairs, the importance of defining Japan's position in the world economy and in the councils of international organizations is underlined. Thus the term *kokusaijin* is bathed in an aura of value, with ideologically diverse groups subscribing to the view that the development of the *kokusaijin* as a desired goal of education.

The diverse meanings assigned to the term, however, reveal the rhetorical character of the support given to any policy directed toward the "internationalization" of the educational system. When discussion moves from support in principle to more specific matters of implementation, the *"kikokushijo* problem" groups express two opposing views. The more traditional groups express a view (which is called *kokunaiha*) that Japanese culture and society provide the primary framework for the perception, evaluation, and assimilation of foreign practices and values. Proponents of this view, while acknowledging the importance of exposure to and understanding of other societies and cultures, assert that a Japanese who is not firmly grounded in Japanese language, history, and tradition has no valid perspective for assessing the relative value of cultural differences in outlook and practices. Accordingly, they have promoted insitutional "solutions" to the *kikokushijo* problem that have assumed without question the importance of integrating the returnees into the existing educational system in order to facilitate their "harmonious" reentry into Japanese society. The term *kokusaiha* is used to designate the contrasting viewpoint that is oriented outwardly toward other societies and their cultures. From this perspective, the Japanese educational system is criticized as parochial and insular, and organized to eradicate the effects of the *kikokushijo*'s "international experience."

In this exchange on the issue of "internationalism" and the promotion of the *kokusaijin*, the *kokusaiha* have become progressively isolated as a minority view, as parents, business interests, school personnel, and others have been mollified by the institutional accommodations to the *"kikokushijo* problem." It remains to be seen how effectively those accommodations are judged to have neutralized the putative social and cultural impediments of the *kikokushijo* status. As they complete their education in Japan and confront the scrutiny of their "educational background" in employment interviews, the *kikokushijo* may find that even the slightest shortcomings remotely attributable to their "foreign experience" may differentiate and exclude them from full and equal participation within the work group.

The emergence of this aspect of the *kikokushijo* experience in Japan has appeared in the past few years in the form of a small group of young adults who have established an organization called "Meta." Organized initially as a "support group" for describing and examining their experiences as *kikokushijo*, members of Meta have developed an analysis of their situation as one of social oppression by institutional practices organized and maintained by the parochialism of the *kokunaiha* point of view. Although it claims less than twenty members, Meta has been the subject of television, newspaper, and magazine coverage through which its spokespersons have presented its claims.

As part of our continuing research on "the *kikokushijo* problem," we propose to monitor the activities of Meta and similar organizations as potential bases for the development of stage three of "the *kikokushijo* problem," representing the "reemergence of claims and demands by the original group(s) . . . expressing dissatisfaction with established procedures for dealing with the imputed conditions . . . ." (Spector and Kitsuse, 1977).

REFERENCES

Kirst, Michael W.
   1981   "Japanese education: Its implications for economic competition in the 1980's." Phi Delta Kappan, (June):707.
Kobayashi, Tetsuya
   1978   "Japan's policy on returning students." International Educational and Cultural Exchange 13:4.
Mills, C. Wright
   1959   The Sociological Imagination, New York: Oxford University Press.
Minoura, Yasuko
   1979   Life In-between: The Acquisition of Cultural Identity Among Japanese Children Living In the United States. Unpublished Dissertation, UCLA Department of Anthropology.
Murase, Anne E.
   1978   "The problems of Japanese returning students." International Educational and Cultural Exchange 13(4):10.
   1979   Survey Report: Japanese Students Returning from Overseas—A Preliminary Study of Four Different Types of Schools. Unpublished manuscript.
   1983   *"Kikokushijo to ippan seito no fuan no hikaku kenkyu: sono kyoku ni okeru imi."* ("A comparison of anxiety levels among returnee and non-returnee students: Implications for education.") In T. Kobayashi, (ed.), Ibunka No Naka Ni Sodatsu Kodomotachi, Tokyo, Japan: Yūhikaku.
Spector, M. & J. I. Kitsuse
   1977   Constructing Social Problems. Menlo Park, CA: Cummings Publishing Co.
Vogel, Ezra F.
   1979   Japan As Number One. Cambridge, MA: Harvard University Press, p. 243.

8 Morality, social problems, and everyday life*

Joseph W. Schneider
Drake University

The definition and study of morality has been traditionally the property of theologians and philosophers, thought of more as a topic within a discipline than as something we routinely experience. When events and issues are defined to involve questions of "morality," we turn or are guided typically to these experts for direction. Although this philosophical literature may be provocative intellectually, it offers little insight for the study of morality as a part of our daily lived experience. Discussions center often on "absolute principles" and "universals"; in short, are abstract and distant from our mundane lives. Moreover, philosophers themselves have lost interest in pursuing these questions of practical ethics (for exceptions, see Bok, 1978; Singer, 1979). In consequence, we know comparatively little about what might be called the roots of the "morality" we see writ large in our public life.

In this chapter I want to suggest a definition of morality that makes it a topic of interest to sociologists, and to sociologists of social problems in particular. I want to illustrate how we might pursue the study of everyday

*I have received helpful comments and suggestions from many people while writing this paper. Special thanks to John Kitsuse, and to Kenneth Brody, Peter Conrad, David Matza, Karen Peterson, Quentin Schultze, Ronald Troyer, and Stephen Wieting. Earlier versions of parts of this paper were presented at the 1980 annual meetings of The Society for the Study of Social Problems and The American Sociological Association. I received support for the preparation of the manuscript from the Department of Sociology at The University of Iowa.

morality, not by reference to abstract intellectual debates, but by turning a careful eye to our own and others' routine conduct. I outline a general interactionist conceptualization of morality taken from recent work in deviance and social problems, review talk as the most available and unequivocal embodiment of morality so seen, and provide an extended example of one way to study everyday morality, using smoking as an instance of putatively moral conduct. Finally, I speculate about the links between morality, social problems, and everyday life, and pose some questions for further discussion.

MORALITY, DEVIANCE, AND SOCIAL PROBLEMS

Common sense suggests that, whatever else it may be, morality is about bad and good, right and wrong, that which is desirable and that which is not. Less familiar is the premise that morality is something people do; it is an accomplishment, a construction by actors engaged in on-going, socially situated interaction. This contrasts with morality as a set of abstract, absolute principles somehow disembodied from experience. Central to this view is the process of valuation and judgment. When we invoke words that carry evaluative meaning, and apply them to persons, behaviors, ideas, and conditions, we contribute—wittingly or not—to a collective process through which such objects are created and recreated as moral phenomena. Morality is first and foremost a matter of meanings and definitions.

While such agency is a fundamental, indeed, distinctive quality of conduct (see Wrong, 1961; Matza, 1969; Kitsuse, 1980), so too, however, is the resistence of the social (as well as physical) world (see Giddens, 1976). We do not enjoy unrestrained creativity in making and changing morality. Such work reflects differences in individual access to and skill in using various "tools," including the recognition and availability of various evaluative "containers" (Burke, 1945) of meaning. Such questions have been studied, albeit incompletely, under the rubric of "power," that is, the proven capacity to impose one's wishes—including versions of right and wrong— on others. Apropos of morality, this occurs sometimes through conflict and domination, much more commonly (and, ironically, even less well understood) in subtle, usually unrecognized ways. The construction, maintenance, and change of morality is profoundly political.

Given the universality of evaluation and judgment in social life, it is surprising that, excepting Durkheim's classic discussions, morality rarely has been given central importance in traditional sociological theory and, most particularly, research. Rather, we have been more likely to assume a particular brand of morality as given, proceeding then to examine in quantified detail that conduct and those persons judged beyond or in violation of it. We have identified "social pathologies," "deviants," and "social problems" as inherently bad and threatening, and have become unwitting professional partisans in battles against a variety of "evils." Little time has been given to reflecting on the political implications of such participation, or the kinds of questions it precludes. The consequences for sociology have been identified most clearly in recent work in the sociology of deviance and social problems.

Beginning sometime in the 1950s and reflecting earlier scattered writings in philosophy, criminology, and social problems, a few sociologists suggested, as a supplement to the pursuit of the causes and control of deviant behavior, that we study how people define various behaviors, situations, and persons as deviant in the first place. Rather than studying only the products of such definitional process—various populations of labeled "deviants" as particular "kinds of people"—these sociologists asked how members of groups create and subsequently apply rules to particular others in specific situations. They also asked about the consequences of such application and enforcement for both definer and those defined.

Malcolm Spector and John Kitsuse (1973, 1977; Kitsuse, 1980; Spector, 1981) have extended this viewpoint to the study of social problems. Just as no act is inherently deviant, no condition is inherently problematic. Social problems are thus constructed in the very acts of naming and claiming associated with such phenomena. It is not the physical assault of a child by a parent, nor the medical removal of a fertilized ovum from the wall of a uterus, nor the percent of cancer-causing particles in the air we breathe that constitute these objects as problems, but rather the *claim* that they are problems (and particular *kinds* of problems) that renders them such. Morality is first and foremost a matter of how things are named.

This view led deviance sociologists to look at the process of concrete interaction between labeler and labeled. Similarly, we should look for the creation and perpetuation of, and challenge to, morality in on-going, situated interaction between claims makers and responders. The nature and source of moral meanings are to be found most clearly in their use.

MORALITY AND TALK

Since morality is a matter of evaluation and judgment, and since most, although not all, evaluation is made through verbal behavior, one focus of research on morality should be the study of moral talk—talk that evaluates and judges; that creates, reinforces, and challenges moral meanings. C. Wright Mills (1940) encouraged such research over forty years ago. He argued that talk, and in particular what he called "motive talk," should be seen not primarily as derivative or reflective of some mysterious inner dynamic that propels our conduct, but as conduct constitutive of the social itself. Accordingly, motives (and values more generally) may be seen best as language resources used to make sense of what we do, both for questioning others and ourselves.

Moreover, such moral talk typically seeks to portray what we have done or are about to do against the background, or in terms, of contextually appropriate ("cultural") meanings. The success we meet, whether toward preventing, mending, or creating social breaches, depends heavily on which motives, upon what language, we use. Others have followed Mills' insight by drawing attention to how people mediate routine experience and the particular abstractions of "society," "culture," and "values" (see Scott and Lyman, 1968; Hewitt and Hall, 1973; Hewitt and Stokes, 1975; Stokes and Hewitt, 1976; Goffman, 1959, 1967, 1971, 1981).

One way to get at this mediation work, in effect, the concrete "work" that "makes" society, is to study the talk people use in various kinds of situations. My concern here is to draw this distinction in terms of what might be called "public" moral talk, on the one hand, and the kinds of evaluative and judgmental words people use in various routine, everyday settings on the other. A relevant example of the former is the language of abstract moral principles—the sort of "morality" we recognize as the subject of public debate and philosophical exegesis (Gusfield, 1981). Compared to everyday morality, it has received the lion's share of popular as well as scholarly attention.

Although abstract moral language may serve an important symbolic function in defining the boundaries of a given culture or group (cf. Erikson, 1966), most of us seem in our daily lives to engage only rarely in explicit debates in the name of this or that "big" or public moral principle. Alfred Schutz (1973) suggested that such routine behavior is premised on a taken-for-granted consensus about what is going on and whether it is bad, good, or neither. While the moral dimensions of these taken-for-granted meanings are influenced perhaps broadly by abstract moral language we learn from parents, peers, teachers, clergy, and others, routine moral meanings reflect more directly the demands of managing adequately the task at hand within specific political and social contexts (e.g., police precincts, courts, bureaucracies, laboratories, nursing homes, schools, airports, sidewalks, parties, and so on).

Even this taken-for-granted, unsignified morality of our everyday lives, however, does not just happen. Such routine settings too have moral contours defined by the interests, goals, and conduct of participants and their reference groups. When we see things as "ordinary" (McHugh, 1970; Dingwall, 1976), "as they should be," indeed, when such questions or definitions simply do not occur to us as relevant, we take a moral consensus for granted. Such everyday morality involves what Jack Douglas (1970) has

called "mystification," what Marx called "false consciousness" and "ideology," and what Gramsci (1971) called "intellectual and moral leadership"
(hegemony). These ideas highlight the fact that certain definitions serve
some groups more than, or even against, others.

One item on an agenda of research on morality, then, might be to
examine the circumstances under which the language of public morality
begins to be used, how that talk differs from more routine moral language,
and to consider the implications of such differences—to the extent they
exist—for participants and larger social networks. A body of closely related
work by deviance and social problems sociologists has focused on the
origins and rise of public moral contests and categories. In addition to and
drawing on Spector and Kitsuse, Joseph Gusfield (1967, 1975, 1981) has
written widely on this process surrounding alcohol and drinking driving;
other relevant studies have examined hyperactivity (Conrad, 1975), child
abuse (Pfohl, 1977), alcoholism (Schneider, 1978; Chauncey, 1980), smoking (Markle and Troyer, 1979) and crime (Fishman, 1978). Peter Conrad and
I (Conrad and Schneider, 1980) have attempted a similar kind of analysis for
what might be called "medical morality." While these and similar studies
contribute to our understanding of the processes through which public and
professional moral work is accomplished, there has been comparatively
little interest in how people attempt to make, sustain, and change moral
definitions by evaluative talk and claims as they go about their daily rounds
(but see Lidz and Walker, 1980; Sabini and Silver, 1982). Toward this end, I
decided to look into the construction of smoking as putatively moral
conduct.

MORAL WORK IN EVERYDAY SETTINGS: THE CASE OF SMOKING

Smoking seems today to be encountered fairly routinely in everyday settings.
At the same time, at least in a public, organizational sense, it is becoming
more problematic (see Nuehring and Markle, 1974; Markle and Troyer, 1979;
Troyer and Markle, 1983). Given this, how do people define smoking, and
how do smokers respond? By studying the talk people use in such definitional work, we can begin to see the social problems process at this "grass
roots" level, both in its own right as well as for how such definitions serve as
the origins and/or reflections of more public social problems activities.

I sent a memorandum to about three hundred fifty people at my university asking those with "negative feelings" about smoking to contact me and
possibly be interviewed for a "smoking study." The forty-three who responded are likely, then, to be more frequent users of negative talk about
smoking than one might encounter in a general population or a representative sample of one. I interviewed twenty-three of these people and sought

out two others for a total of twenty-five "anti-smoking" respondents. Fifteen are men, ten women; their occupations, except for the two additional people I contacted, are from within the university community, and include maintenance workers, full professors, and administrators. I sent another memo soliciting smokers to "give their viewpoint." Twenty-six responded, of whom I interviewed eleven, six men and five women. I make no claims for the representativeness of this sample. Because of its middle class skew, respondents may have *more* access to symbolic ammunition for as well as against smoking, along with skills in making claims. At the same time, however, they may be *less* likely actually to make them, due to sociability norms and a concern with "proper" interpersonal forms of interaction.

In response to unstructured, open-ended questions about smoking, these people offered a variety of situated stories. In addition, they used a good deal of what might be called "loose talk," specifically loose *moral* talk: largely unsituated, evaluative descriptions. While Deutscher's (1973) well known distinction between what people "say" and "do" should be respected, I think such unsituated, diffuse talk should not be ignored. At minimum, it may be seen as a background or pool of meaning against or from which specific instances of claims and responses may be drawn. While the responses from smokers provide a balance, in effect, the "other side" of the process, I am concerned here primarily with claims against smoking and how they are made.

Loose Moral Talk about Smoking

When I began interviewing those opposed to smoking, I expected a lot of talk about the detrimental effects of smoking on health: that it causes cancer, emphysema, heart disease, and so on. These people did use this vocabulary, but typically almost in passing, in vague, general ways, saying that smoking is "unhealthy" and "not good for you." By contrast, these non-smokers drew more commonly on a vocabulary of personal offense to convey their disapproval—in short, that smoke "bothered" them. Such talk came in two "containers": that smoke "smelled bad," "awful," "offensive;" and that smoking was "dirty" or "messy."

These definitions of smoking commonly took precedence over health and medical vocabularies. One man, for example, said flatly: "It isn't mainly because of health [that I oppose it] but because I don't like the smell":

> I'll look at the medical evidence, but . . . another reason is just hedonism: do what you like and avoid what you don't like. That's why I could never smoke. I could experiment with hallucinogenic drugs before I would start smoking.

Not only is cigarette smoking something this man could not imagine himself doing, it is also an offensive intrusion. Although her words were perhaps more intense than others', one woman spoke for many when she called smoke a "vile and hateful thing," and smokers "rude" and "inconsiderate":

> The most offensive thing about it is the odor . . . and it does bother my eyes.
> It's the most odious thing. With drinking, eating, or even shooting drugs . . .
> those things don't infringe on others, but smoking does—even on complete
> strangers. It's a vile and hateful thing.

This intrusiveness of smoke, particularly indoors, lived longer than the cigarette. It "spoiled" such places for some time to come. One man said that, as
a result of having smokers in his home, "you can't air out the room, your
clothes, home, furniture—the environment is spoiled for a period thereafter." Smokers themselves were defined as "polluted" and, as such, to be
avoided. One woman said, only partly in jest: "I try to cultivate friends who
smell good." And a man said he got his wife to stop smoking by "making
innuendos" and telling her "there is nothing feminine about it—it is a real
turn-off to get next to a woman and smell stale cigarette smoke."

Beyond smell, smoking was defined as "dirty," "messy," as something
that produces "dirt," or, more generally, as visually disturbing (cf. Douglas,
1966). I asked one man what it was about smoking that he disliked. He said:

> Well, I think the saying that "It's such a filthy habit" says a lot—that has a high
> priority with me—the ashtrays, burns, and so on. The aesthetics of smoking
> are very high with me. I guess second would be personal control—it's high.
> Health is higher for some than for me. And those who do things to excess—
> anything—will pay for it later.

Another, a maintenance worker, said he stopped smoking several years ago
when he heard "all that stuff about cancer." He added, quickly, however: "I
really don't like ashtrays, the mess, and all that stuff anyway." And smoking
was seen as incongruous with certain settings, activities,and categories of
people. Beyond smell, for example, there were repeated references that food
and cigarettes should be kept firmly separated, particularly during eating,
and that smoking "looks terrible," or "bad" or "worse" for "old people," and
particularly older women.

Having defined smoking as a "vile and hateful thing," as "unhealthy,"
"bad," "offensive," "rude," and "dirty," these nonsmokers were only a short
step from considering the issue of agency, of who is "responsible" for such
offense. As their comments foreshadow, the "character," "will power," and
"control" of smokers themselves were seen as somehow flawed or weak.
Not unlike the "puzzle" of repeated alcohol intoxication (cf. MacAndrew,
1969), continued smoking, given these definitions, could be "made sense
of" only as the product of irrationality and/or lessened "control" over self
and conduct. Nonsmokers drew most typically on the vocabulary of "habit,"
"addiction," and "lost control" to understand smoking. While this kind of
talk blurs the issues of responsibility and blame, it also retains an unequivocally moral dimension. Agency aside, to be "addicted" or "habituated" is to
occupy an undesirable state.

This vocabulary ranged from relatively mild references, such as, "It's a habit," and "They do not realize . . . they are so immersed in it they don't see how contaminated the environment becomes," to more stern descriptions: "They're hooked and can't stop. Maybe they don't want to stop. They have a blind spot. It's selfishness—they are concerned with their own needs over another's." A woman who called herself a "reformed smoker" said:

> I think they [smokers] have a problem with self discipline and some even have a death wish. I think they are not very happy with themselves and they smoke to prove it. I see it as a weakness of will, I guess.

She said, as others had, that she felt "very virtuous" when she stopped smoking.

With such talk of "virtue" and "will," it is perhaps not surprising to find an explicitly religious vocabulary to describe the "wages" of smoking. A woman whose husband had stopped smoking to become a minister put it this way:

> No man can serve two masters. People who smoke are slaves to tobacco, cigarettes. I believe in freedom, and when you can't say "no, I won't smoke," you're not free; you're a slave.

Other religious talk about smoking was that it is "wrong" because it "defiles the Temple of the Body" and thus violates a Biblical prohibition.

Finally, smokers were characterized as "unintelligent," based on their pursuit of this "irrational" and unreasonable" conduct. A man who described his own behavior toward smoking as "tyrannical" said: "I stigmatize people who smoke . . . drop them down a level of intelligence. They deny all the evidence. To me it just seems unintelligent"; a woman added: "A mature and intelligent person wouldn't need it . . . it's like drinking, a crutch."

The smokers I interviewed used moral vocabularies quite parallel to those just described. Since the effects of smoking on a smoker's health have been touted more than its effects on nonsmoking others (e.g., the issue of "second hand smoke"), there was more talk, offered earlier in the interviews, about smoking as "bad for me," "bad for my health," "makes me cough," "gives me shortness of breath," and so on. All mentioned the potential or actual deleterious impact of smoking on their well-being. They spoke of "wanting to quit," or "cut down," or knowing that they should. At best, their definitions of smoking and "theories" to explain it combined perceived benefits and risks. After listing a variety of negative things about smoking, one man said: "I don't like it . . . but I do. Do you understand?" A woman called it a "terrible habit that I enjoy. I guess the pleasure just outweighs the pain."

The themes of "smell" and "dirt" were also present. The talk of smell, however, was not of their own smoke, or even that of others, but rather of "stale" smoke and "dirty ashtrays" left in a closed space. None said their own smoke "smelled bad"; to the contrary, some even said that it was a "good" smell. They all were aware, however, that the smell and physical offensiveness of smoke were "problems" or potential problems in others', particularly nonsmokers', eyes.

This was clear in talk about how "considerate," "careful," and "sensitive" they were about their smoke, where it drifts, and who might be "offended" by it. There was much talk, for example, of how they would police themselves in social situations, smoking only "if it was permitted," and then only "if others are smoking," "ashtrays are made available," or "people don't mind."

They also catalogued various "dirt" considerations, such as "messy ashtrays," "burns" in carpets and clothes, ashes and cigarette butts carelessly deposited. One man called acquaintances who put out cigarettes on the floor at work "uncouth" and "gross," and a woman offered a distinction between what she called "clean" and "dirty" smokers. The former, of which she numbered herself a member, were "careful about when and where they put cigarettes out"; the latter were not. Others spoke of how "terrible" or "crazy" smoking "looked." One woman said: "I don't think it looks very good. It isn't very attractive"; and another said: "When I stopped [smoking], I began to realize just how crazy it looks for people to have this thing hanging out of their mouths burning. It does look crazy." And finally, one man, a pipe smoker, talked of the importance of "smoking etiquette" and how rarely it is observed: "There is a smoking etiquette, you know, and if more smokers tended to be mindful of their smoking and observe good etiquette, then perhaps there wouldn't be so much of a problem. Some people do not observe social graces. I try to do that." This idea that there are "other" smokers who are "messy," "dirty," and "inconsiderate," and then "me," appeared throughout these interviews.

As to why they smoke, most said that smoking is a "habit," even an "addiction," something that can be overcome only with greater "will power" than they had currently. Some spoke specifically of this as a "character flaw" that "bothered" them. One said: "It [his continued smoking] doesn't make me feel very good about myself." Most talked of how they had, at one time or another, tried to stop smoking for good. Accompanying descriptions of smoking as habitual or addictive were various accounts of the "glue" holding conduct and self together: "stress and tension," "pressure," "anxiety," social or peer expectations, "something to do with my hands," "it relaxes me," and "I just enjoy it, I guess."

To defend continued smoking against the background of growing moral disapproval using accounts of "will power" and "habit" (by far more commonly used than "addiction") may well accomplish a variety of goals for these smokers. On the one hand, it aligns them with what appears to be increasingly popular disapproval of smoking; "I don't like it" and "I wish I could stop"; "It's unhealthy, I know." At the same time, however, it provides something of a buffer against blame—at least superficially so. Talk of "habit" and problems of "will power" are intimately familiar to most of us. As such, it is a viable currency for "selling" accounts of self as at least in part a "victim" of circumstance.

Claims-Making in Public, Rule-Free Settings

Given the range and intensity of this loose moral talk, we might expect descriptions of situations in which those opposed to smoking actually made claims against it. But moving from loose talk to direct claims is apparently hard work, fraught with concerns for potential negative consequences. There were very few stories of such claims making, but a variety of justifications for why, even when confronted by another's "bothersome" smoke, these people rarely asked the smoker to stop. This seemed to be true particularly in public settings populated mostly by strangers and without posted no-smoking rules.

Avoiding Smoke and Claims.   A common strategy in such situations was to avoid both the smoke and claims making by altering something about the environment to minimize the effect of the smoke, or simply to move away. Accounts such as "Well, it wasn't really *that* bad," "there were just a few people smoking and I was only going to be there a short time," and "it was just easier to put up with it than to say something to them" were common. Others said they "opened a window," "turned on a fan," or "just moved away." Interestingly, according to the smokers' accounts, this kind of attention to spatial location, aimed at reducing the "bother" their smoke might cause, is precisely what they themselves do in such situations, seeking seats or positions near windows, by open doors, or in the path of a stream of air moving through a ventilation system.

Some went to greater lengths, drawing on situational norms or typical practices as resources. One man told of how he and his wife have a "strategem" they use in airports:

> We occupy an entire row of seats and between us we put coats, packages, and so on, on the unoccupied seats. Then we observe people who come toward the seats to see if they are smoking. If they are, we tell them it is a non-smoking area and that the seats are reserved.

He reported that they "have never been challenged." Another man told of how he had successfully avoided telling a friend and colleague "down the hall" that not only does he dislike cigarette smoke, but avoids coming to his friend's office because of it.

> I devise ploys to get him to come down here [to his office]. We are friends and for 6 years I haven't said anything to him about it—never said "I don't like to come down there because of the smoking and smell"—but I make up reasons not to. For example, I say, "It's more efficient here"—that there are materials here that we will need . . . or that I am expecting a student . . . have to stay by the phone.

He called himself a "wishy-washy guy" about asking people not to smoke. When I asked him if he had encountered resistence to such avoidance, he said: "No, but sometimes I do go down there—when his logic is more compelling and I can't think of something."

Such definitions and strategies were mirrored in smokers' comments. As described, they portrayed themselves as very mindful of their smoke, holding that if only they "knew" their smoke was bothering someone, they would stop or take remedial steps. There was a point, however, at which these smokers said they would assert themselves and their choice to smoke. If nonsmoking others were seen as "wanting" to be "bothered," that is, if, as one man put it, "they are upset just because they don't want me to smoke, and they could move elsewhere," then these embattled smokers said they would hold their ground. One man said, almost courageously: "I might even tell them to go to hell!"

Reactions of Strangers: The Threat of Assault. The grounds non-smokers offered for avoiding such claims in these settings dealt with concerns over how smokers might react; embarrassment and fear of physical assault were paramount. One man said: "I like to avoid scenes and embarrassing situations"; and another: "I wouldn't want people to yell or bring attention or get into a big argument. It would be embarrassing." Others said they just preferred to avoid "conflict" and "confrontation," that it was "just easier" to say nothing.

Another concern was what to do, in effect, if the smoker simply ignores the claim and continues to smoke, rendering both claim and claimant ineffectual. The question seemed to be, "What do I do then, fight?" A woman said: "It's not just that people might get mad, but that they might not respect the request." A man commented more generally:

> I suppose one reason people hesitate is that if you say something to someone [a stranger] and they say, "Up yours, I'm going to smoke anyway, there's no law against it," you can't do anything then . . . . What can you do? Grab the cigarette out of the guy's mouth? Kick him in the shins? What are you gonna do?

Beyond this threat to face, people spoke directly of a fear of physical reprisal. One man said: "I don't want to be hurt—I don't want someone to take a swing at me as a result of asking them not to smoke, particularly with strangers." Another said, frankly:

I suppose it's a 90 pound weakling sort of thing. If I were 6 foot tall and weighed 200 pounds, I might do it. It takes a lot for me to go up to a stranger and tell him his smoking bothers me. It has to be more than unpleasant for me . . . it has to move to suffering before I would do that.

Such concern conjures an image of smokers as, in effect, "ready to fight" if their smoking is challenged. Although, undoubtedly, there are smokers who may react this way, those I spoke with seemed just as hesitant to defend their smoking assertively as nonsmokers were to challenge it, particularly in the absence of some authority or posted rule. While they said they "wouldn't like it" if so challenged, few smokers said they would resist and join the issue. Similarly, none told of ever in fact doing that. To do so would, at least given these data, require making their smoking grounds for something considerably more weighty—a contest over the "rights" of one group over against those of another.

Smokers Rights: The Emergence of Public Contest
It is precisely in such public settings of rule ambiguity—what some have called a form of normlessness or anomie—that nonsmokers and smokers begin to use a vocabulary of abstract, principled morality—that of one's "right" to smoke or be free of smoke. When I asked those opposed to smoking why they would or (more commonly) would not make claims against smokers in such settings, and, of smokers, why they would or would not "feel free" to smoke, both chose the issue of "rights" to frame their answers. And at least in these data, nonsmokers were more quick to give smokers the right to smoke than the latter were to claim it.

One man said, for example: "I suppose you hesitate. It's not an area where smoking is prohibited and it's the feeling that the law tells this person that he has a right to do this." Another explained why he said nothing to a smoker whose smoke was "bothering" him in a restaurant:

I figured it is their right to smoke and it is a public place. I have the right to leave or move and I don't feel you can tell someone in a public place what they should do. You have no authority there.

And another, a smoker, said he was "happy to say" he had never been asked not to smoke or stop smoking in such a situation. When I asked why he was "happy" about it, he answered: "Well, then I would be torn between whether I have the right to smoke or they have the right to ask me not to." Talk of one's right to smoke or be free of smoke was, however, much more common in the comments of the nonsmokers I interviewed. Moreover, such talk focused overwhelmingly, at least for public, rule-ambiguous situations, on the right of the smoker to smoke uninterrupted.

One way to make sense of this apparent difference is to consider a scenario in which a such claim might be made. It would require the nonsmoking person to invade the smoker's public anonymity and space (a rhetoric used frequently by nonsmokers to describe smokers), intruding on another's doing and thoughts. As Goffman (1981) has suggested in his recent discussion of public talk, this is no mean intrusion. Moreover, having made it, the nonsmoker must pursue a line of talk and action that attempts to control the conduct of the smoker, to bring it into line with what he or she thinks ought to be. The smoker, by contrast, is the party wronged, the self interrupted. The burden of proof, so to speak, rests on the intruder, and, as we shall see below, the success of the intrusive project is in no sense a certainty. In short, it is a good deal more work to make a successful claim in such a situation than to "give" the smoking other the right to smoke.

The major and universal exception to this, given the comments of the smokers, is if their smoke is "really bothering" another—even in such rule-free situations. In every case when a smoker spoke of his or her right to smoke, it was always conditional on not "seriously bothering"—meaning to cause physical discomfort to—another. In short, when the definitions held by smoker and nonsmoker were couched as "interests" and the conflict was joined, the "big," public moral issue of "rights" entered into these people's talk. Neither, however, was particularly anxious to pursue the moral issue so framed.

Using Others' Rules: The Shield of Authority

When we move from public situations of rule ambiguity regarding smoking to those in which rules exist, how do people who discover rule violations respond? How, in turn, do violaters react to rule-based claims? One might expect that such legitimation is all strongly "anti" smoking people need to make successful claims. As it turns out, it is not so simple.

When I first asked nonsmokers whether or not they had ever asked a smoker in some nonsmoking place to stop smoking, many said they had. Further conversation revealed that what they did was report the smoker to an on-site "official" of the restaurant, airplane, supermarket, or setting. When I asked why they had not made the claim themselves, they said, for example: "I wouldn't take that on myself . . . that's the law of the restaurant and they are in charge," and, "That's management's job." One man said: "I usually look for the proprietor and tell him that the person is smoking. Then I'm not involved. If the time is short, it's not worth the agony of them saying something nasty."

Virtually all said, however, that the rule made claims-making easier—in principle, if not in fact. One young man said:

> [In the no smoking section] . . . it's not me being the "heavy." I don't make the rules . . . the regulation had already been made. In places where there is no

regulation, I would be seen as the authority figure—infringing on their rights, I guess.

Rules do infringe. They are made and applied typically in an attempt to control, or at least to symbolize, effectiveness aside, how one *should* behave and/or think. Those who make rules, those "responsible" for them, have presumed the prerogative to do just that. Those, on the other hand, who use rules, those Becker (1963) identified as "rule enforcers," are usually free of this moral burden. At minimum, enforcers have such responsibilityshifting accounts available; "I'm just doing my job. I didn't make the rules." On the other hand, using someone else's rules brings to the user the weight of authority as well as constituting a validation of and support for that authority. A preexisting rule, in contrast to claims making in rule-ambiguous settings, seems to shift the burden of defending the conduct, if continued, to those engaged in it. One man spoke directly to this, in the case of laws:

> If there is no law against it, all you have going for you is a need for your own personal comfort—you have nothing going for you. I don't know if you could just stand up in a group and complain about what someone else is doing if that's all you have. I'm not sure that's enough. If there is an ordinance, that takes the onus off the individual—you have a rule that someone else has made. Part of it is escaping the issue, I suppose. If you have the strength of the law, you can say: "Don't smoke because of the law," as opposed to saying: "Don't smoke because I don't like it."

"It takes the onus off the individual." The "onus" of what? one might ask. This weight appears to be in large part, and at least for individuals, that of the moral presumption itself. It is perhaps not surprising to find smokers hesitant to claim their right to smoke in rule-free places.

There were, however, people who did make direct claims against smokers in rule-supported settings, such as on airplanes; in restaurants with segregated seating; occasionally in other kinds of places, such as an elevator or a grocery store. In these settings, however, claims were couched not in the kind of loose but "strong" moral talk discussed earlier, but rather in the vocabulary of rule breaking itself, framed typically with a verbal or physical reference to a "no smoking" sign near at hand. It seemed almost that in directing attention away from themselves and to the posted rule, these cautious claims makers were saying, "You see, but it's not *my* rule."

A moment's thought about behavior in public, particularly given recent negative definitions of smoking, should be sufficient to predict smokers' reactions to posted no-smoking rules. They do not smoke. With the exception of one man who said he "used to" smoke in classrooms while teaching, standing directly under a no-smoking sign, none of the smokers said they would intentionally smoke in a no-smoking area. In fact, they gave such rules, and rules in general, considerable weight as effective controls in their lives.

Making Rules: Hard and Risky Work

What happens to claims-making when we move from public settings to those in which, through ownership, position, or relationship, the claimant can make rules? The data thus far might make one cautious about predicting that, at last, these nonsmokers will have their way. But isn't one's home one's "castle"? A place to do what we want and keep outsiders at bay? And one's car and office, aren't these places where prerogative gives us perfectly legitimate grounds to control the kind of conduct that occurs and expect others to respect this control? But rules do not just happen; they are made and often must be invoked and/or enforced.

Making Claims and Giving Offense.   Both smokers and those opposed to smoking certainly were aware of the prerogatives that go with ownership. In conversation about smoking at home and in their or others' cars or offices, they asserted these "place rights" as legitimate grounds for rules against smoking or feeling free to smoke. One man said about a home prohibition: "It's our home and I think we can do what we want there"; a woman added: "In my car, I figure I can ask people not to smoke. I have never asked anyone not to smoke in someone else's car—I figure I am on their ground; I am the guest." And smokers universally expressed sensitivity to the definition of smoking in others' homes as potentially problematic, saying they "curtail" their smoking or "just don't smoke there"—"unless I know they are smokers, or they would give me an ashtray and tell me to smoke." This hesitance was based on the definition of that space as, in one smoker's words, "their territory." None suggested they would chafe under restrictions based on these prerogatives, or that it was "wrong" that such rules be made.

But even here, further talk revealed more complexity. Even though nonsmokers defended their prerogatives to ban smoking at home and in their cars, none said they ever had actually put it to smokers in quite such blunt terms, choosing often to make vague remarks about "smell," "irritation," "bad lungs," and so on. To invoke specifically the place rights they asserted to me would be too close to a challenge, too much a violation of sociability.

The greatest concern about making rules against smoking in one's home was the risk of "offending" the smoking guest. At minimum, guests are to be treated with civility, free from unwarranted attack and criticism; variously catered to, depending on the nature of the relationship.

Aside from not wanting to offend a smoking guest, nonsmokers were concerned that, in making such claims, they were risking the friendship itself, courting the possibility of being rejected in return. These people were willing to tolerate a good deal of "bothersome" smoke in the name of sociability. A man explained why he recently had loosened the smoking prohibition in his home:

> I do a lot with my friends. Bob, here in the department, smokes, and I don't think he would come over if I kept that rule. And parties—that's where it really has negative consequences. It's not party-like to lay this big rule on people. When you are at a party, you are supposed to have a good time.

Justifications by nonsmokers in the name of "hospitality," "friendship," and not wanting to offend went on and on, even though no one could ever recall actually having lost a friend to a smoking claim.

Even those who prided themselves on being "vocal" and "assertive" about their antismoking ideas made exceptions to their own rules. A story about the "babysitter" for one man's daughter illustrates this point:

> Jane's babysitter smokes. She has asked us, and we say, "Go right ahead." She's 67 years old and a lovely woman. We don't judge her—have never hinted to her not to smoke. She's like a guest in our home; if you invite them in, you accept them, warts and all.

"Warts and all." This affirms the kind of "carte blanche" that guests may assume or be attributed. To, as the man above put it, "lay on rules" under such circumstances would be to risk one's reputation both as a friend and one who "knows how to entertain, how to treat people."

One of the reportedly most active claimants against smoking told the following story:

> We had, for a while, a sign on our front door that said "no smoking" or "thank you for not smoking." My wife has asthma and smoke really bothers her. There is a group of people, one social group that we see that we like very much—and many of them are heavy smokers. We don't ask them not to smoke and don't use the sign for them because we think it might compromise the friendship. We like them, and realize that they are addicted to it, and it would be very embarrassing for them to ask them to stop—they probably couldn't anyway. We have no alternative. If we want to be in the group, we have to suffer.

Even given his wife's asthma and an earlier account of how he enforced the smoking prohibition against others in his home, this man and his wife could find no legitimate language to use against their friends' smoke. The quasi-medical "addiction" perhaps assuages his own discomfort at the gap between this conduct and the "strong" moral stance he took earlier. "After all," he added, "they probably couldn't stop anyway."

Smokers told similar stories about how, "when I come over, they [nonsmoking friends] will get out their one ashtray and I will smoke." And while smokers asserted they certainly would smoke in their own homes if they chose, they also told of restrictions around family members who "don't like it." One man said he stopped smoking when his wife's asthmatic relative visited. He said he "didn't mind," but admitted, "I was a little put out since it was my own home."

With the prerogatives of ownership and control comes the "onus" named above: responsibility for making rules. Not only must we make the rules for these places, and often deal directly with enforcement, we must "be responsible" in a more fundamental, personal sense. Such rules do not become just rules, but rather *our* rules; they can come to represent, and even stand for, us in others' eyes, just as violation of rules may become grounds for how the violater is defined. We become, in short, the kind of person who would make and enforce, or break and denigrate, such rules. These considerations were not lost on those who had or had thought about making rules and claims against smoking. Even in these "castles" of their own construction and control, nonsmokers were reticent.

An example of this caution is the use of signs. In those few cases where people attempted to maintain smoke-free homes, cars, and offices, no-smoking signs of one variety or another were seen as helpful tools that allowed their users to make claims without having to actually *say,* "Please don't smoke here." I asked one woman, who had such a sign on a foyer mirror just inside the front door, whether she had ever pointed it out to any of her smoking guests. She replied, somewhat increduously, "Why, no! It's right there in front of them. How can they miss it?" And another sign user, this time on the outside of the front door, said he and his wife rarely say anything about the sign when they display it. Others told of how they tried to place buttons and signs in prominent places that would be "hard" for others to miss.

Giving Good Reasons.   Visual aids aside, when it was clearly *their* rule, people were prepared to give what they considered the "best" reasons as grounds. Virtually all claims based on claimant-authored rules and "requests" in rule-ambiguous settings were grounded in references to physical irritation, health, and/or "scientific facts" about the perils of smoking. While such grounds may not be paramount in the loose moral talk described earlier, these people are not fools. One man said that, whenever he had to ask someone not to smoke in his office, he would talk about the "poor ventilation" and his "bronchitis condition." Another, who maintained a smoking prohibition at home, said if he "had to" give a reason for the rule, "I would say my wife's asthma." Another described how he would tell people that he has "a set of bad lungs," but admitted there was in fact no such medical diagnosis. A self-diagnosed "allergy" was used by one woman to keep her visiting mother from smoking, and so on.

When people went on "campaigns" against the smoking of intimates and friends, they would use "medical findings" as grounds for claims. One man said he had convinced his fiancee to stop smoking by, among other things, "giving her research findings about lung cancer—facts and scientific stuff that supported my view, and I ignored the stuff that didn't." Similarly, a man who said "health" was not a major priority in his dislike of smoking said: "The health thing never came into it until I started tapering off. That was before the national campaigns came along—before the Surgeon General's Report. So, when they came along, I was really for it." This man said he "uses" such information when he does what he called "missionary work" to convince others they should not smoke. Finally, another commented on the significance of medical scientific data on smoking:

> Well, I can use it in an argument, I guess. I suppose there is something to it. It has some bearing on the issue, but it must be an individual thing. It is not guaranteed that you will get cancer if you smoke, just that the chances are better.

While this tack was not a guarantee of success, such health value mongering often seemed to work, particularly if claimants alluded to the effects of smoke on them. As one smoker commented to me: "I mean, what can you say? There's no defense against the health argument."

Claims and Authority in the Workplace.   Not surprisingly, authority differences at work seemed to affect smoking and claims against it. Those with less authority were, in general, less willing to make claims against smokers, or to smoke against the wishes of those more powerful. A departmental secretary described how she often asks students not to smoke as they sit waiting to see professors, telling them it is not "right" to leave their smoke behind when they go. When she mentioned that sometimes professors come into the office and smoke, I asked if she treated them the same. She said: "No, being in a position of working, you realize that you don't tell professors not to smoke." She said she managed such situations by "arranging to run an errand, just to get out." Another woman, an accountant, said that her supervisor smoked in the office and it "bothered" her because of her allergy. She said she had "mentioned it to her," bought an air-freshener for her desk, but was not willing to press the issue: "I need the job. I work with her every day and it is necessary for us to work closely together. She is my superior on the job and I have seen her reactions to others who offend her."

My conversations with smokers revealed a similar sensitivity, or at least a reported one, to authority differences and smoking. One man recounted how the dean of his college had asked him, during the job interview, "What would you say if I asked you not to smoke?" The man said he misunderstood, thinking the dean meant in the man's office: "I said we would have to re-negotiate." Uncomfortable with his possible insubordinate remark, he added: "I clarified it later, though. He meant around him. That's fine." And a woman who worked as a second level administrator told of how her superiors had declared the office a no-smoking area and put up signs to that effect. She said she does not smoke in her office or anywhere in the area. When I asked her how she felt about that, she said: "Well, right now I'm dying for a cigarette. My husband [also a smoker] says he doesn't know how I get through the day."

Those with authority said they sometimes could use their position as a foundation for making and enforcing—often quite subtly—rules about smoking. A nonsmoker hesitant to make rules against smoking in her home said: "I have asked people not to smoke here in my office. In my office, or at work, I think I have more personal leverage."

Smokers demonstrated similar awareness of how authority could be used to define smoking as legitimate or, in one case, as grounds for breaking a posted no-smoking rule. One man, a therapist, drew both on his authority and a suspected difficulty of his clients to make claims against his smoking:

> After the first session [during which he smokes] I will ask if they find my smoking offensive. I say: "Would it be all right with you if I smoke?" They have to come back with a negative response in order to get me to stop. I suppose there is something about the power of the therapist and the client not being able to say "Yes."

Another told of how he had defied a no-smoking sign at work that he himself had ordered posted:

> I was standing there . . . with no smoking signs all around me. [A person] came up to me and said: "You are smoking in a no smoking area." I said, "I know, I ordered the signs!" He just backed off.

This man said he did not stop smoking as a result of the claim.

But authority and definitions of smoking interact with other considerations. As reported, virtually all smokers said that, regardless of prerogative, if their smoke "really bothered" someone, they would stop. For smokers, this was considered a "good reason" for a claim against their smoking. Stories from nonsmokers about smoke in the workplace reflected the importance of being able to give what they considered good reasons for antismoking claims, even when made against subordinates. For instance, a biology professor talked about his defense of a no-smoking rule in the laboratory:

> I tell students they should not smoke because the smoke could contaminate some of the microorganisms or it could interact with some chemicals in the air and might be dangerous. I don't know that that is true, but it sounds good.

I asked why he would say that rather than simply asking them not to smoke because he found it personally offensive. He said: "Well, it would mask that as the ultimate reason, which I guess I wouldn't want to give."

Another man, employed as a psychiatric attendant at a local hospital, described how he made a no-smoking rule that was binding on fellow workers, almost all of whom had more authority:

> We had report every morning at 7:30 and would all have to get in this small room and there were several smokers. It was really terrible. I asked that there be no smoking during this report period.

Wasn't that difficult, I asked, given your position as attendant?

> Oh, no. I got very assertive there. That was an important thing there—to express your feelings. The staff sort of practiced assertiveness on one another.

When I asked him later, after he described what a "shy" person he is, how he could have made that claim, he said: "The atmosphere made it not too terrible . . . it has to do a lot with where I'm working. It helps or makes it hard to be assertive."

Moral Work and Reputation

One striking parallel between the talk of smokers and nonsmokers is a concern for how claims making might reflect on the self. Social scientists, and we sociologists in particular, have written a good deal on this issue for those against whom moral claims are made. It is an important part of what Matza (1969) has called the impact of signification—specifically, ban and apprehension—and what Lemert (1951), before him, described as "societal reaction" and its importance for the development of secondary deviation. Concerned to portray the impact of such signification on the deviant, we have given less attention to how the signification process itself is accomplished, particularly as it occurs outside formal or official processing organizations, and even more particularly when we turn attention to the concrete scenes and situations of our everyday lives.

The data on the moral construction of smoking I have presented here certainly suggest that questions of identity and reputation are relevant not only to "becoming" and "being" deviant, but also to the construction of such moral definitions and their specific, situational applications. Nonsmokers' comments, such as "It's very hard to tell someone something negative about them" and "I don't think you should tell somebody what to do," reflect a hesitance to make negative claims against putative "normals" in everyday settings. Such rule making and application is defined generally as a presumption limited to those having some kind of "official" or legitimate control. In a society in which we "prize" individual rights—rhetorically, at least—there is much skepticism of rule makers outside such institutional and/or professionally dominated situations. As one smoker said, angrily: "After all, who do they think they are?"

Moreover, smokers' talk also reflected the morally suspicious and deteriorating status of smoking in the society. Recall that virtually all offered some negative talk about it, various accounts for why they do it (usually before I asked them), and were at pains to define themselves as "considerate," "thoughtful," and "sensitive" about how smoking might "bother" others. Some expressed "guilt" or "embarrassment" in facing an interview about smoking. One said: "This is difficult for me . . . to talk about something that I know I shouldn't be doing." This surely is ban at work. As for apprehension, those few who reported such experience said either that they obligingly stopped smoking and said they were "sorry" for the offense, or, at minimum, expressed to me a sense of having been "wrong" for continuing to smoke in defiance of the claim.

And those who had made attempts at rule and claims-making against smoking said they had second thoughts. They told me they wanted to avoid being "obnoxious," "crusaders," and, most fervently, "self righteous"—in effect, to avoid being what Becker (1963) called a "moral entrepreneur." One man, after reciting a list of accounts for making no claims at home, added: "I choose to have my guests enjoy themselves over my own comfort . . . . and I don't want to assume that 'holier than thou' stance. I hate to be a prick." A woman said it is "an awkward thing" to ask people not to smoke in her home, "like I don't know how to approach it. I think it would reflect badly on me." A man who had relaxed his home prohibition explained why: "Well, I thought maybe I was being an asshole about it." This same man said he would be hesitant to ask someone not to smoke in a nonsegregated place, particularly if he were in the company of people he has just met. "They . . . might get the wrong impression of me," he said. What kind of impression would he want to avoid, I asked. "Self righteous, rigid . . . those kinds of things." Finally, another spoke of what he called "something in our day that says it is not permissible to judge others": "At a Republican caucus . . . it was very crowded. It was assinine [for the person] to smoke. I don't know why no one said anything. People don't want to seem self righteous." What did he mean? "Smugness; persons assuming a morally superior position. I don't care for persons who exhibit no humility and seek to dictate to others."

Such fears are apparently well founded. Even though all but one of the smokers acquiesced to claims against their smoking, when I asked them how they felt about such claims, some admitted that they were "angry." When they talked further about their feelings, the grounds for this anger were expressed through remarks such as: "Well, I think it was really the way they did it that bothered me. It was very blunt. Very disapproving." One woman told of how she responded to a brusque statement from another woman at a football game. The latter, seated in front of this woman, turned suddenly and said: "I certainly hope you are not going to burn my husband's coat with that!" The woman, affronted, shot back: "Well, I certainly don't intend to!" In no case, however, was affront taken when the claims against smoking were based on or seen to arise from medical or health-related grounds. One man spoke directly to this distinction:

The non-smokers who have a physical reaction to smoke—you're just sensitive to that and you stop. I don't care for self-righteousness for any cause. People who are sensitive to smoke because they want to be—because you're doing something they don't like . . . that I don't like.

When asked by a woman to stop smoking in a restaurant waiting area, one respondent said she stopped immediately: "She was very polite. I have enough friends with asthma [the claimant did not mention any health problems] and so I am careful. I felt guilty for making her uncomfortable." Similarly, although knowing there was a bona fide health concern, a professor described a "very reasonable," "serious," and even "courageous" student who made a claim against the former's smoking in class: "I knew he wasn't just making an issue of it, or making it up." Even when no grounds were given, claimants who were "nice," "polite," and "reasonable" increased the chance of success both of affecting the undesirable conduct and complimenting themselves.

ON EVERYDAY MORALITY AND SOCIAL PROBLEMS

I have argued that to study social problems is to study evaluation and judgment, and that social problems as "objects" are such definitional processes that occur not only on a public stage, but in the routine scenes and settings of our daily lives as well. While we have begun to examine some of the public, organizationally grounded aspects of social problems as social accomplishments, we have yet to focus attention on such evaluative activity writ small. I have considered definitions of, and claims about, smoking toward gaining insight into this kind of social activity.

Although certainly not news, the gap between what people said to me about smoking and what they actually had done about it in various routine settings seems a discrepancy pregnant with research possibilities. In their loose moral talk, nonsmokers offered strongly negative definitions of both smoke and smokers. No one, including smokers, defended smoking on its own merits. Against this "rich" background of negative meaning, however, few reported ever having actually made a verbal claim against a smoker in some face-to-face situation. Smokers, by and large, said they were very mindful and considerate of nonsmokers and how smoke might offend, being willing to, and actually having stopped or refrained from, smoking in various situations. Even in places where predictions based on positional or so-called "structural" prerogatives might suggest it, claims against smokers and smoking were rare. Given the variety and intensity of the loose moral talk and the rarity of the actual claims made, how are we to understand the former?

One direction for future work might be to pursue the nature and use of such loose moral talk in routine situations, across various kinds of social relationships. What is going on, for instance, when people wax indignant about this or that alleged condition or conduct to associates, friends, family members, or available others, while being careful *not* to confront those involved or responsible with such claims-making talk? It may be that such loose moral talk is one way we define, both for ourselves and others, the moral contours of our personal lives and the larger social world. It may be a "low-risk" way to be a moral actor, indeed, even a "moral entrepreneur," in a world in which explicit moral enterprise seems too threatening, ineffective, or unavailable. While we may think better of actually lodging a claim to another's face, it is considerably easier to "talk big," using explicit moral language about problematic persons and/or conditions.

Beyond this difference between loose and actually applied moral talk, we should study the kinds of moral vocabularies used in everyday settings and how they differ from those used in more public, "official" cases. For smoking, the former was very much a vocabulary of interpersonal offense and concern for sociability. More public moral vocabularies, such as those framed in medical/health and legal "rights" language, were seen as *useful* primarily in an explicit conflict of interests, or to persuade. The people I interviewed were hesitant to make smoking a rights issue when involved in a face-to-face encounter. To do so would be to raise the stakes and gravity of what was happening beyond comfortable bounds. These and similar issues suggest we need to examine in more careful detail the connections between public moral vocabularies in which claims are made and the evaluative talk used in routine, everyday situations. Are the latter merely reflective of the former, or do they provide a reservoir of negative sentiment crucial to the effectiveness of subsequent public and official claims? In the case of smoking, for instance, to what extent is the rapid public devaluation of smoking, couched primarily in terms of medical and health costs, facilitated by an already extensive disapproval on an everyday, interpersonal, and experiential level? When we suggest that smoking has only recently become "deviant," it may be that we ignore a long-lived set of negative definitions that have existed around this conduct in routine settings.

A third and closely related set of questions suggested by these data focuses on how routine moral work or claims making is or is not done. Given the definitions of social problems embraced here, such claims-making is obviously of great importance. It is clear, recent talk of "assertiveness" and "openness" in relationships aside, that making claims against others is difficult work, fraught with fears of lost face and even physical assault.

Again, however, this is not news. Everett Hughes (1962) spoke to this question in his well-known discussion of "good people" and "dirty work," and Howard Becker's distinction between rule creators and rule enforcers both turn on the difficulty, or at least costs, associated with moral work. For Hughes, the "good" German people could define themselves as such only to the extent they could distance themselves from and allocate responsibility to the S.S. Hughes argued that these good people, in various and often not so subtle ways, supported the moral definitions in which the S.S. operated. Becker described how the functionary can simultaneously enforce rules and at least partially escape the "onus" of responsibility discussed earlier. So-called "structural" considerations aside, it appears making and enforcing rules is difficult work, particularly when there is no responsibility-shifting convention to invoke. We need to study this moral work more carefully, both in rule-free as well as rule-bound settings and relationships. While Becker's discussion of moral entrepreneurs is widely and ritually cited, there have been few if any attempts to examine such conduct up close and to ask how it is done and experienced by those doing it. Finally, in light of Hughes's and Becker's comments, we should study the links between such moral crusaders and those of us who draw on their definitions and vocabularies, in both support and rejection of them. Are we like the "good" German people discussed by Hughes, only too anxious for someone else to do the desired but "dirty" moral work on which our definitions of self and social experience rest? These and similar questions about moral work in everyday settings provide a largely untapped research agenda for students of social problems.

REFERENCES

Becker, Howard S.
    1963   Outsiders. New York: Free Press.
Bok, Sissela
    1978   Lying: Moral Choice in Public and Private Life. New York: Random House.
Burke, Kenneth
    1945   A Grammar of Motives. New York: Prentice-Hall.
Chauncey, Robert
    1980   "New careers for moral entrepreneurs: Teenage drinking." Journal of Drug Issues
        10:45–70.
Conrad, Peter
    1975   "The discovery of hyperkinesis: Notes on the medicalization of deviant behavior."
        Social Problems 23:12–21.

Conrad, Peter and Joseph W. Schneider
   1980   Deviance and Medicalization: From Badness to Sickness. St. Louis, MO: C. V.
            Mosby.
Deutscher, Irwin
   1973   What We Say/What We Do: Sentiments and Acts. Glencoe, IL: Scott, Foresman.
Dingwall, Robert
   1976   Aspects of Illness. New York: St. Martin's.
Douglas, Jack D. (ed.)
   1970   Deviance and Respectability: The Social Construction of Moral Meanings. New
            York: Basic Books.
Douglas, Mary
   1966   Purity and Danger. London: Routledge & Kegan Paul.
Erikson, Kai T.
   1966   Wayward Puritans. New York: Wiley.
Fishman, Mark
   1978   "Crime waves as ideology." Social Problems 25:531–43.
Giddens, Anthony
   1976   New Rules of Sociological Method. New York: Basic Books.
Goffman, Erving
   1959   The Presentation of Self in Everyday Life. New York: Anchor.
   1967   Interaction Ritual. New York: Anchor.
   1971   Relations in Public. New York: Basic.
   1981   Forms of Talk. Philadelphia, PA: University of Pennsylvania Press.
Gramsci, Antonio
   1971   Selections from the Prison Notebooks of Antonio Gramsci. Edited and translated by
            Quintin Hoare and G. N. Smith. New York: International.
Gusfield, Joseph R.
   1967   "Moral passage: the symbolic process in the public designations of deviance."
            Social Problems 15:175–88.
   1975   "Categories of ownership and responsibility in social issues: Alcohol abuse and
            automobile use." Journal of Drug Issues 5:285–303.
   1981   The Culture of Public Problems: Drinking Driving and the Symbolic Order. Chicago,
            IL: University of Chicago Press.
Hewitt, John P. and Peter M. Hall
   1973   "Social problems, problematic situations and quasi-theories." American So-
            ciological Review 38:367–74.
Hewitt, John P. and Randall Stokes
   1975   "Disclaimers." American Sociological Review 40:1–11.
Hughes, Everett C.
   1962   "Good people and dirty work." Social Problems 10:3–10.
Kitsuse, John I.
   1980   "Coming out all over: Deviants and the politics of social problems." Social Prob-
            lems 28:1–13.
Lemert, Edwin
   1951   Social Pathology. New York: McGraw-Hill.
Lidz, Charles W. and Andrew L. Walker
   1980   Heroin, Deviance and Morality. Beverly Hills, CA: Sage.
MacAndrew, Craig
   1969   "On the notion that certain persons who are given to frequent drunkenness suffer
            from a disease called alcoholism." Pp. 483–500 in S. C. Plog and R. Edgerton
            (eds.), Changing Perspectives in Mental Illness. New York: Holt, Rinehart and
            Winston.

Markle, Gerald E. and Ronald J. Troyer
    1979   "Smoke gets in your eyes: Cigarette smoking as deviant behavior." Social Problems
            26:611–25.
Matza, David
    1969   Becoming Deviant. Englewood Cliffs, NJ: Prentice-Hall.
McHugh, Peter
    1970   "A common-sense conception of deviance." Pp. 61–88 in J. Douglas (ed.), De-
            viance and Respectability. New York: Basic Books.
Mills, C. Wright
    1940   "Situated actions and vocabularies of motives." American Sociological Review
            6:904–13.
Nuehring, Elaine and Gerald E. Markle
    1974   "Nicotine and norms: The re-emergence of a deviant behavior." Social Problems
            21:513–26.
Pfohl, Stephen J.
    1977   "The 'discovery' of child abuse." Social Problems 24:310–23.
Sabini, John and Maury Silver
    1982   Moralities of Everyday Life. New York: Oxford.
Schneider, Joseph W.
    1978   "Deviant drinking as disease: Alcoholism as a social accomplishment." Social
            Problems 25:361–72.
Schutz, Alfred
    1973   Collected Papers, Vol. 1. The Problem of Social Reality. The Hague, Netherlands:
            Martinus Nijhoff.
Scott, Marvin B. and Stanford M. Lyman
    1968   "Accounts." American Sociological Review 33:46–62.
Singer, Peter
    1979   Practical Ethics. Cambridge, MA: Cambridge University Press.
Spector, Malcolm
    1981   "Beyond crime: Seven methods for controlling troublesome rascals." Pp. 127–158
            in H. L. Ross (ed.), Law and Deviance. Beverly Hills, CA: Sage.
Spector, Malcolm and John I. Kitsuse
    1973   "Social problems: A reformulation." Social Problems 21:145–90.
    1977   Constructing Social Problems. Menlo Park, CA: Cummings.
Stokes, Randall and John P. Hewitt
    1976   "Aligning actions." American Sociological Review 41:833–49.
Troyer, Ronald J. and Gerald E. Markle
    1983   Cigarettes: The Battle Over Smoking. Rutgers, NJ: Rutgers University Press.
Wrong, Dennis H.
    1961   "The oversocialized conception of man in modern sociology." American So-
            ciological Review 26:183–93.

Author index

Italic page numbers indicate bibliographic citations.

Subject index